IMAGES
of America

HENDERSON COUNTY

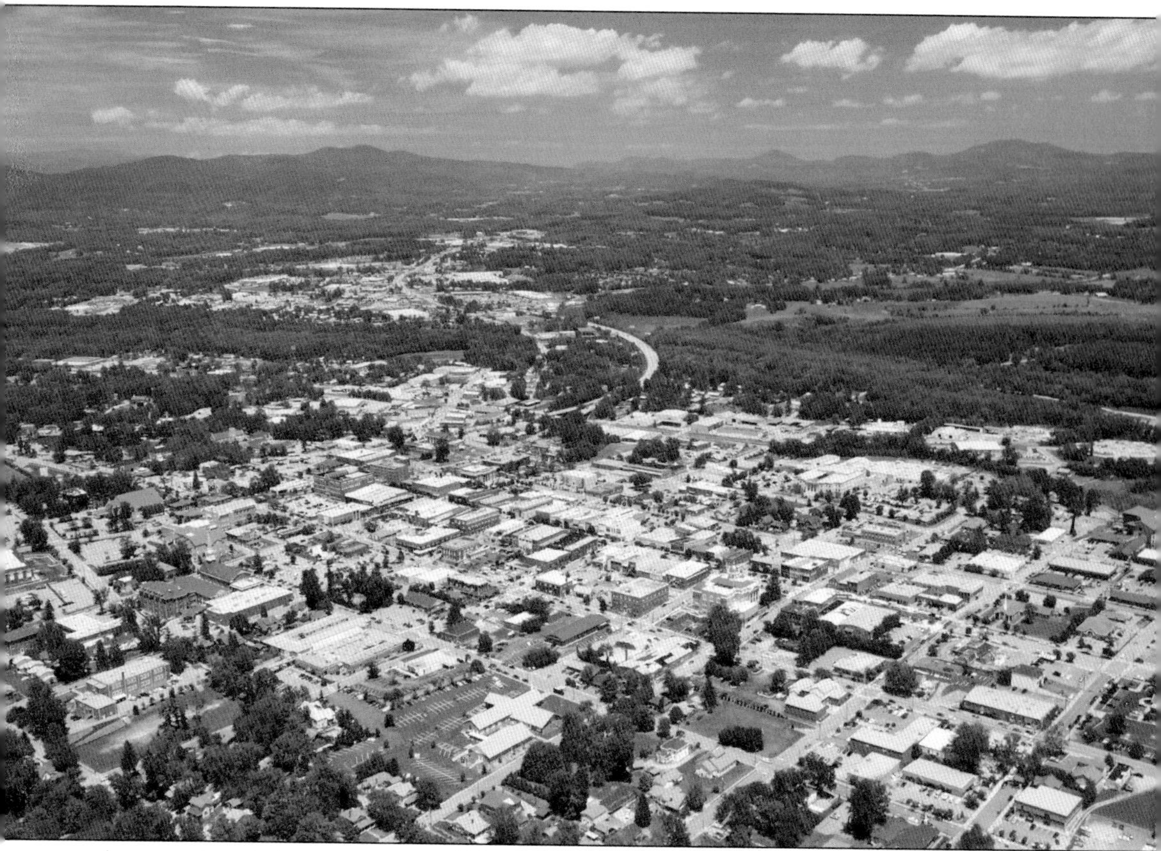

An overview of the county seat of Henderson depicts downtown Hendersonville situated on a rolling plateau circumscribed by a vastness of mountains. The city's Main Street once stretched "wide enough for a coach drawn by a team of four horses to turn around without backing, and then turn again"—a dictum of Judge Mitchell King, who donated 50 acres for the town in 1841. By 1978, four lanes had been reduced to two in a serpentine reconfiguration. (Courtesy of Tim Culberson of Aerial Photo Professionals.)

On the Cover: Two gentlemen enjoy an outing on the French Broad River in 1887. Some of the earliest colonists in what became Henderson County chose the fertile banks of the French Broad River for their settlements. The French Broad ranks as the third-oldest river in the world and counts as one of only a few rivers that flows south to north. (A.F. Baker photograph, courtesy of the estate of Louise H. Bailey.)

IMAGES
of America

HENDERSON COUNTY

Terry Ruscin

ARCADIA
PUBLISHING

ISBN 978-1-4671-2981-7

Published by Arcadia Publishing
Charleston, South Carolina

Printed in the United States of America

Library of Congress Control Number: 2018945929

For all general information, please contact Arcadia Publishing:
Telephone 843-853-2070
Fax 843-853-0044
E-mail sales@arcadiapublishing.com
For customer service and orders:
Toll-Free 1-888-313-2665

Visit us on the Internet at www.arcadiapublishing.com

Dedicated to the gifted and dedicated board and volunteers of the Henderson County Genealogical and Historical Society and to Theron Larnce Maybin Sr.

CONTENTS

Acknowledgments

Thank-yous go to the many who contributed to this project by sharing treasured family photographs, granting interviews, making connections with people in the know, and for their roles as sounding boards. Special thanks go to Elsie Tate Aiken, Morris Bagwell, Joseph Bailey Jr., Bill Barnwell, Fred Beddingfield, Drew Brannon, Buddy Brock, Ray Bryson, Pat Waldrop Buck, Sarah Brown Cannon, Christy Corn, Knox Crowell, Tim Culberson, Jim Davenport, Shirley Jackson Davidson, Faye Edney, the Etowah Heritage group, Jo Ann Fain, Phillip Heavner, Daphne Hedden, the Henderson County Genealogical and Historical Society, the Henderson County Heritage Museum, Louise Jackson Hill, Marilyn Horne, Barbara Hudson, Bobby Justus, Carolyn Justus, Marcia Mills Kelso, Ruth Kidd, Melinda Pilgrim Lowrance, Tammy Manley, Don McCarson, Paula Machen, Mary Lib McLeod, Larry H. McKay Jr., Lois McKinnish, Diane and Fred McMullen, Dorothy Means, Jeff Miller, Ruth Montgomery, Alex Nelon, Jean and Leon Pace, Arthur Pearsall, Hortence Potts, Patsy Pryor, Stan Shelley, Gayle Hamilton Stepp, Bonnie Heffner Stewart, Ella Surrette, Carl Taylor, Margaret Thomas, Marylin Jones Thomas, Jim Toms, A.B. Wexler, Barbara Weese Willis, Patricia Walker, Sid Williams, and Richard Wilson.

INTRODUCTION

Nestled in the eastern Blue Ridge escarpment of the Southern Appalachian Range in Western North Carolina at latitude 35.3726 degrees north, longitude 82.4319 degrees west, Henderson County supports a diverse geography, clime, and populace. The Eastern Continental Divide—the rim of the Blue Ridge—transects the county. Waters west of the divide drain toward the Mississippi River and the Gulf of Mexico; waters east of the divide drain toward the Atlantic Ocean. The county's altitude ranges between 1,400 and 5,000 feet, with an average elevation of 2,200 feet, and the county seat of Hendersonville stands at 2,129 feet near its geographical center.

Six rivers flow within the county: the French Broad and Mills (west of the divide) and the Rocky Broad, Hungry, North Pacolet, and Green (east). More than 40 peaks—including Bald Rock, Bearwallow, Burntshirt, Little Pisgah, the Pinnacle, Sugarloaf, and Tater and Turkey Knobs—encircle the county seat of Hendersonville.

Henderson County was formed from Old Buncombe in 1838, but not until 1851 did Buncombe County cede most of the land comprising the town of Fletcher and some of Hoopers Creek to Henderson. When first created, the new county included most of today's Transylvania County and a section of today's Polk County, with the horseshoe bend of the French Broad River near its geographical center. Part of Polk County sprang from Henderson in 1855 and most of Transylvania County from Henderson in 1861.

Members of the North Carolina General Assembly and Western North Carolinians Phillip Brittain, John Clayton Sr., and Montreville Patton struck an accord in 1833. If named for North Carolina Supreme Court chief justice Leonard Henderson (1772–1833) of Granville County, a new county would be formed from Old Buncombe. In 1837, the general assembly appointed 11 citizens—Richard Allen, John Clayton, Samuel Chunn, Reuben Deaver, Asa Edney, Epaphroditus Hightower, John Jarret Sr., Robert Jones, John Miller, Benjamin Wilson, and John Yount—to organize the new county.

The act to lay off and establish a county by the name of Henderson in Western North Carolina passed on December 15, 1838. The wording of the court of pleas and quarter sessions minutes reads in part, "That all the southern part of Buncombe County beginning on the top of Pisgah Mountain on the Haywood line . . . from . . . the dividing ridge between Hominy Creek and Mills River to the dividing ridge between Mills River and Avery's Creek . . . to the head of Israel's Branch . . . down said Branch to the French Broad River; from . . . opposite the mouth of Cane Creek . . . crossing the river to the mouth of Cane Creek . . . up Cane Creek to the Buncombe Turnpike Road . . . to the top of the Ridge between Cane Creek and Mud Creek . . . taking the main dividing ridge between Cane Creek and Clear Creek waters to the top of the Bear Wallow Mountain on the Rutherford line . . . to the South Carolina line. From thence with the South Carolina line to the Macon line . . . with the Macon line to the Haywood line . . . with the Haywood line to Pisgah, the Beginning, Be & the same is hereby erected into a separate and distinct county by the name of Henderson."

Those present and presiding at the session were Richard Allen, Reuben H. Ballard, William Brittain, John Clayton Sr., John Clayton Jr., Marvel Mills Edney, Lincoln Fullam, Meredith Freeman, Charles Greer, James Hamblin, John Hamilton, John Justice, Samuel King, Joseph B. Thomas, and John Woodfin.

Before 1842, magistrates held courts of pleas and quarter sessions in the home of Hugh Johnson (1838), at the Mills River Academy (1839, 1840, 1841), and at "Osborne's old store house" (1841). By 1842, sessions convened in the new courthouse at Hendersonville.

No town existed in the county before 1841, at which time a referendum election was held to determine the placement of a county seat. A dispute ignited concerning where to locate the seat and build a town. The controversy persisted from 1838 to 1841 between two opposing sides, the River Party and the Road Party. The River Party desired a town near the French Broad River at today's community of Horse Shoe. The Road Party preferred a location alongside the Buncombe Turnpike, a stagecoach route and main thoroughfare through the region at the time. The 1841 election determined the placement of the new town and county seat, with the Road Party winning by 463 to 354 votes.

Judge Mitchell King (1783–1862) of Flat Rock and Charleston conveyed 50 acres, and John Johnson (1787–1848) of the Horse Shoe and Mills River communities and James Brittain (1750/55–1831/32) of Mills River gave an additional 29 acres for the new town. Hendersonville would soon rise from a plateau circumscribed by marshlands and mountains.

James Dyer Justice (1787–1857) surveyed the land, and Charles de Choiseul (c. 1821–1862) laid out the streets and designed the new town. The first building on Main Street went up in 1841, a wooden two-story multipurpose structure located at the corner of Main Street and Chestnut Street (today's First Avenue East). By 1842, the first formal courthouse had been completed. The town of Hendersonville incorporated in 1847.

The townscape soon blossomed with livery stables, harness shops, general stores, a stagecoach inn, boardinghouses, and homes. Commercial enterprises shared the same blocks with dwellings alongside the broad expanse of Main Street.

Even before its establishment, Henderson County drew a multiplicity of personalities and disciplines, from visionaries, trendsetters, and speculators to legislators, business moguls, farmers, and orchardists. The earliest settlers included William Capps, Lambert Clayton, John Peter Corn, William Dalton, Joseph Henry, Noble Johnson, Hiram King, Samuel King, Abraham Kuykendall, Matthew Maybin, John Merrell, James Miller, William Mills, James Murray, Jeremiah Osborne, and Jacob Shipman.

The nature of the county's topography and inherent isolation impeded its progress until the first Western North Carolina Railroad excursions of the Spartanburg–Asheville line reached the region in the late 1800s. Transportation schemes not only opened avenues for technological advancement but also boosted the average standard of living. The region earned fame as a destination resort, the outcome effecting land speculation, which burgeoned over the following decades. Textile mills and logging operations dotted the valleys and slopes. Inns sprang up to lodge sojourners, and certain of those vacationers, taken with the majesty and setting of mountain-fringed vistas, snatched up vast parcels of acreage in what promoters publicized as the "Land of the Sky." Since its pre–Revolutionary War epoch of a sparsely populated and unspoiled milieu, Henderson County has attracted industry, agriculture, and recreation, and it hosts protected forests, campgrounds, retirement communities, and thriving towns and cities. By 2016, the county's population had exceeded 114,000.

The county's major population centers comprise the city of Hendersonville, the towns of Fletcher, Laurel Park, and Mills River, and the village of Flat Rock. Townships include Blue Ridge, Clear Creek, Crab Creek, Edneyville, Green River, and Hoopers Creek. Bat Cave, Chestnut Hill, Mountain Page, Naples, Tuxedo, and Zirconia count among the unincorporated communities. Census-designated communities include Balfour, Barker Heights, Dana, East Flat Rock, Etowah, Fruitland, Gerton, Horse Shoe, Mountain Home, Tuxedo, and Valley Hill.

Home to the annual North Carolina Apple Festival, Henderson County boasts top-producing orchards, floriculture, wineries and breweries, and world-class golf courses and master-planned communities amid accessible natural resources and four seasons of color and clime. The county's spectrum of historic architecture has ranged from log dwellings to Romanesque, neoclassical, Victorian, and Greek Revival styles.

The story of Henderson County's formation and its seminal years has been recounted by many from Sadie Smathers Patton to Louise Howe Bailey. The intention of this book is not to repeat what has flowed from the pens of bygone scribes but rather to share countywide images, several of them never previously published in book form. Illustrated herein is but a sampling of the many business concerns, institutions, and personalities that helped shape the character of Henderson County, North Carolina.

One

The County Seat

River or Road?

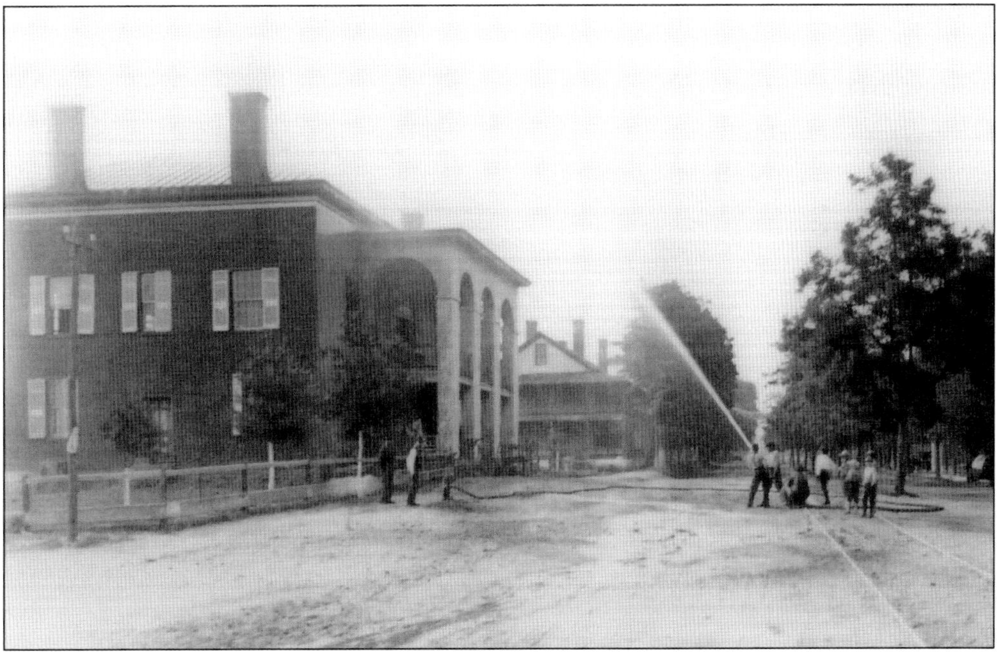

Members of the Hendersonville Fire Department test water pressure in front of the 1842 courthouse. John Mann Kimzey (1809–1876) built this courthouse for $366.70. The building featured a flat roof and arched portico. A more elaborate structure designed by Richard Sharp Smith (1852–1924) replaced Kimzey's building on the same block in 1904–1905. (A.F. Baker photograph, author's collection.)

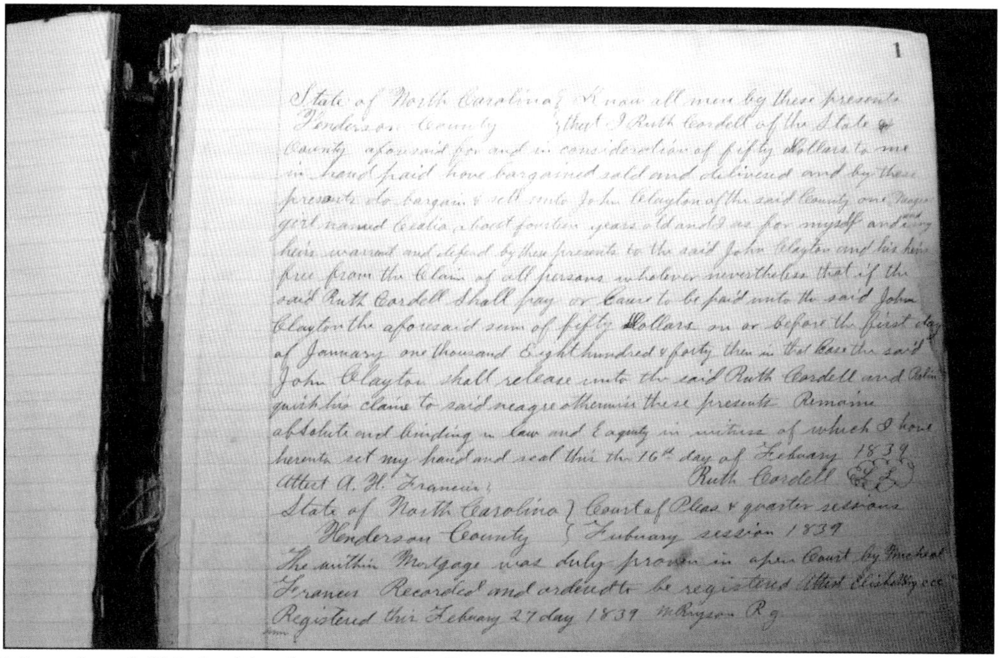

1

State of North Carolina } Know all men by these presents
Henderson County } that I Ruth Cordell of the State &
County aforesaid for and in consideration of fifty Dollars to me
in hand paid have bargained sold and delivered and by these
presents do bargain & sell unto John Clayton of the said County one Negro
girl named Cealia about fourteen years old and do for myself and my
heirs warrant and defend by these presents to the said John Clayton and his heirs
free from the Claim of all persons whatever nevertheless that if the
said Ruth Cordell shall pay or Cause to be paid unto the said John
Clayton the aforesaid sum of fifty Dollars on or before the first day
of January one thousand Eight hundred & forty then in that Case the said
John Clayton shall release unto the said Ruth Cordell and Robin
quit his claim to said negro otherwise these presents Remain
absolute and binding in law and Equity in witness of which I have
hereunto set my hand and seal this the 16th day of February 1839
Attest A. H. Francis   Ruth Cordell (Seal)
State of North Carolina } Court of Pleas & quarter sessions
Henderson County } February session 1839
The within Mortgage was duly proven in open Court by Micheal
Francis Recorded and ordered to be registered Attest [illegible] c.c.c.
Registered this February 27 day 1839 M. Bryson R.g.

More than 1,000 deed books occupy the Register of Deeds office in the Henderson County Courthouse. The first entry (*Record of Deeds*, book I, page 1; registered February 27, 1839) was not for an exchange of land but for "one negro girl named Cealia about 14 years old." (Photograph by the author.)

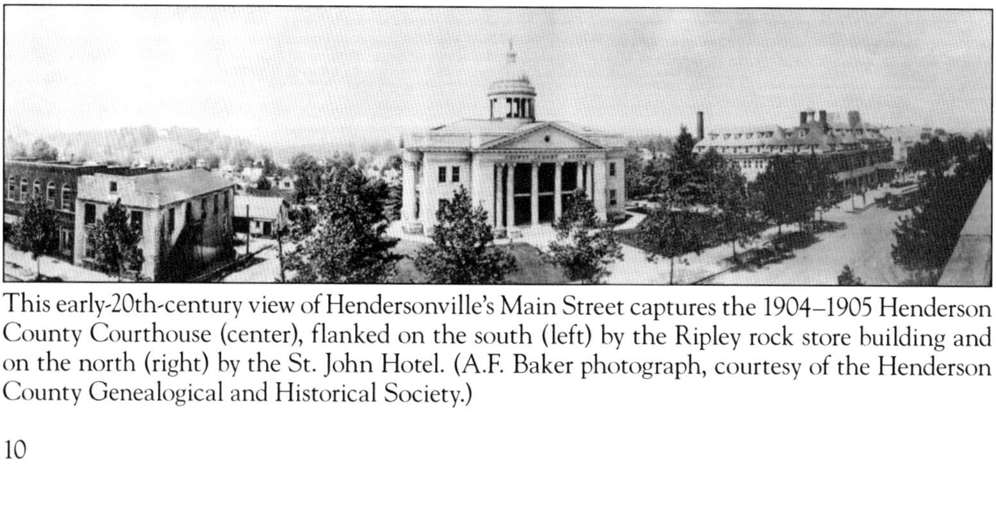

This early-20th-century view of Hendersonville's Main Street captures the 1904–1905 Henderson County Courthouse (center), flanked on the south (left) by the Ripley rock store building and on the north (right) by the St. John Hotel. (A.F. Baker photograph, courtesy of the Henderson County Genealogical and Historical Society.)

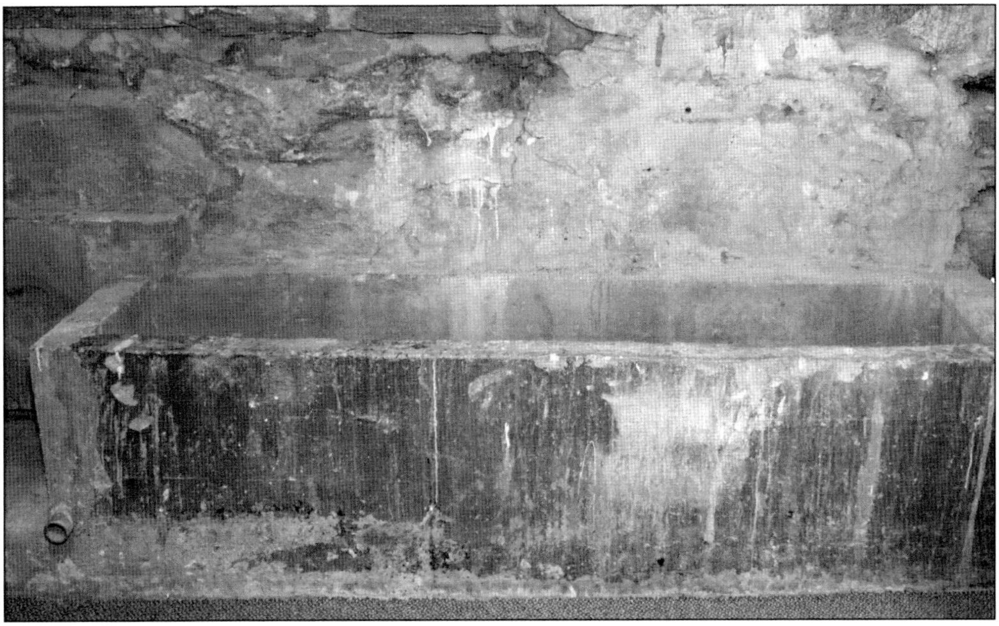

The trough for watering horses at Henderson County's historic courthouse reminds modern visitors of an era when travel from the far reaches of the county to the county seat by horseback or carriage exhausted the good part of a day. (Photograph by the author.)

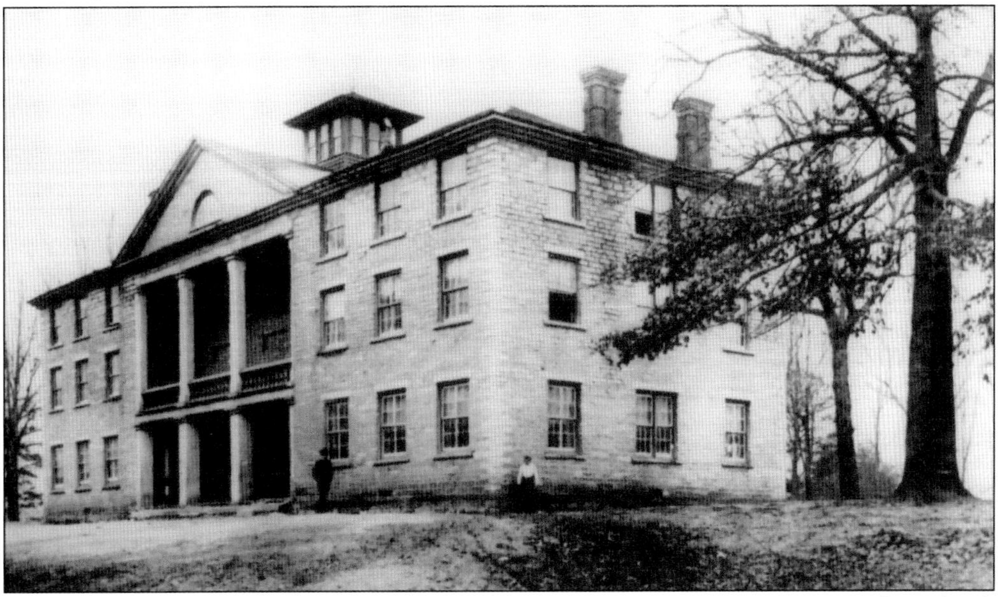

Named for Emily Chubbuck Judson (1817–1854), the wife of a Baptist missionary, this school, chartered in 1861 as Judson Female College, later became coeducational. The Western North Carolina Educational Company established a school in the building, which opened in 1882. In 1894, the Reverend George H. Detwiler (1854–1914) leased it for his nonsectarian Christian school. The City of Hendersonville sold the property to Dr. Guy Dixon (1877–1952), who operated a sanitarium in the building. In 1963, the city razed the structure, which stood at the northwest corner of Fleming Street and Third Avenue, to make way for a federal housing project. (Courtesy of the Henderson County Genealogical and Historical Society.)

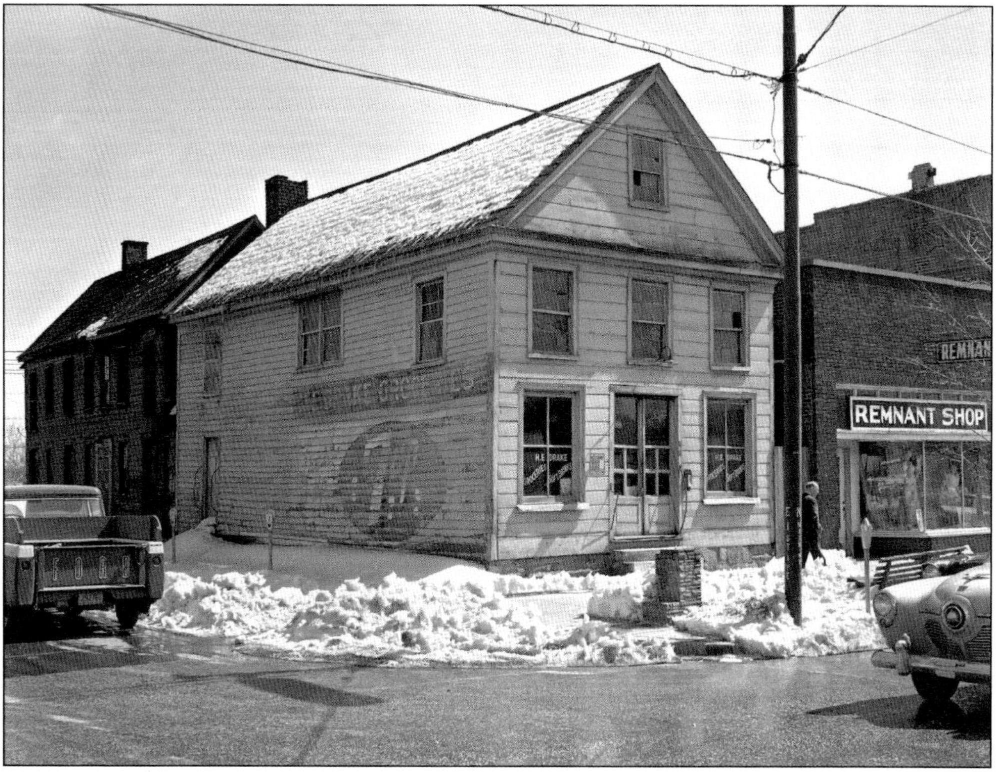

This frame building stood at the southeast corner of Chestnut Street (First Avenue) and Main Street. The structure, built in 1841, served as Hendersonville's first store and post office, an apothecary shop, an infirmary, Baker's Art Gallery, a saloon, and M.M. Shepherd Dry Goods. The last occupant, Hezekiah Elezer "Skin" Drake (1890–1964) operated a general store in the building, which was razed in 1962. Boarders lodged in the structure behind the store. The jockey lot—a produce exchange—occupied the back lot, facing King Street. A brick office building now stands on the footprint of the old structures. (Lucile Stepp Ray photograph, courtesy of the Henderson County Genealogical and Historical Society.)

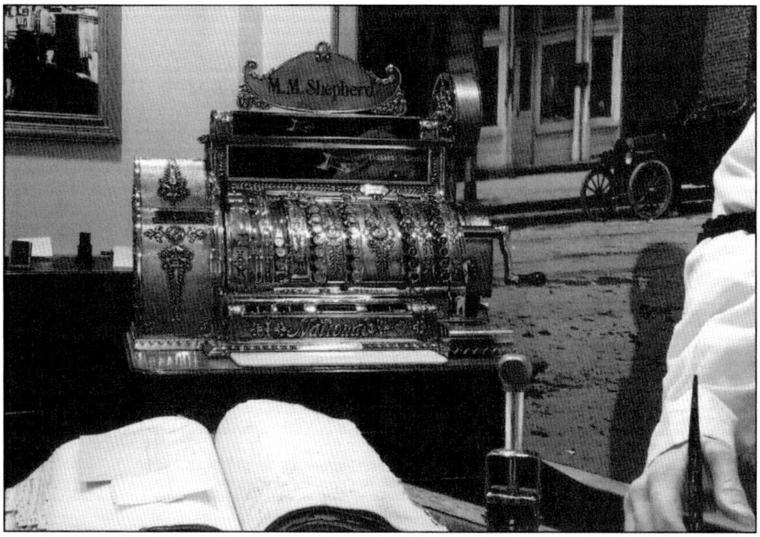

The M.M. Shepherd Dry Goods store's cash register may be found on display at the Henderson County Heritage Museum. (Photograph by the author.)

Hendersonville's first city hall stood on the east side of Main Street between Fourth and Fifth Avenues. This 1893 Romanesque-style structure accommodated a 400-seat opera house, city offices, and police and fire departments. Bells sounded from the turrets. By 1914, Raleigh condemned the building, which was razed in 1925. (A.F. Baker photograph, courtesy of the Henderson County Genealogical and Historical Society.)

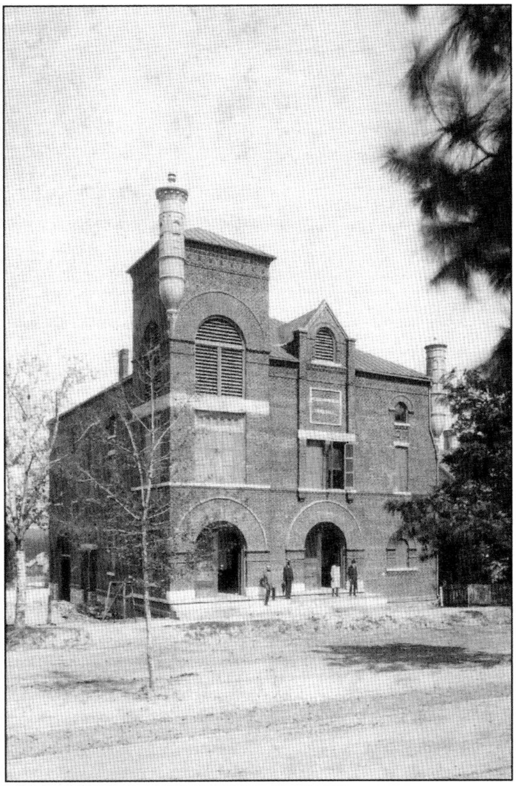

In this 1925 photograph of the Hendersonville Police Department, from left to right are (first row) Volney Condorcet Voltaire Shepherd (in a straw hat), Bill Powers (child), and Otis Powers; (second row) Fred Edney, Clarence Edney, Gaston Freeman, Jess Maxwell, Seth Edmundson, Will Davis, and Jeter Lewis. (Courtesy of the Henderson County Genealogical and Historical Society.)

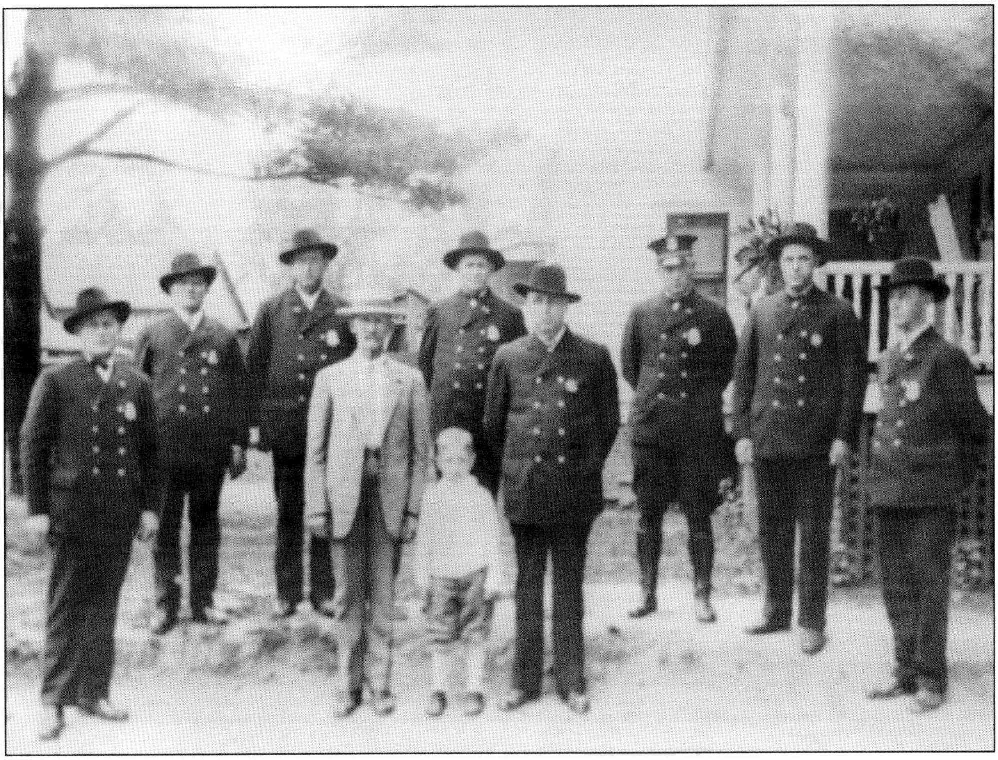

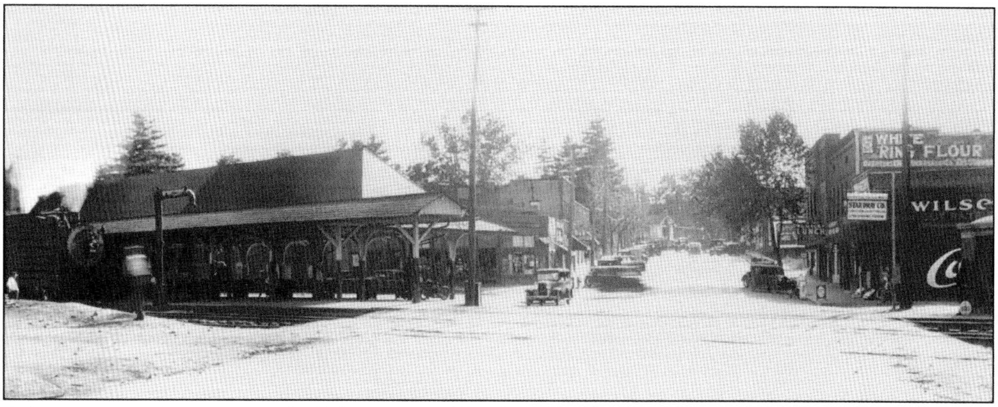

A locomotive-drawn train, far left, stops at Hendersonville's Southern Railway station. The first passenger train pulled into town on June 21, 1879, followed by a celebratory arrival from Spartanburg, South Carolina, on July 4, 1879. Passenger service ceased in 1968. (Author's collection.)

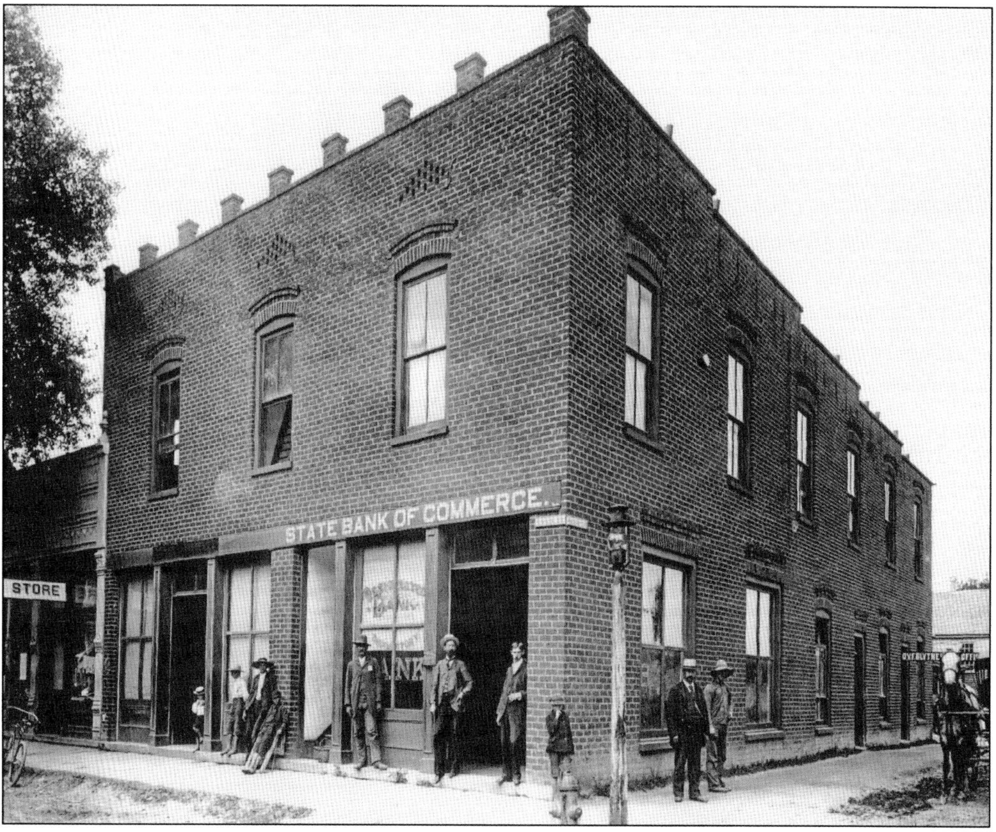

The Cole Bank building, named for its founder, Dr. George Henry Phillip Cole (1856–1924), hosted the first official bank in Hendersonville. This 1880s structure stands at the southwest corner of Fourth Avenue and Main Street. Tenants have included the State Bank of Commerce, a post office (1905–14), Rose Pharmacy, and currently, Mountain Deli and the Doll Clothes Factory. (Courtesy of the Henderson County Genealogical and Historical Society.)

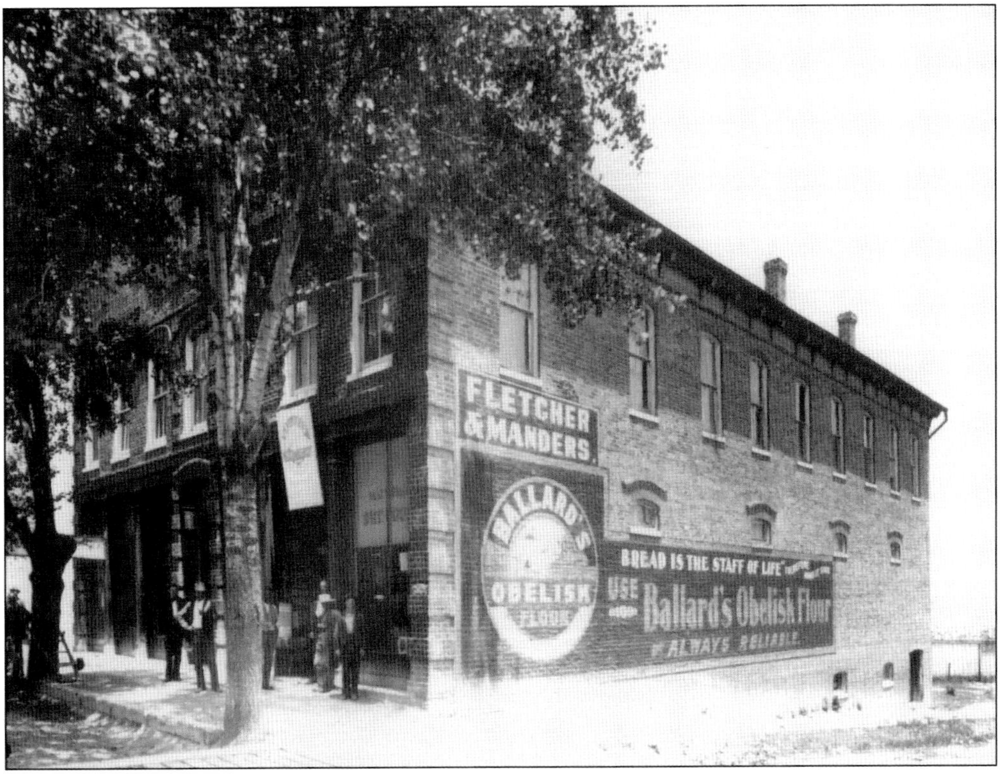

Confederate veteran Capt. Marion Columbus Toms arrived in Hendersonville at the end of the Civil War to work for Valentine Ripley in his general store. The business would later become Ripley & Toms. Toms's new store building, pictured here, was constructed in 1906 at Main and College Streets (Third Avenue East). The building housed M.C. Toms's Dry Goods. Hannah Flanagan's Pub currently occupies the street level. (Courtesy of Jim Toms.)

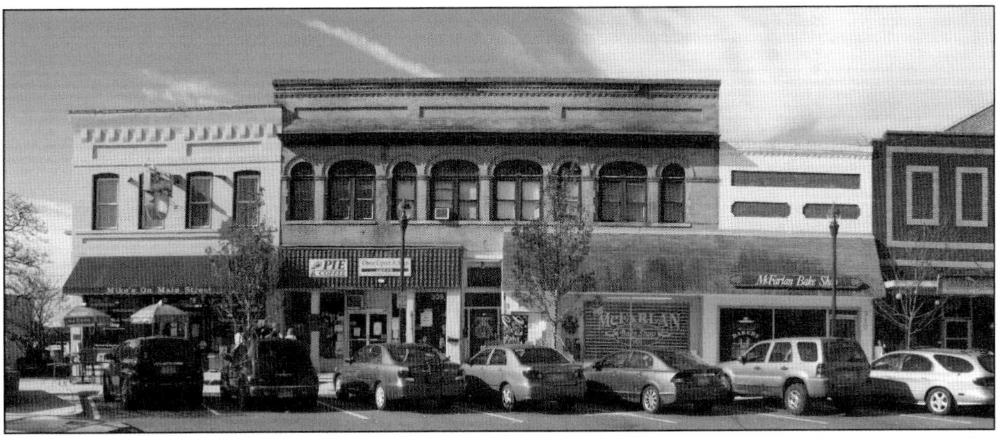

This building at 302–309 North Main Street replaced an older wooden structure known as the "Twyford/Stepp-Bailey-Clarke building and a vacant lot between it and the Justus Pharmacy," according to a *French Broad Hustler* notice on September 19, 1907. Richard Sharp Smith designed the building. Tenants have included surveyor G.W. Justice, Citizens Bank of Hendersonville, Duke Power Company, and the telephone company. McFarlan Bake Shop now occupies the street level. (Photograph by the author.)

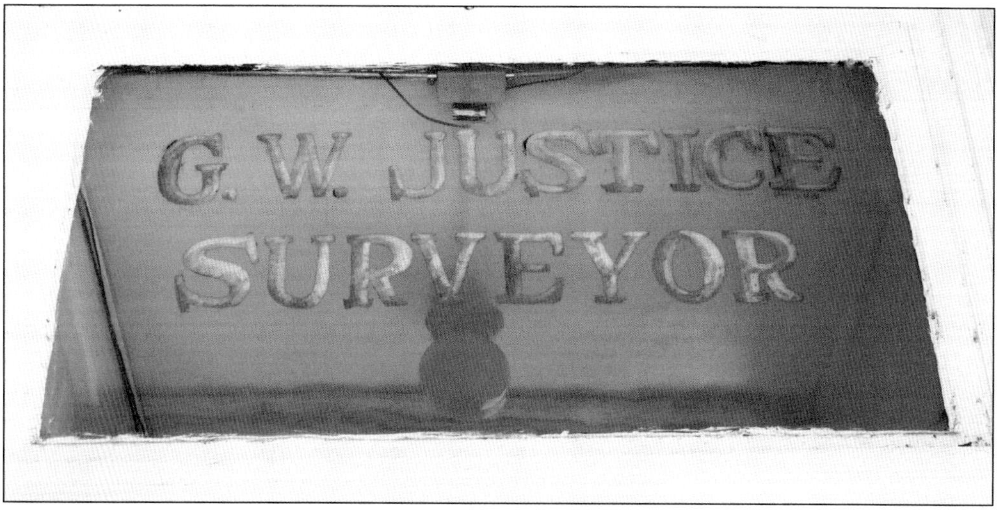

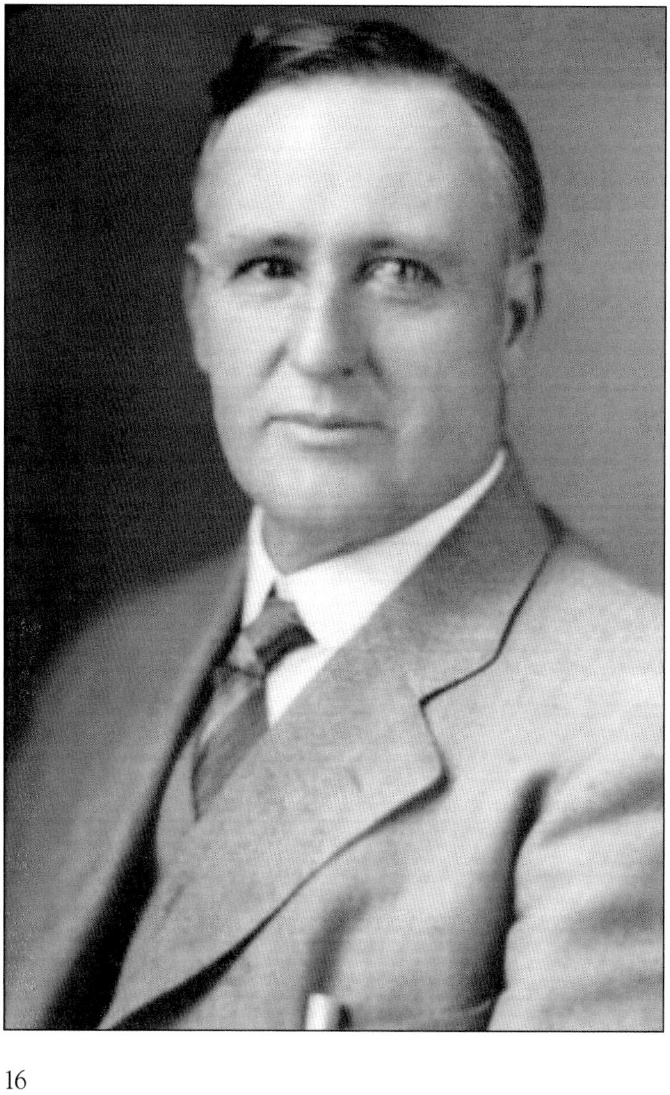

Lettering painted on a transom window at 309 North Main Street can still be seen. George Washington Justice (1877–1948), pictured at left, kept an office upstairs. Justice worked as a surveyor, county commissioner, civil engineer, and Hendersonville's first city manager. Justice's work included surveying the tract of land that would become Oakdale Cemetery. (Above, photograph by the author; left, courtesy of Leon and Jean Pace.)

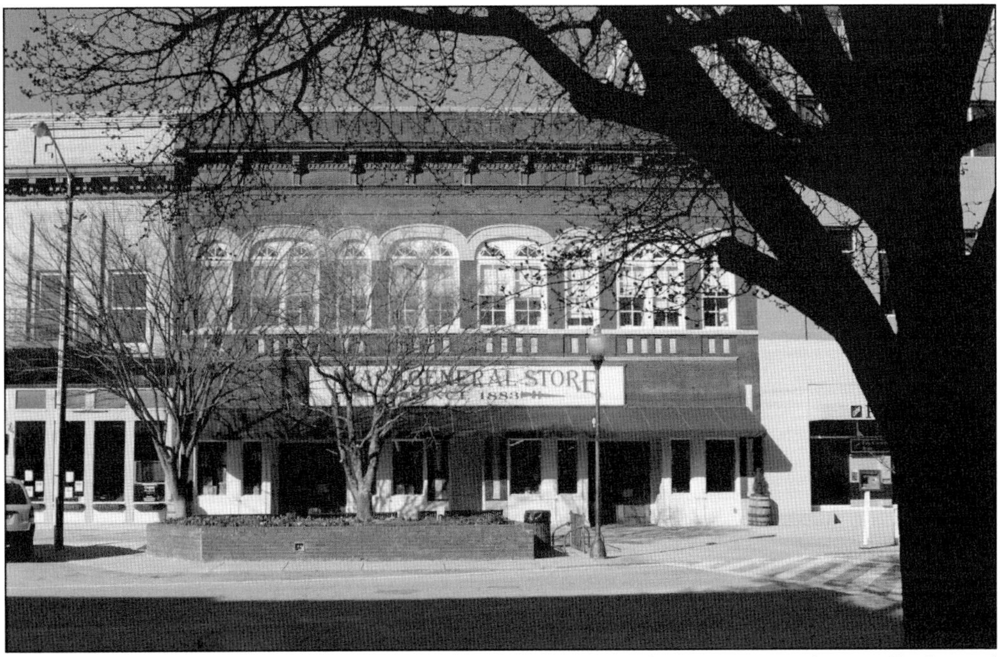

The c. 1910 Syndicate Building, at 529 North Main Street in downtown Hendersonville, hosted several businesses, including Maxwell & Brown and S.J. Harris's Pure Food Store. Early-20th-century advertising discloses that Maxwell & Brown sold "fancy groceries." The building also hosted John Henry Hines (a harness maker), Freeze Drug Store, Potts 5¢ & 10¢, Woodmen of the World (a benevolent secret society), and Jack Schulman's Clothing. It currently houses Mast General Store. (Photograph by the author.)

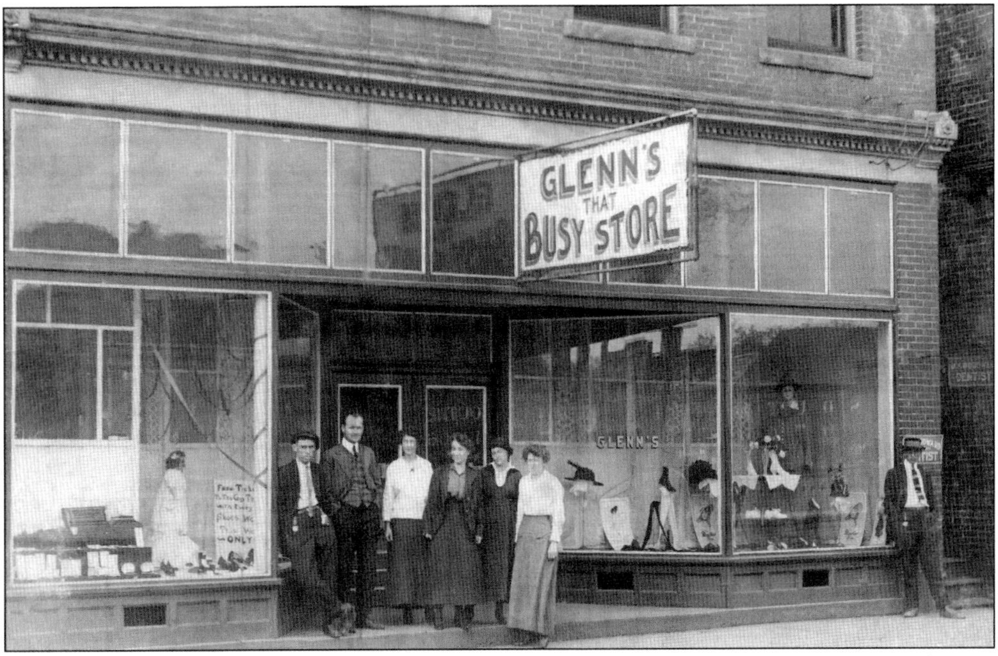

The c. 1915 Glenn's Store occupied 427 North Main Street with John Glenn (1864–1923) as its proprietor. (Courtesy of the Henderson County Genealogical and Historical Society.)

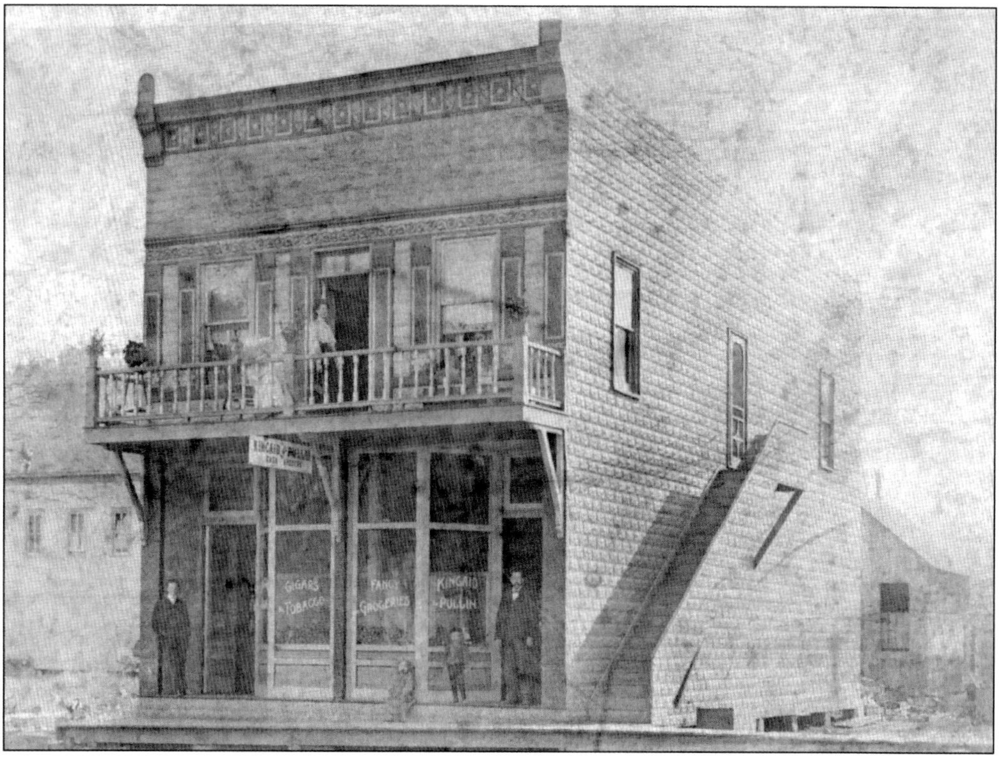

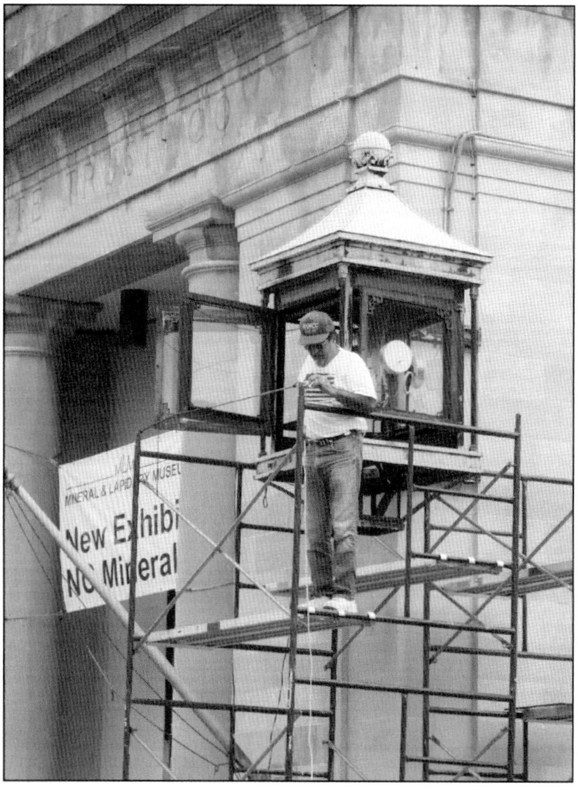

Kincaid and Pullin Cash Grocers stood at 612 North Main Street. Early city directories list Forest Houston Kincaid (1878–1928) and John David Pullin (1871–1950) as proprietors of this store. By the 1920s, directories recorded the establishment as "Kincaid & Son (Forest H. and Houston P.)." (Courtesy of the Henderson County Genealogical and Historical Society.)

Wayne Arcuri of the National Association of Watch & Clock Collectors helped refurbish the 1927 McClintock Clock in September 2013. The clock graces the Erle Stillwell–designed Citizen's National Bank building, which has hosted various banking institutions at the northeast corner of Fourth Avenue and Main Street since its completion in 1921. The Henderson County Genealogical and Historical Society and the Mineral and Lapidary Museum currently occupy the building. (Photograph by the author.)

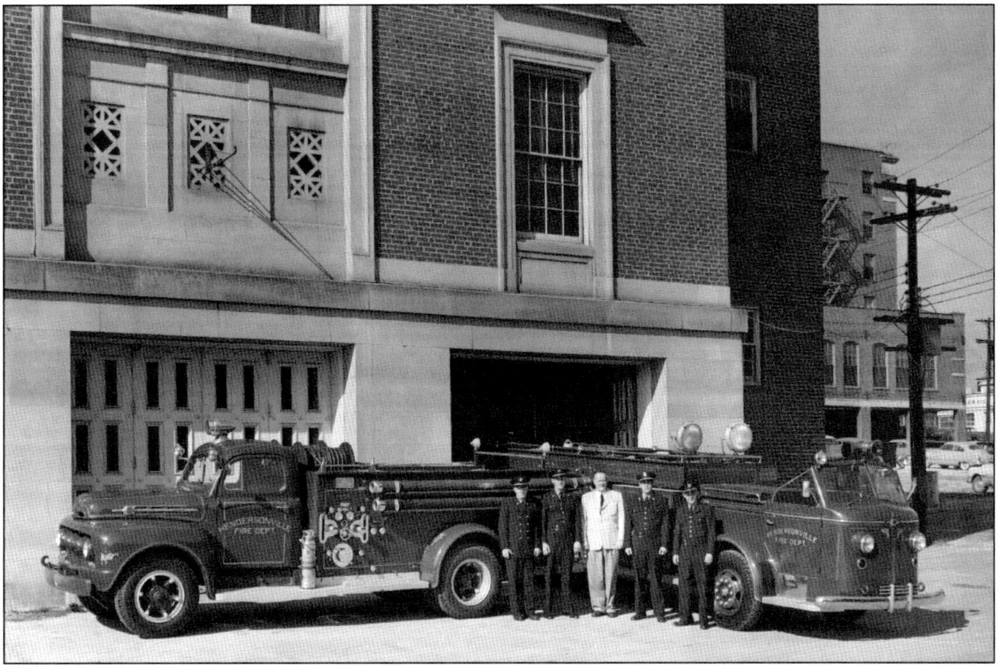

Hendersonville City Hall at one time included a fire department with bay doors opening onto King Street. Albert Victor Edwards (1891–1971), pictured at center, was the longest-serving mayor in Hendersonville (1932–1969). The fire department occupied Hendersonville's first city hall on Main Street from 1893 to 1925 before moving to this building, designed by Erle G. Stillwell (1885–1978), which was dedicated in 1928. The fire department moved to new quarters at Boyd Park in 2001. (Ed Hunnicutt photograph, courtesy of the Henderson County Genealogical and Historical Society.)

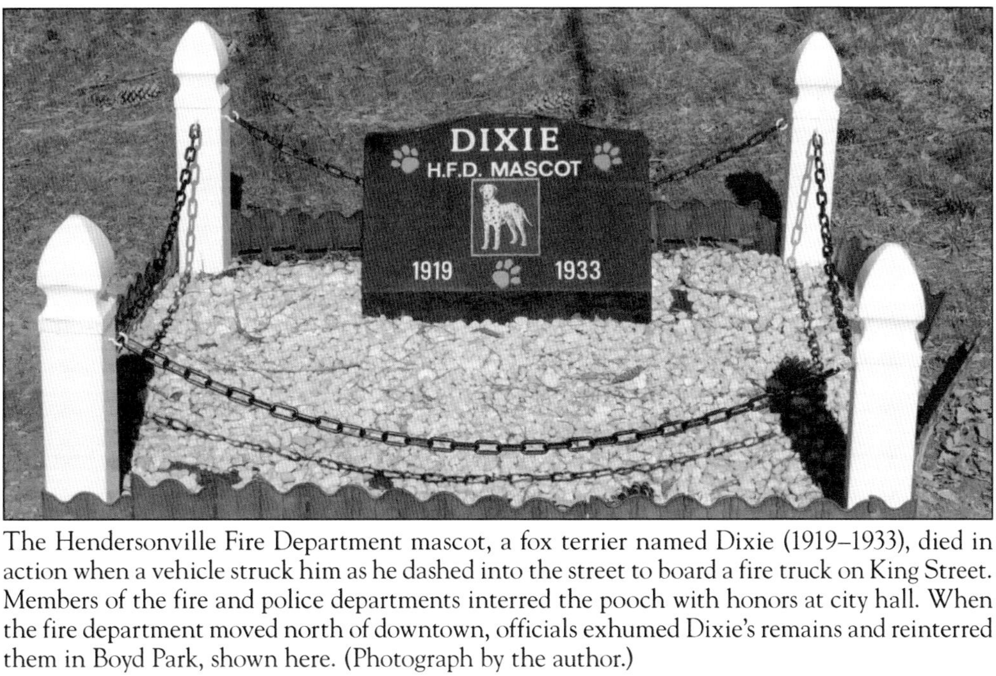

The Hendersonville Fire Department mascot, a fox terrier named Dixie (1919–1933), died in action when a vehicle struck him as he dashed into the street to board a fire truck on King Street. Members of the fire and police departments interred the pooch with honors at city hall. When the fire department moved north of downtown, officials exhumed Dixie's remains and reinterred them in Boyd Park, shown here. (Photograph by the author.)

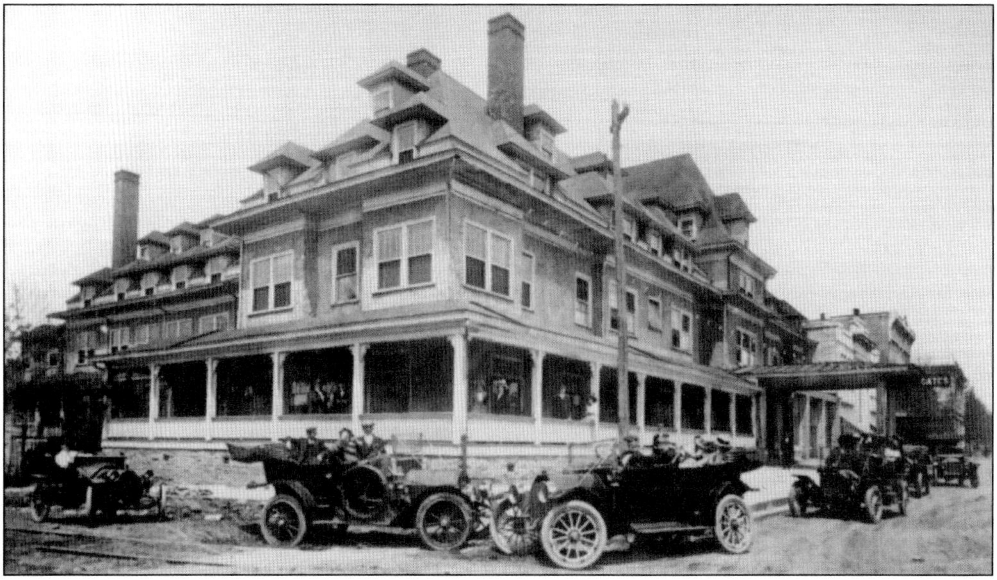

The grand hotel at the northwest corner of Hendersonville's Main Street and Second Avenue began as a much smaller stagecoach inn: the Ripley House, owned by Valentine Ripley (1807–1879). Successive owners expanded the inn with 150 guest rooms and a pebble-dashed exterior and renamed it the Globe, the Imperial, the Gates, and finally, the St. John. George Vanderbilt lodged there during construction of his Biltmore House. (Note the trolley tracks in the lower-left foreground.) The hotel burned to the ground in 1915. Today, the Nuckolls Building (1945), the former Cooley Brothers dry-cleaning building, and Four Seasons Hospice Home Store occupy the site. (Courtesy of Knox Crowell.)

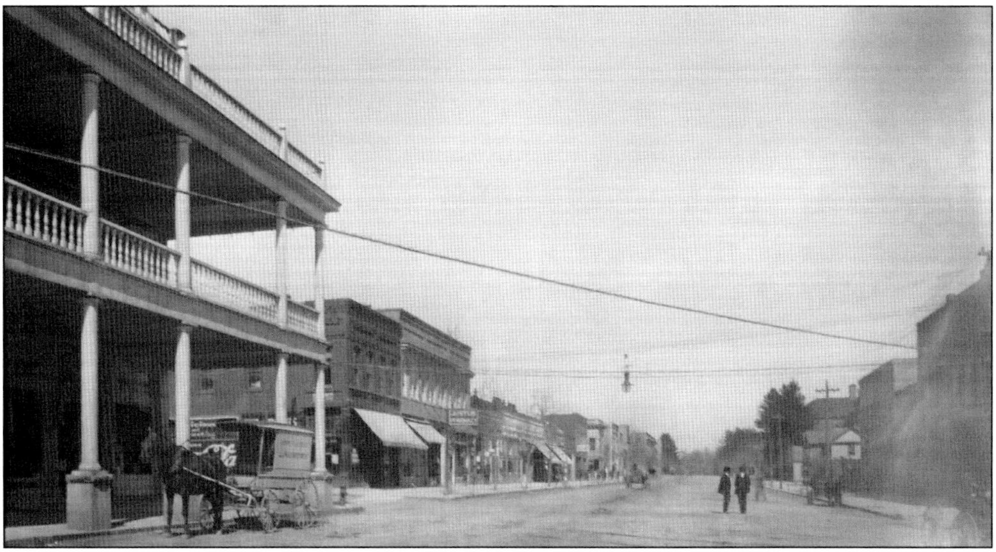

Called the Blue Ridge Inn when built in the late 1800s, this hotel later operated as the Majestic Hotel. It stood at the southwest corner of Third Avenue and Main Street. Dr. William Hicks Justus (1857–1933) took over the business of Dr. Columbus Few (1848–1923), a pharmacy that once occupied a corner in the street level of this hotel. Justus later built his own pharmacy building—Justus Rexall Store, pictured here just right of the hotel—on the next corner north, occupied today by Mike's on Main. (A.F. Baker photograph, author's collection.)

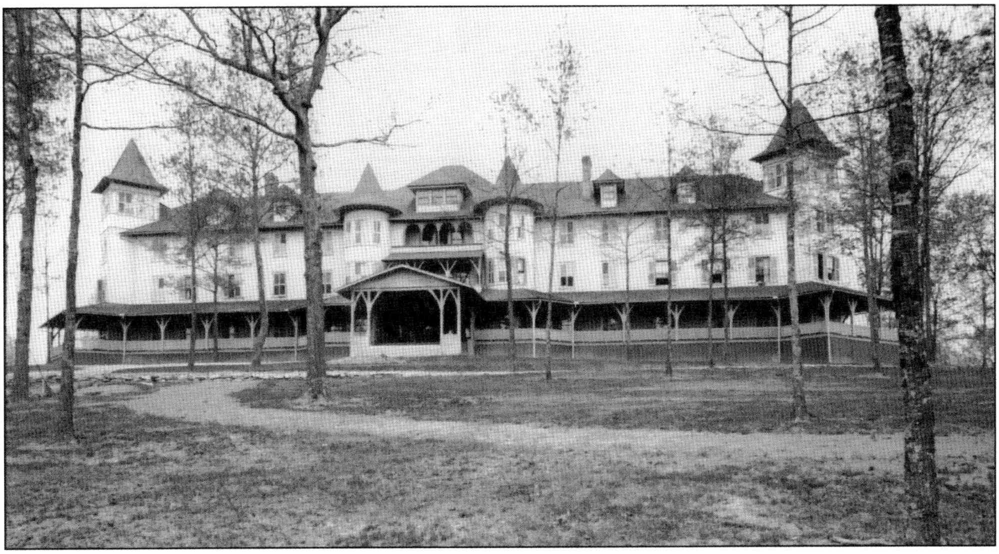

David Henry Wheeler (1830–1906), a South Carolina financier, owned the Wheeler Hotel. The hotel, completed in 1895, featured 100 rooms, a livery stable, and a dance pavilion. Owners renamed the hotel Carolina Terrace and then the Terrace. The dance pavilion burned in 1927, and the hotel burned to the ground in 1930. Bruce Drysdale Elementary School, opened in 1960, now stands on this site. (Courtesy of the Henderson County Genealogical and Historical Society.)

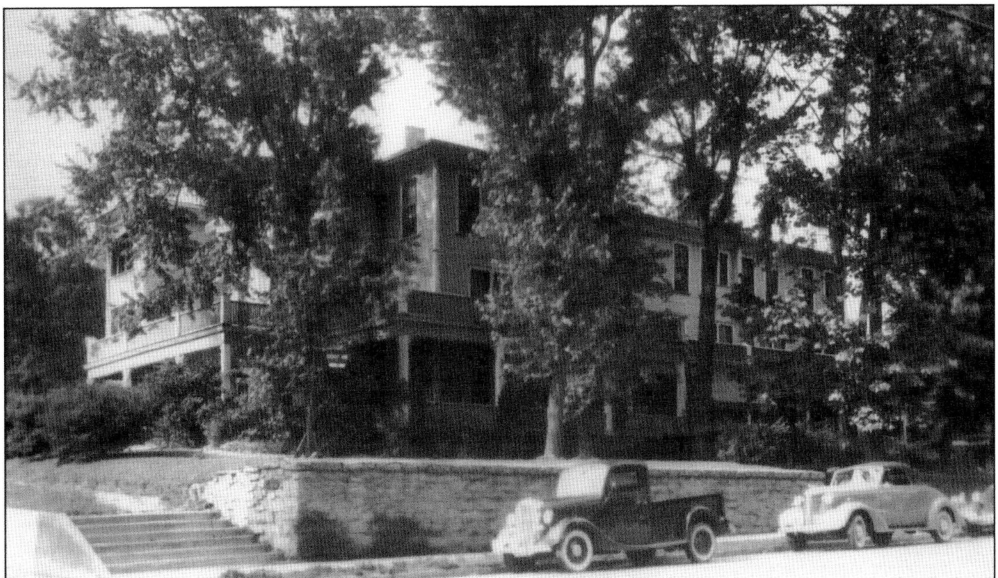

A popular inn during the Roaring Twenties and beyond, the Kentucky Home once stood near the corner of Fourth Avenue and Washington Street. The hotel quickly became renowned for celebrity lodgers and its excellent table fare, prepared by owner Annie M. Gover (1870–1954), a widow from Kentucky. In its heyday, this facility served as the city's only year-round hotel. Boxing champion Jack Dempsey and his movie queen wife, Estelle Taylor, lodged there in the spring of 1926 when promoters hired Dempsey as a publicity attraction to boost land sales in Laurel Park. City officials razed the building in 1962 to make room for a parking lot. (Courtesy of the Henderson County Genealogical and Historical Society.)

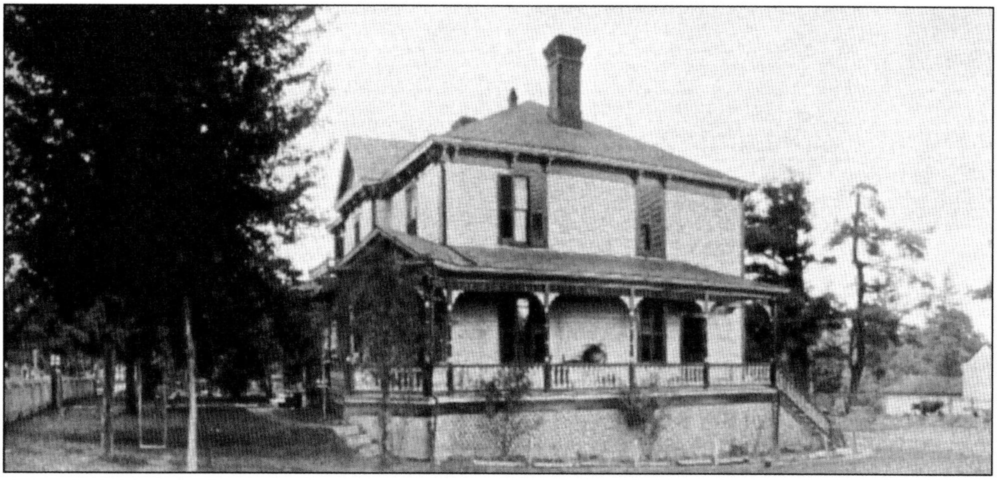

Since 1929, the Skyland Hotel has stood on the site of this Victorian home owned by Dr. William Hicks Justus, owner of Justus Rexall Pharmacy. (Courtesy of Margaret Justus Prim.)

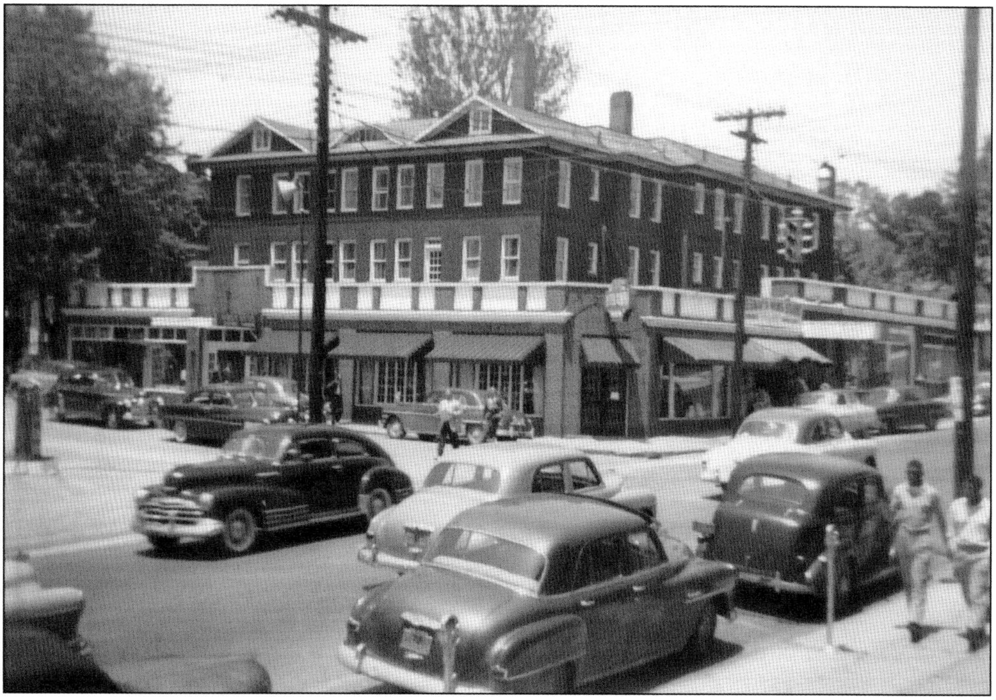

The 32-room Hodgewell Hotel stood at the northwest corner of Fourth Avenue and Church Street. Erle G. Stillwell designed the street-level shops for Samuel Thompson Hodges Jr. (1873–1930). Hotel stories were added later. Louella Ames of St. Petersburg, Florida, bought the property and named it Hotel Ames. Jennie Bowen purchased the hotel in 1944 and renamed it the Bowen. Street-level shops included a real estate office, the radio station WHKP, a newsstand, and an optometrist's office. Bowen's Land O' Sky Fashions shop also occupied one of the spaces. After the hotel closed in 1962, the City of Hendersonville bought and razed it to make a parking lot. (Courtesy of the Henderson County Genealogical and Historical Society.)

The 1951 North Carolina Apple Festival queen's court float glides past Efird's Department Store on Main Street at Fourth Avenue East. Pictured on the left are the State Trust Company/ First Citizens Bank building (1921) and the McClintock Clock (1927). (Courtesy of the Henderson County Genealogical and Historical Society.)

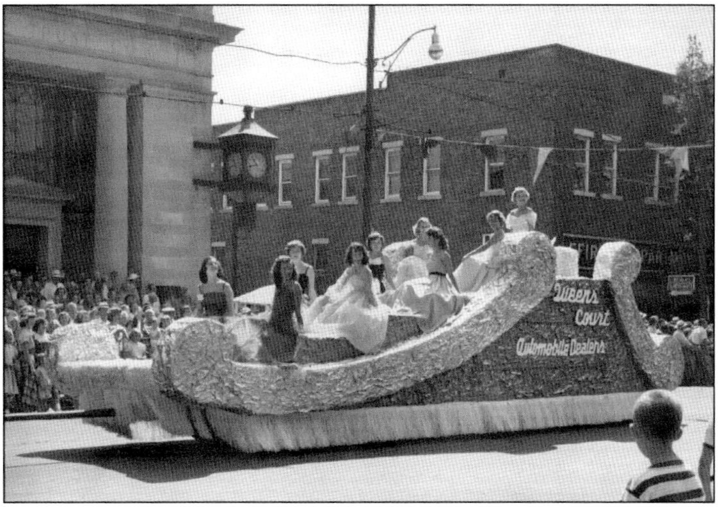

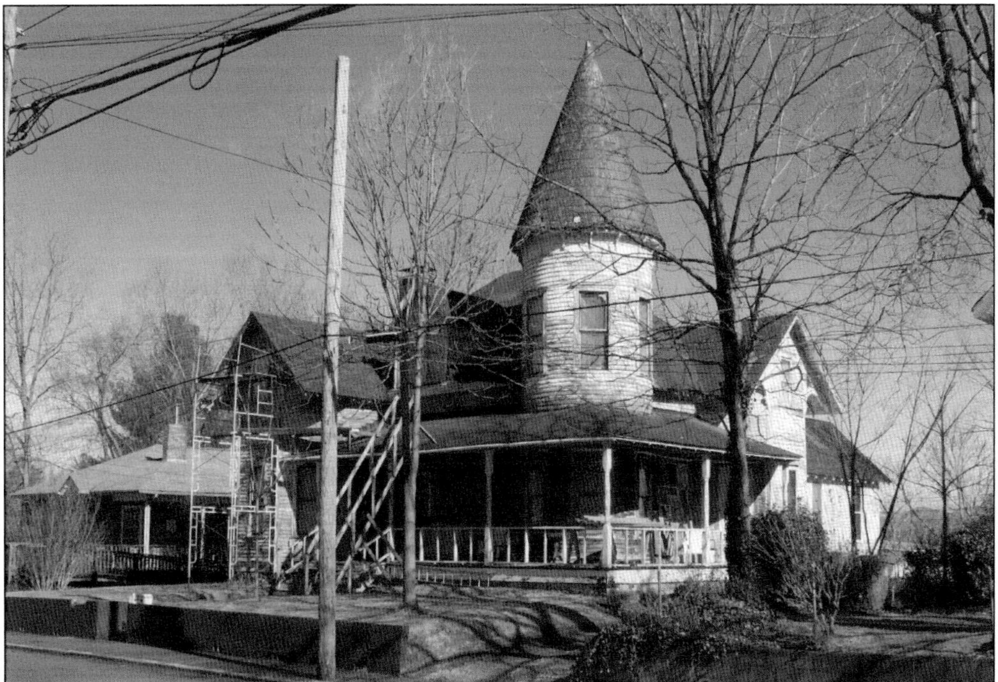

Otto Ebenezer Blythe (1868–1955) built this Queen Anne home for Capt. Joseph William Bailey (1868–1942) on Seventh Avenue. Ulysses M. Orr (1877–1955) later moved the house with log rollers to North Grove Street—a move attributed to inflated tax values in the Seventh Avenue business district. Augusta C. Burton Robards (1838–1926) and then William Preston Lane (1846–1928) next owned the house. The Lanes accepted boarders and named this home the Colorado. Robert Patterson Freeman (1875–1974) and Margaret Esther Freeman (1880–1967), who next owned the home, were among the first in Hendersonville to have a telephone, electric lights, and running water. Their son Thomas Benjamin Freeman (1907–1999) later operated his Mountain Beverage Sales from the home. (Photograph by the author.)

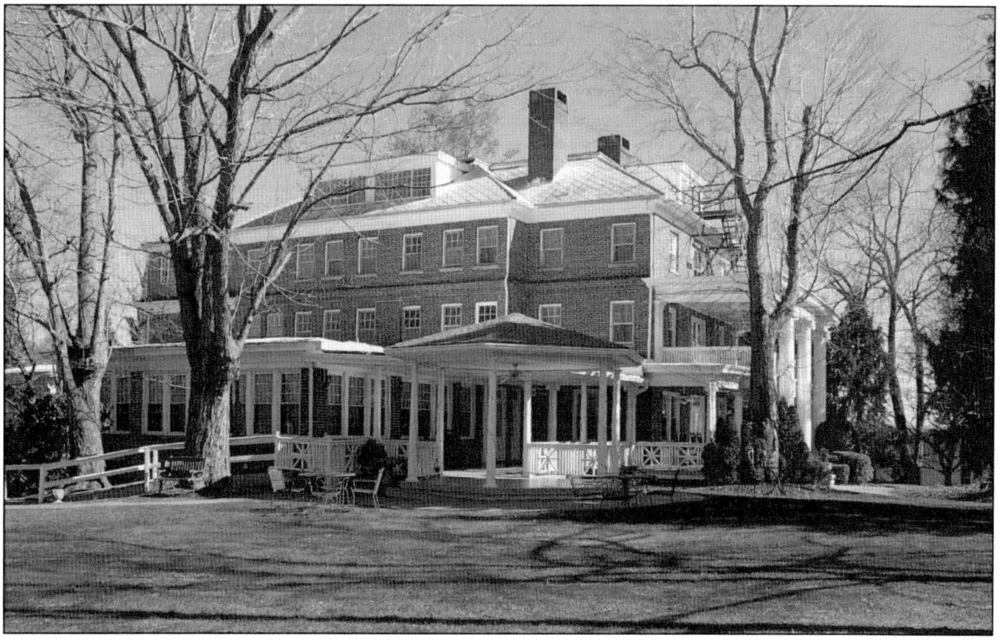

The Hendersonville architectural firm of Meyer & Stillwell designed the Cedars in 1913. Erle G. Stillwell designed the later additions. In 1914, Capt. Joseph William Bailey had this boardinghouse built on Seventh Avenue West at the prompting of his wife, Jennie. The building currently supplies a venue for receptions and club meetings. (Photograph by the author.)

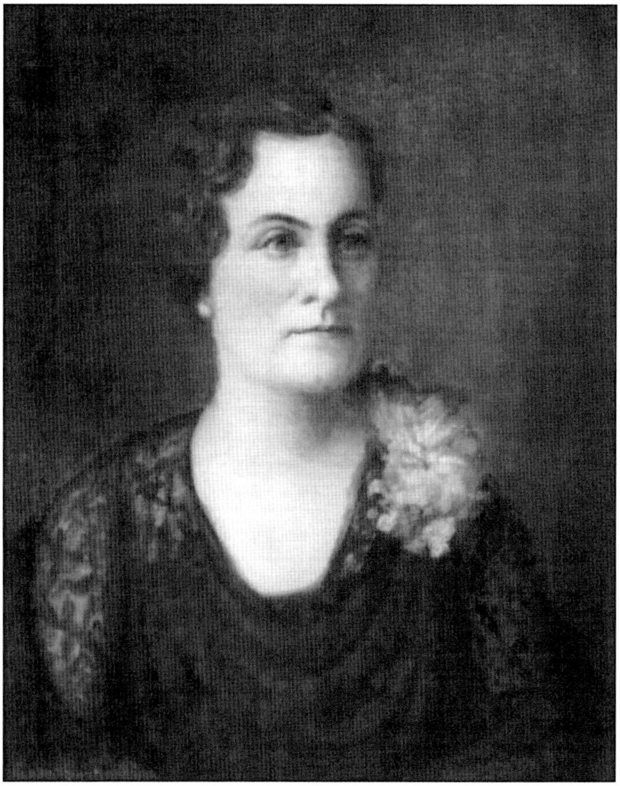

Acclaimed for her welcoming personality, Jennie Collins Bailey (1874–1965) owned and operated the Cedars guest home. An early member of the Hendersonville Women's Club, she involved herself in civic affairs. She married Southern Railway agent Joseph William Bailey (1870–1942). (Painting by Cornelius Hawkins, courtesy of Tommy Shipman.)

Oklawaha, the Victorian home of Capt. Marion Columbus Toms, stood atop the elevation still known as Toms Hill above the "Busy Bend" of Kanuga Road. Three lily ponds graced the foot of the hill in what was known as Toms Park. The ponds were filled in after 1957, after which a mini-train on a circular track was installed for children. In 1965, shuffleboard courts replaced the train. The Toms Park Activity Center, built in 1990, occupies the space today. The center was renamed Whitmire Activity Center in 1999 to honor former mayor Boyce A. Whitmire Sr. (1905–1989). (Photograph by Hugh Jon Barbour, courtesy of the Henderson County Genealogical and Historical Society.)

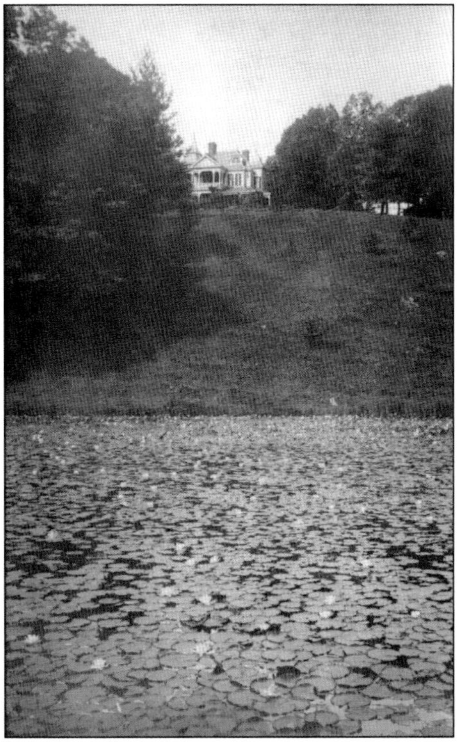

Dr. Joseph Grayson Waldrop (1847–1913), his wife, Nancy Anna Carpenter Waldrop (1863–1941), and their 11 children pose in front of their home Maple Grove on Washington Street. After Dr. Waldrop died, Nancy operated Maple Grove as a boardinghouse. (Courtesy of Pat Waldrop Buck.)

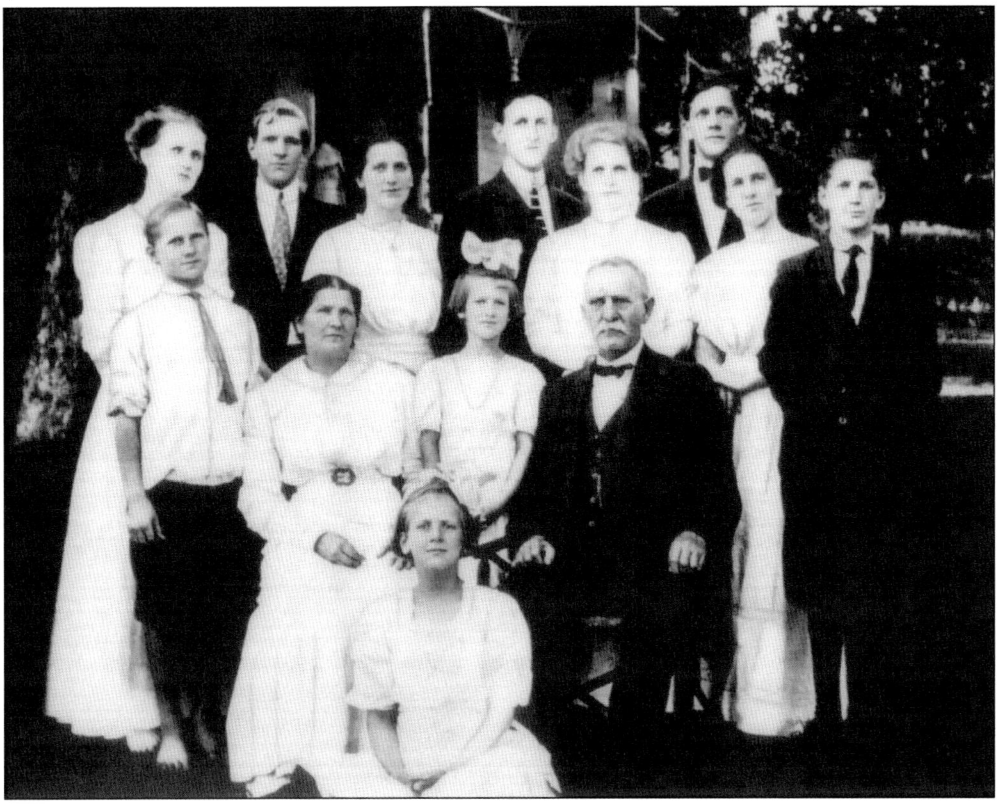

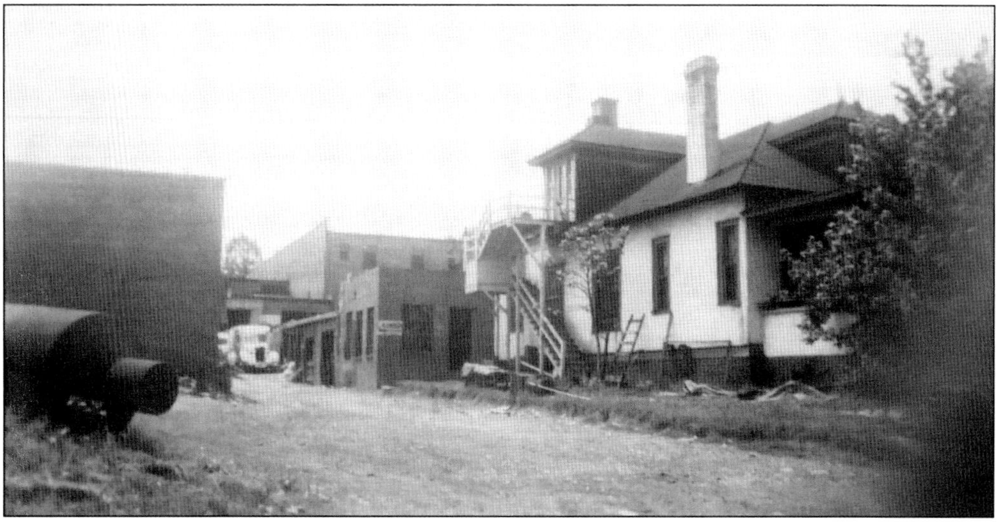

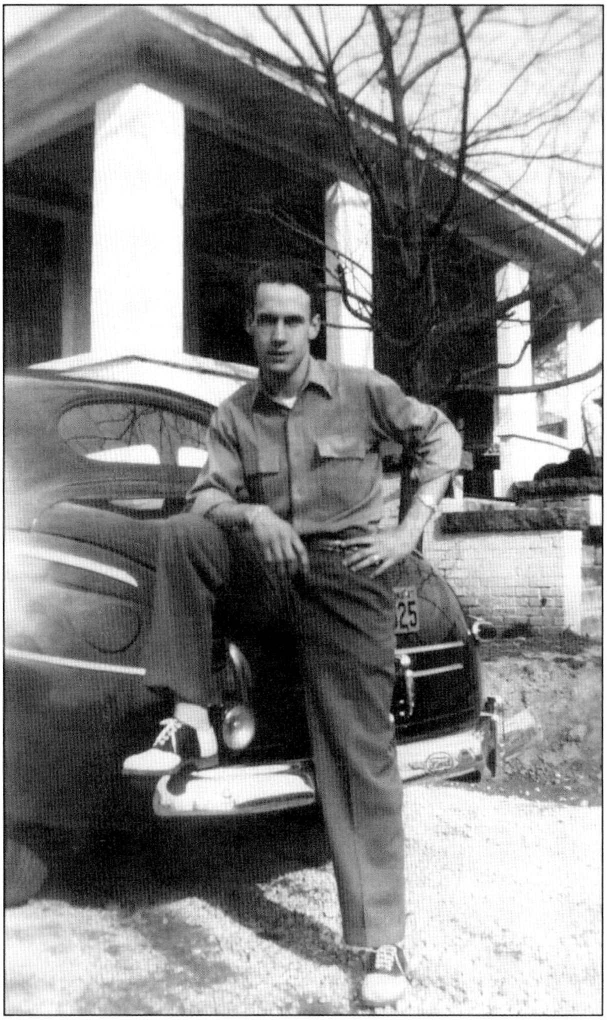

A c. 1919 home known as Honeymoon Cottage once stood near the northwest corner of Fourth Avenue and King Street. The stucco-swathed home featured a sleeping porch in its attic. The house was later moved to a lot on the east side of King Street and was razed in 1974. (Courtesy of Jeff Miller.)

Hubert Eugene "Bert" Miller (1921–2002) poses in front of his childhood home, Honeymoon Cottage. Bert carried on the dry-cleaning business founded in 1915 by his father, Norman W. Miller Sr. (1892–1974). (Courtesy of Jeff Miller.)

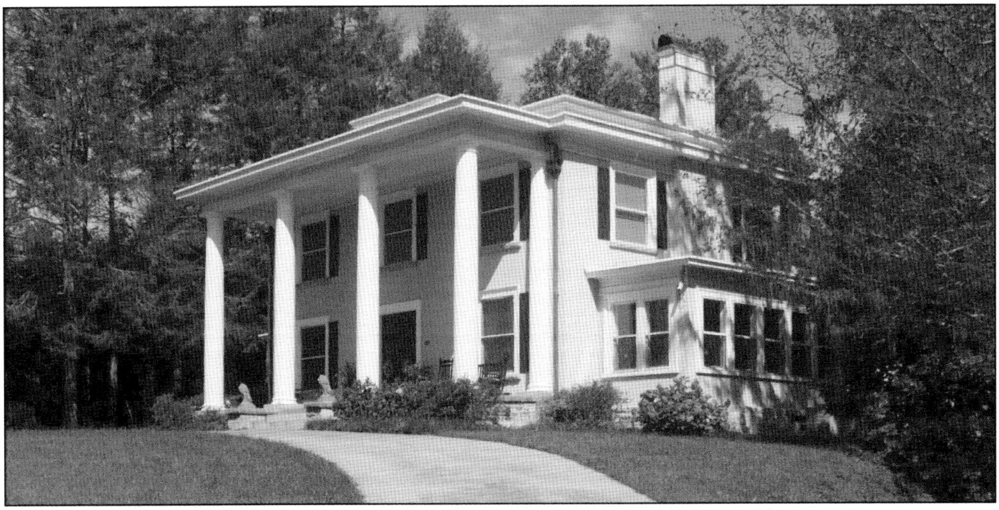

Birdie Bella West (1887–1978) owned La Vogue Millinery on Hendersonville's North Main Street. The shop was later renamed La Vogue Hat Shop and then La Vogue Women's Wear. Birdie carried hats from prominent milliners as well as her own designs and specialized in wedding veils. When West lost her shop because of financial difficulties, a pair of gentlemen bought her this neoclassical mansion—Westhaven on Fifth Avenue West—from which West sold her merchandise and let out rooms. (Photograph by the author.)

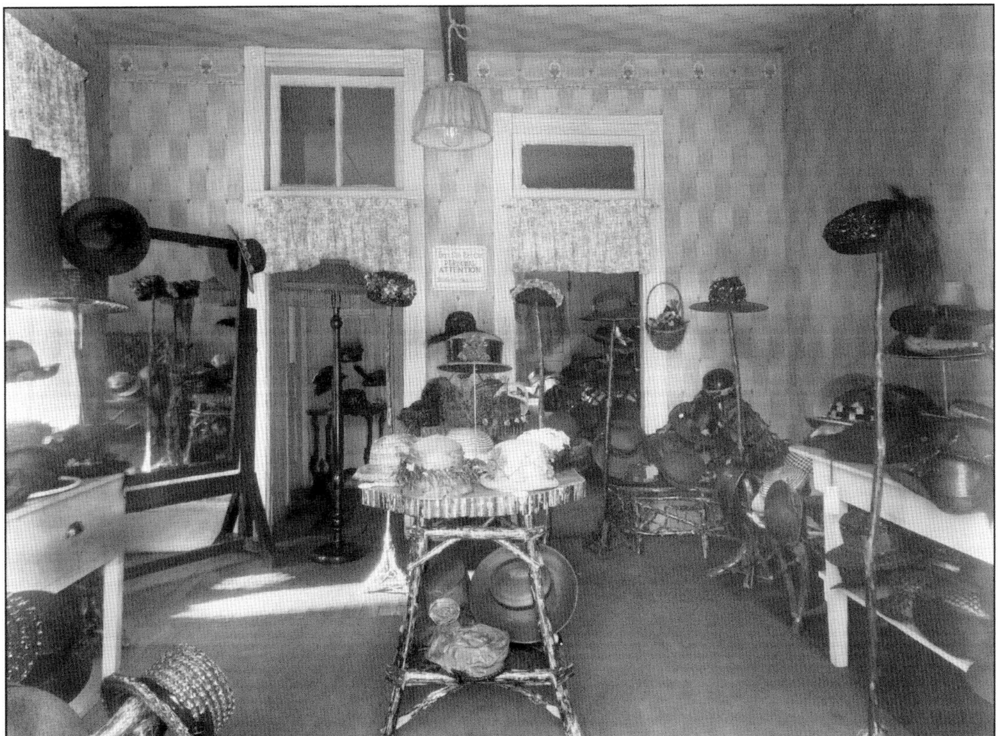

After moving her business from Main Street, Birdie West operated her millinery shop from this dining room in the mansion known as Westhaven. (Courtesy of the Baker-Barber Collection, Community Foundation of Henderson County, Henderson County Public Library.)

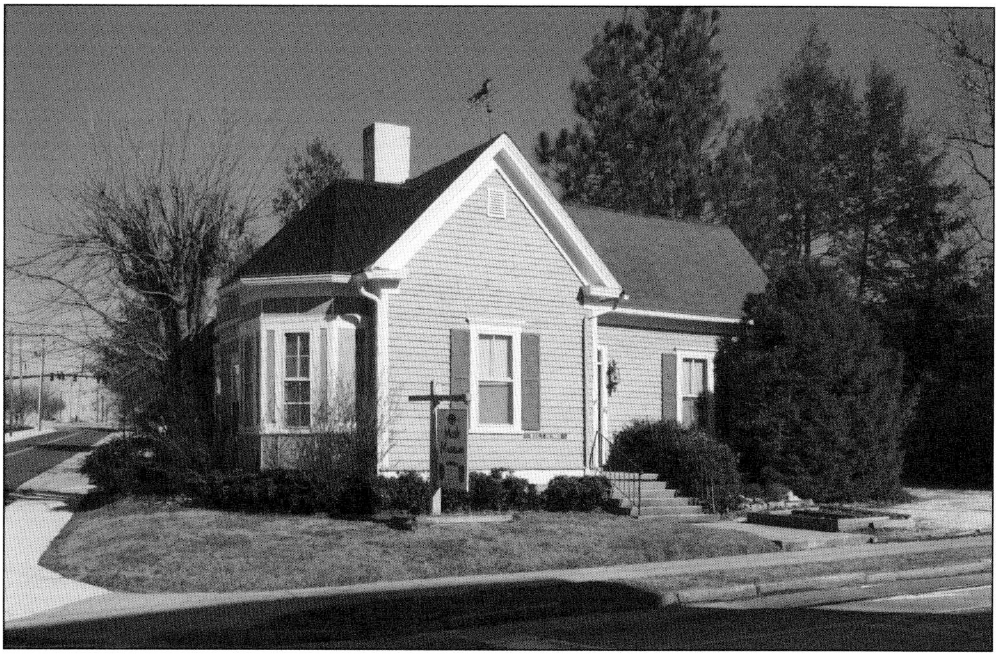

The Fifth Avenue Mask Museum no longer stands on the corner of Fifth Avenue West and Buncombe Street. The home, built in 1903 in the Folk Victorian style and most recently home to Ellen Cole Hobbs (1922–2015), was razed in 2016. The spirited Hobbs offered tours to view her artifacts from North and South America, Asia, and Africa. The collection enfolded more than 500 masks, international textiles, and dolls in native costumes. Hobbs taught art at Hendersonville High School for 30 years and retired in 1985. She was also a pilot and champion sailor. (Photograph by the author.)

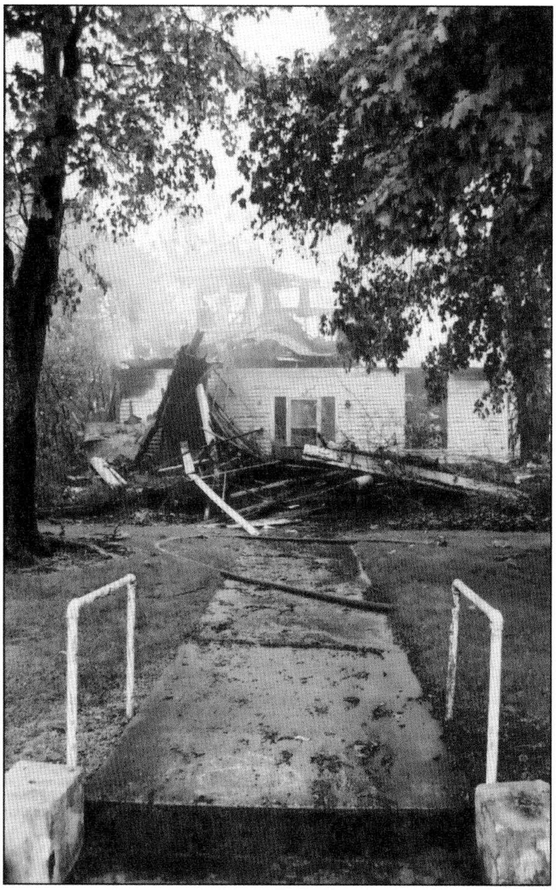

Destroyed by fire overnight on May 4 and 5, 2007, the home of Michael Schenck (1876–1948), former Hendersonville mayor (1907–1908) and senior associate justice of the North Carolina Supreme Court (1934–1938), stood at the southeast corner of Fourth Avenue and Washington Street. Erle G. Stillwell designed the house. (Photograph by the author.)

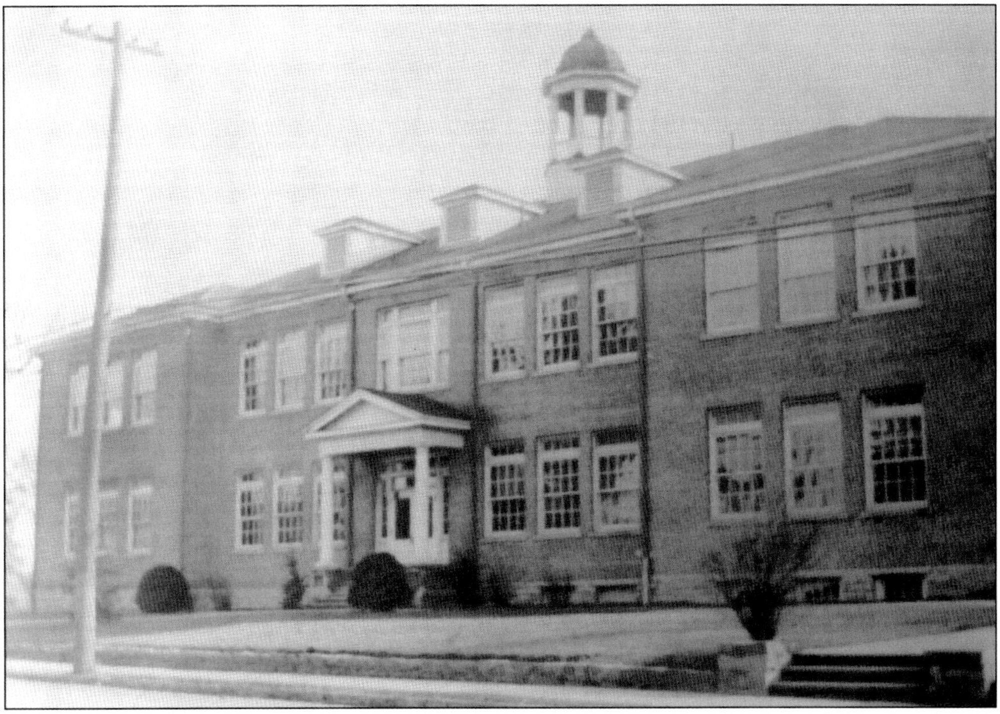

Hans C. Meyer (1875–1946) designed the Hendersonville Graded School, later the Rosa Edwards School, in 1911. The institution opened in 1912 for all grades; in 1919, high school students transferred to the Noterman House. Classes were discontinued from the Rosa Edwards School in 1972. The building has housed the Henderson County Board of Education administration offices since 1993. (Courtesy of the Henderson County Genealogical and Historical Society.)

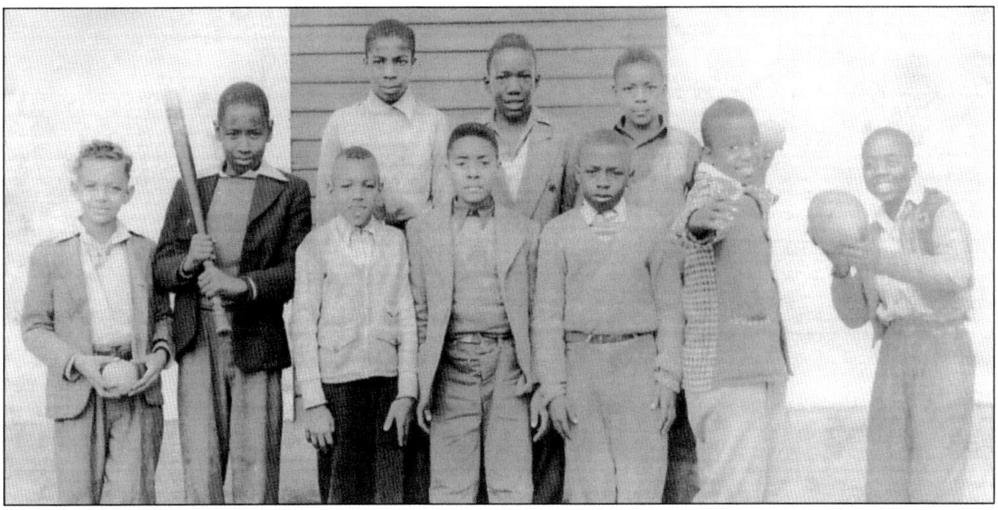

Pictured around 1945, Sixth Avenue School students are, from left to right, (first row) James "Sonny" Pilgrim Jr., William King, unidentified, Robert "Bobby Joe" Hutchinson, James Alvin Gash, Robert Gash, and Henry Glover; (second row) Clarence Brown, unidentified, and Bobby Waters. The school, completed in 1916, stood on the northeast corner of Sixth Avenue and Valley Street. It closed in 1950, replaced by the Ninth Avenue School. (Courtesy of the Henderson County Genealogical and Historical Society.)

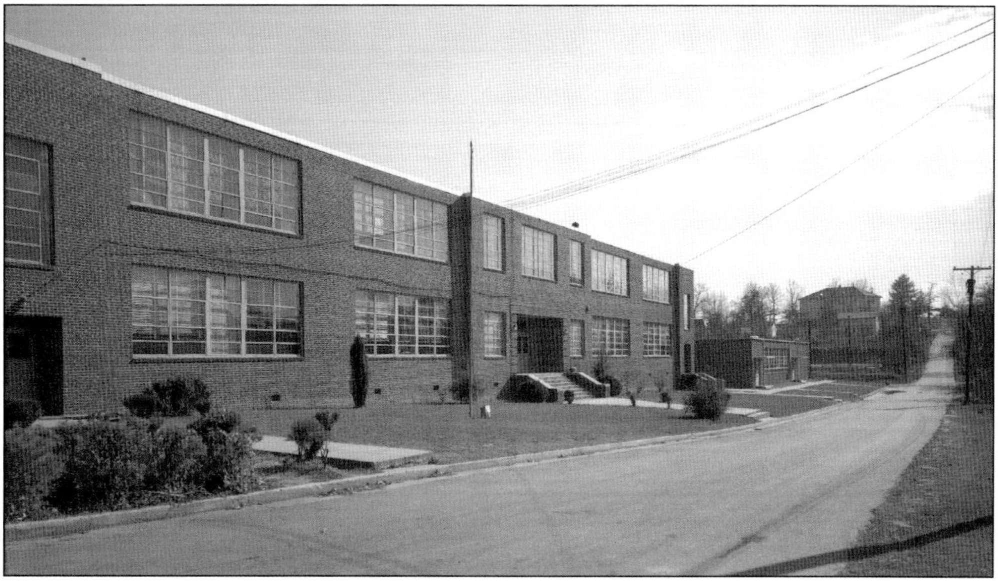

Ninth Avenue School, opened in 1951, offered grades 1 through 12 for black students. The last graduating class held its commencement on May 27, 1965. It became a junior high school in 1966 for children of all races. (Courtesy of the Baker-Barber Collection, Community Foundation of Henderson County, Henderson County Public Library.)

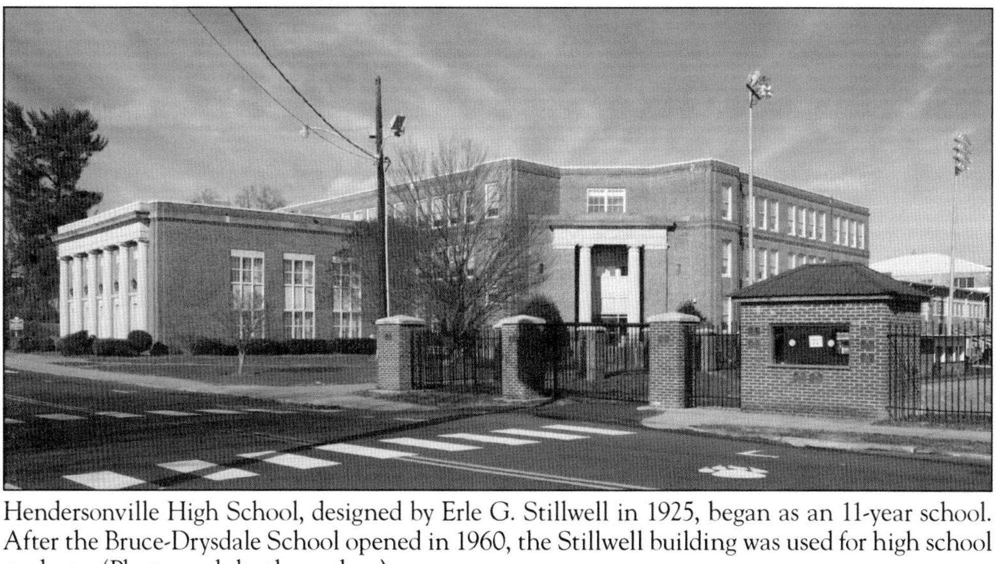

Hendersonville High School, designed by Erle G. Stillwell in 1925, began as an 11-year school. After the Bruce-Drysdale School opened in 1960, the Stillwell building was used for high school students. (Photograph by the author.)

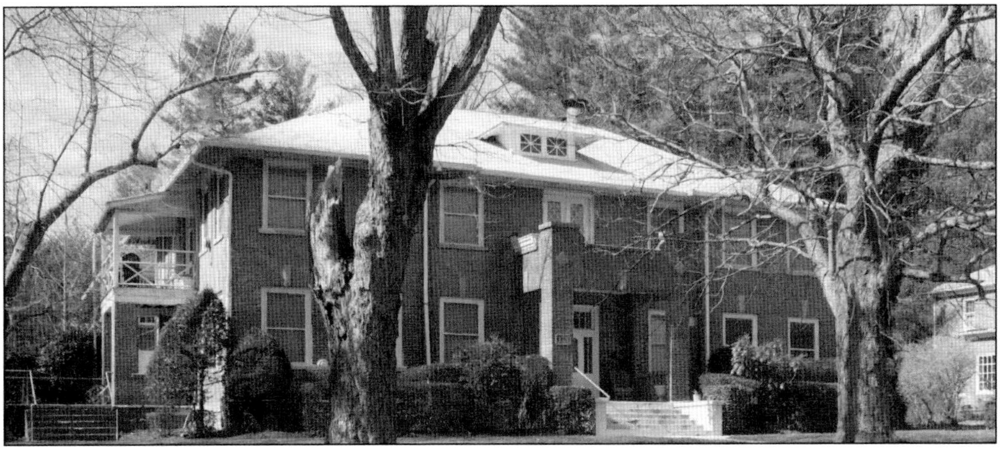

Hendersonville's first hospital, Patton Memorial, was repurposed as an apartment house, pictured here. (Photograph by the author.)

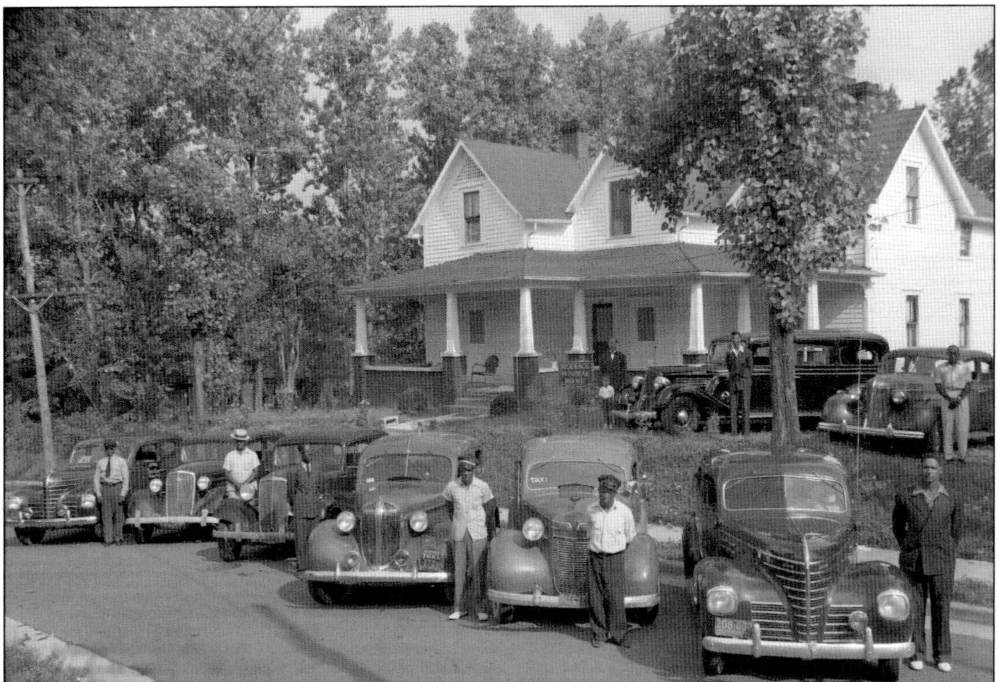

James Pilgrim Sr. (1915–1988) founded Pilgrim's Funeral Home in 1934. The man and child standing near the sign are James Pilgrim Sr. and James "Sonny" Pilgrim Jr.; Alexander Pilgrim stands to the right, by the hearse. (Courtesy of Melinda Pilgrim Lowrance.)

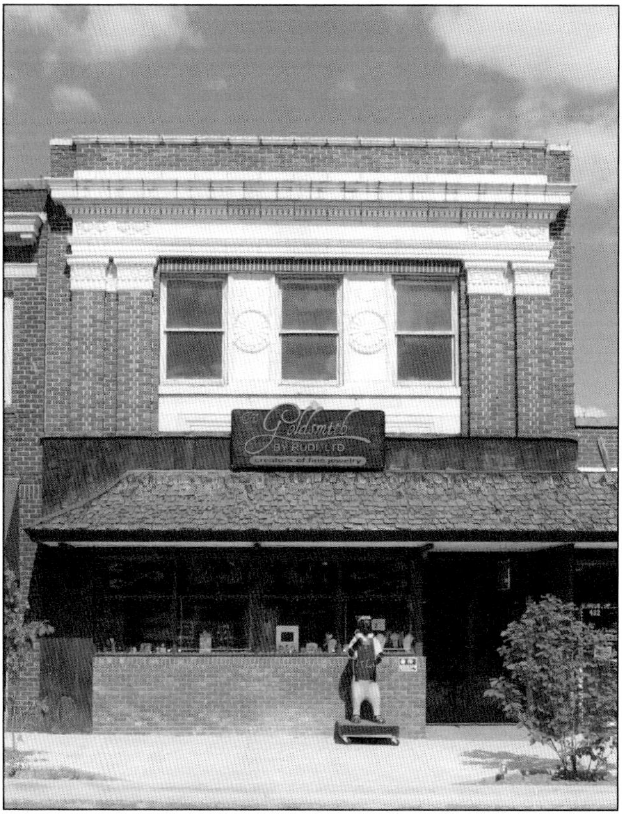

Architect Erle G. Stillwell transformed this 1915 store into a theater in 1921. The building currently housing Goldsmith by Rudi previously hosted a movie house named the Queen, later renamed the State and the Fox. The Fox ceased operations in the early 1960s. (Photograph by the author.)

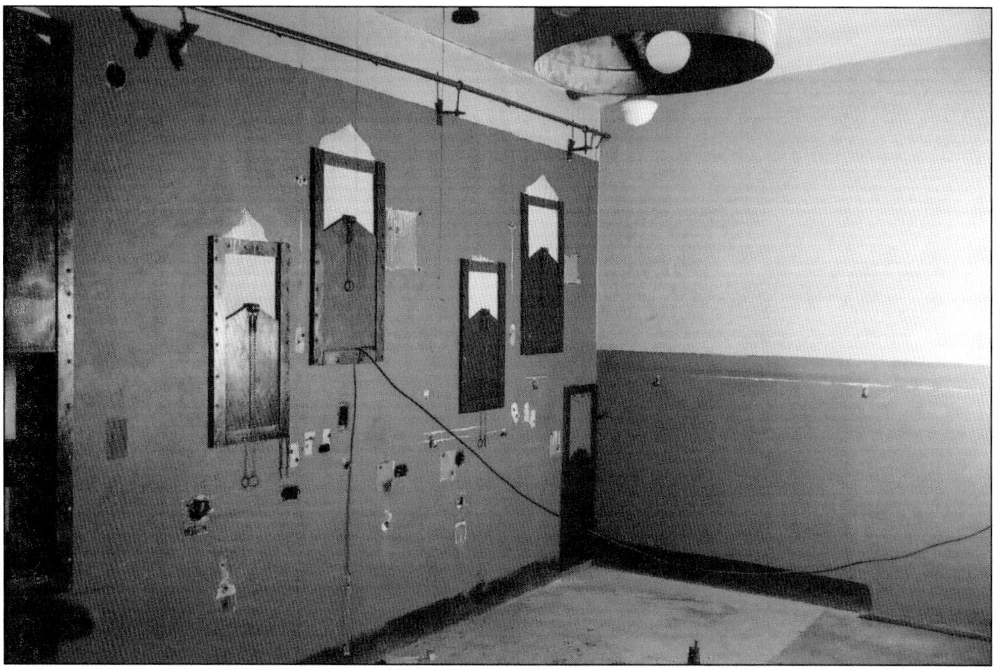

The projection booth in the Queen/State/Fox Theatre remains intact above the Goldsmith by Rudi jewelry store, which has occupied the building since 1975. (Photograph by the author.)

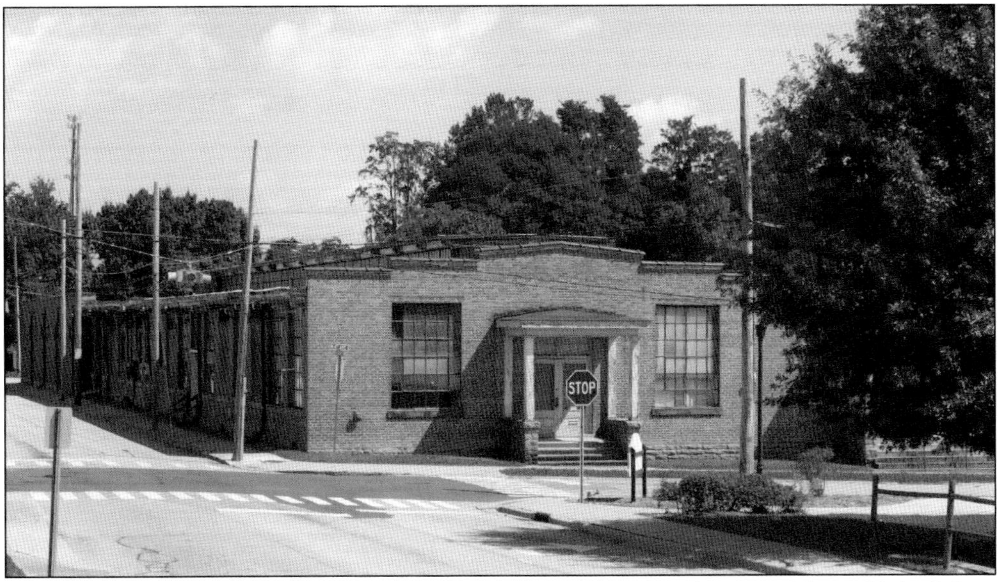

Capt. James Parks Grey (1860–1942) and his son, James P. Grey Jr. (1892–1969), established Grey Hosiery Mill in 1915. The elder Grey's brother, Charles Lester Grey (1868–1951), joined the company in 1919. The mill originally produced knee-length ribbed stockings for children, manufactured on 32 knitting machines, and employed approximately 25 people. In the 1940s, production changed to women's seamless hosiery, producing 66,000 pairs weekly. The mill employed 250 people in its peak years. Holt Hosiery Mills of Burlington, North Carolina, purchased the operation in 1965. Production halted in 1967. The building has since hosted several concerns, including a marketplace and a temporary home for the Henderson County Public Library. (Photograph by the author.)

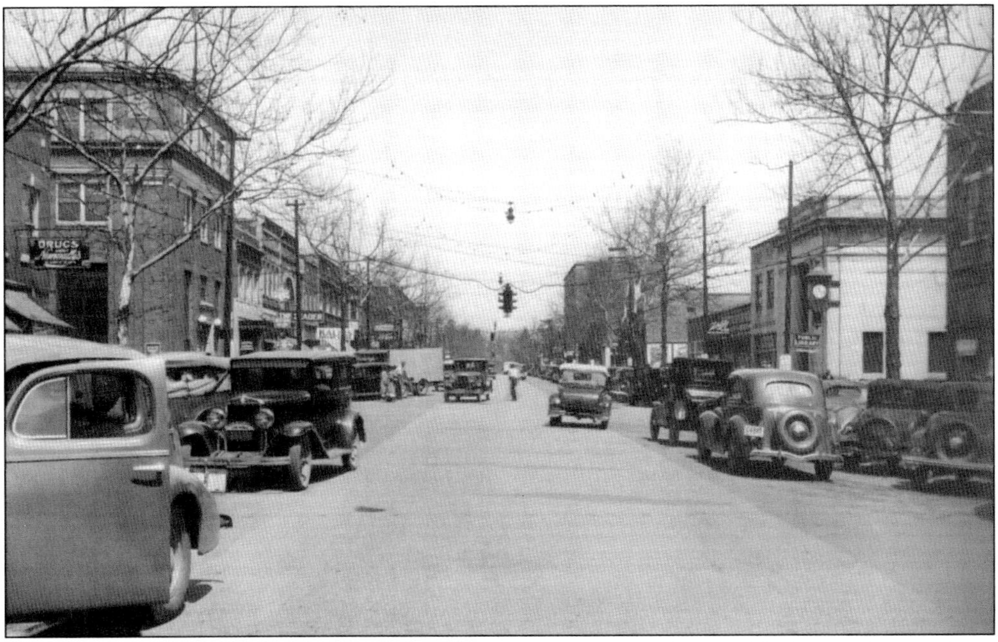

This 1937 view of Hendersonville's Main Street depicts swags of colored lights overhead, which were switched on only in December. (Courtesy of the Henderson County Genealogical and Historical Society.)

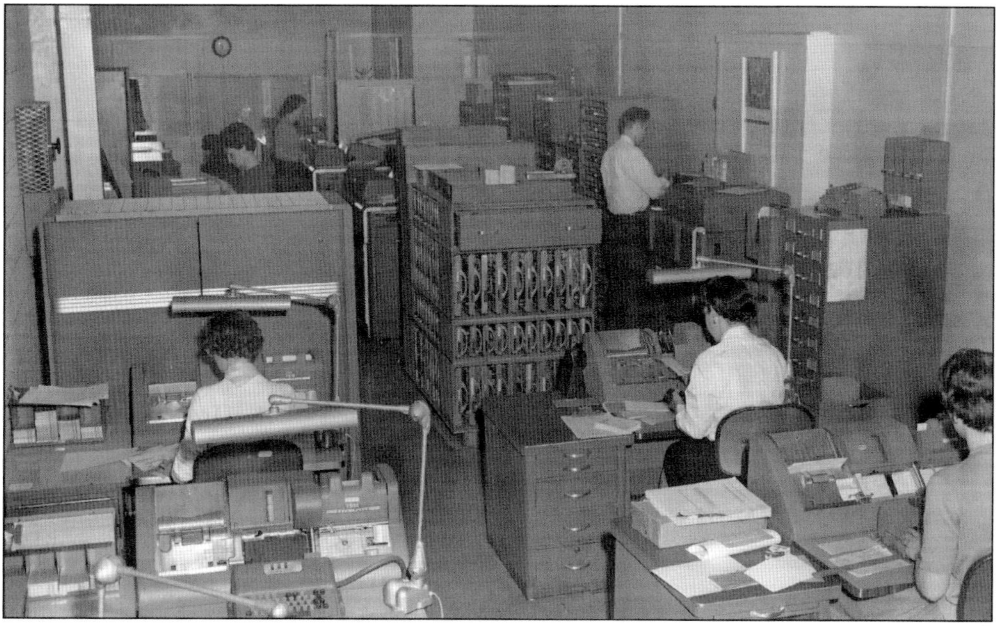

Robotyper Corporation opened a manufacturing plant in the former Joines Motors (1920) and Wetmur Motor Company (1926) building at East Allen and King Streets in 1951. The company produced robotic machines with a punch-card memory system, facilitating several typewriters to operate in sync. The Hendersonville plant closed in 1967. The building also housed part of the Chipman-LaCrosse Hosiery Mill operations (1930s) and, later, county school board offices (1969–1993) and the Henderson County Land Development Department. (Ed Hunnicutt photograph, courtesy of the Henderson County Genealogical and Historical Society.)

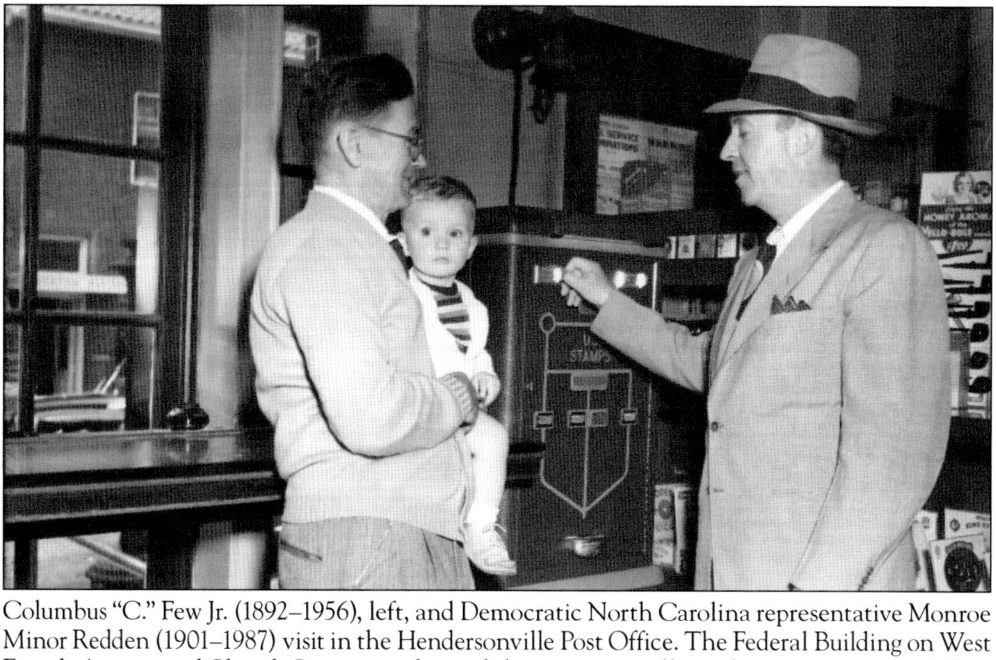

Columbus "C." Few Jr. (1892–1956), left, and Democratic North Carolina representative Monroe Minor Redden (1901–1987) visit in the Hendersonville Post Office. The Federal Building on West Fourth Avenue and Church Street once housed the main post office, where customers could buy tobacco products as well as stamps. (Courtesy of Margaret Thomas.)

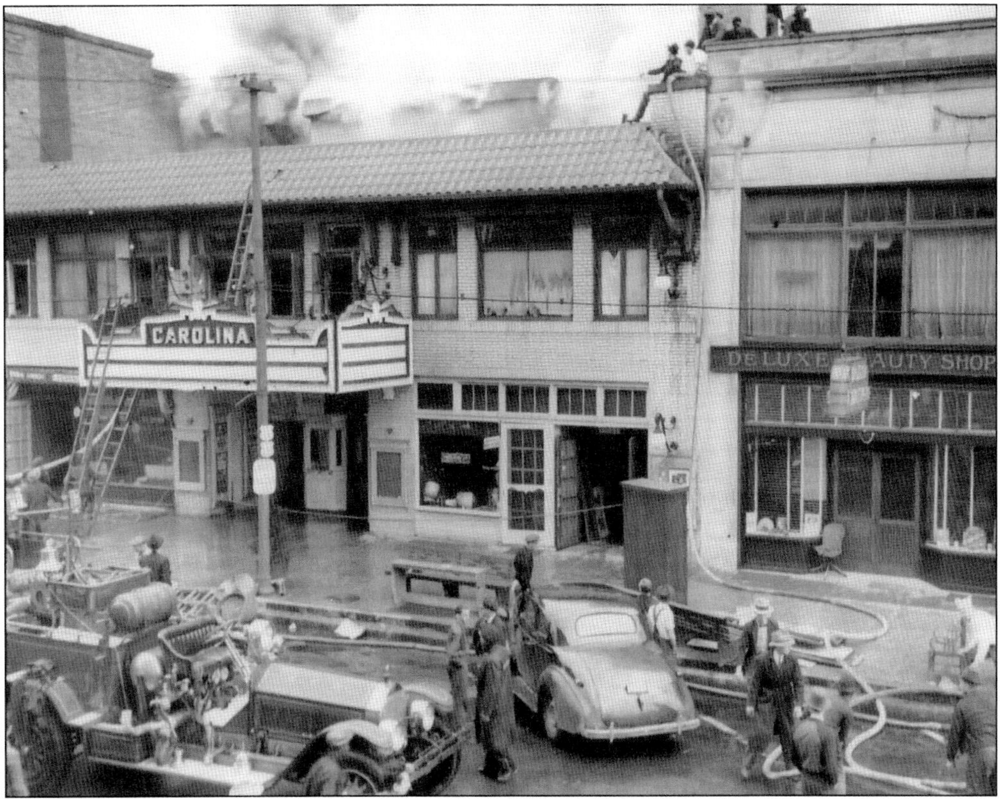

The Rex Theatre stood at this location on the west side of Main Street between Fifth and Sixth Avenues in 1924. It burned in 1932. The Carolina Theatre, designed by Erle G. Stillwell, replaced the Rex. The Carolina burned on May 10, 1940, pictured here. The theater was soon restored. It operated until 1986, when it closed and was demolished. An office building replaced it. (Courtesy of the Henderson County Genealogical and Historical Society.)

The Belk Simpson Company department store burned on February 23, 1953. Belk restored the space and continued operating there until moving to the Blue Ridge Mall in 1983. Today, Black Bear Coffee Company and Hands-On Children's Museum occupy this space in the Rosdon Mall, on the east side of Hendersonville's Main Street between Third and Fourth Avenues. The building to its left housed Sherman's Sporting Goods in one of its former locations. (Courtesy of the Henderson County Genealogical and Historical Society.)

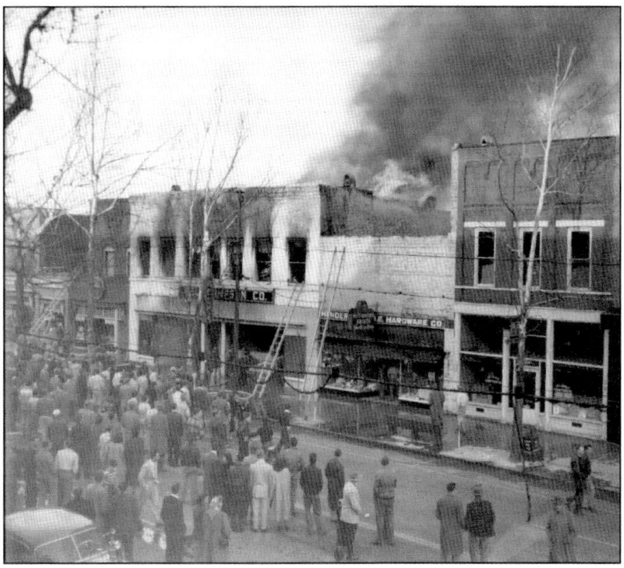

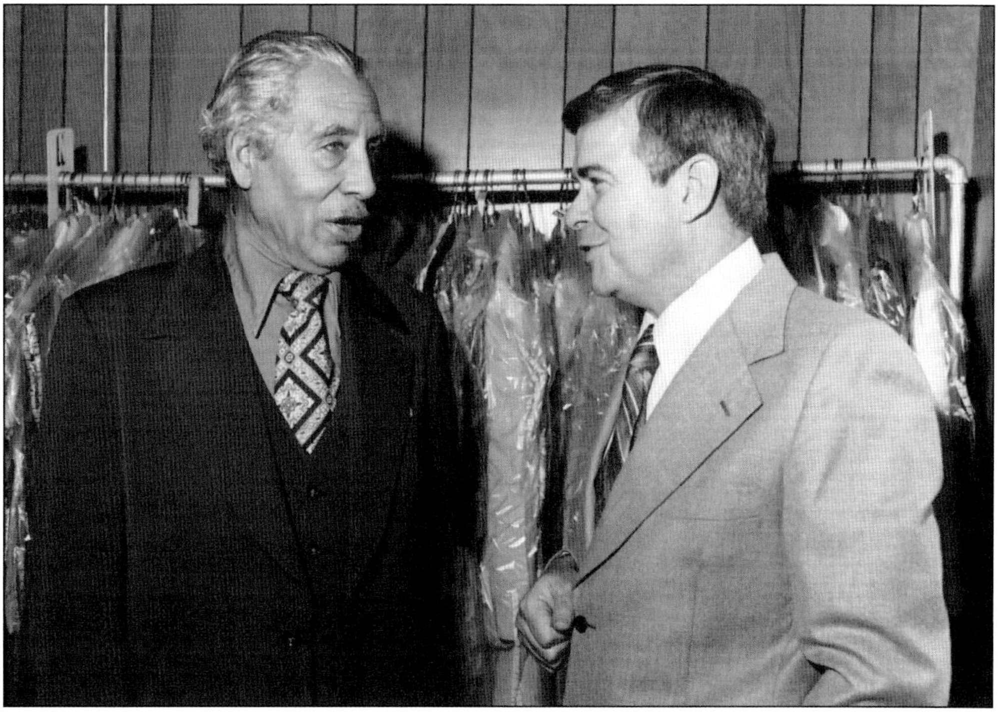

George B. Lazarus (1880–1962), left, and Democratic North Carolina senator Royce Phelps "Bo" Thomas (1932–1997) enjoy a chat in the Lazarus & Company department store at 317 North Main Street in Hendersonville. (Courtesy of Margaret Thomas.)

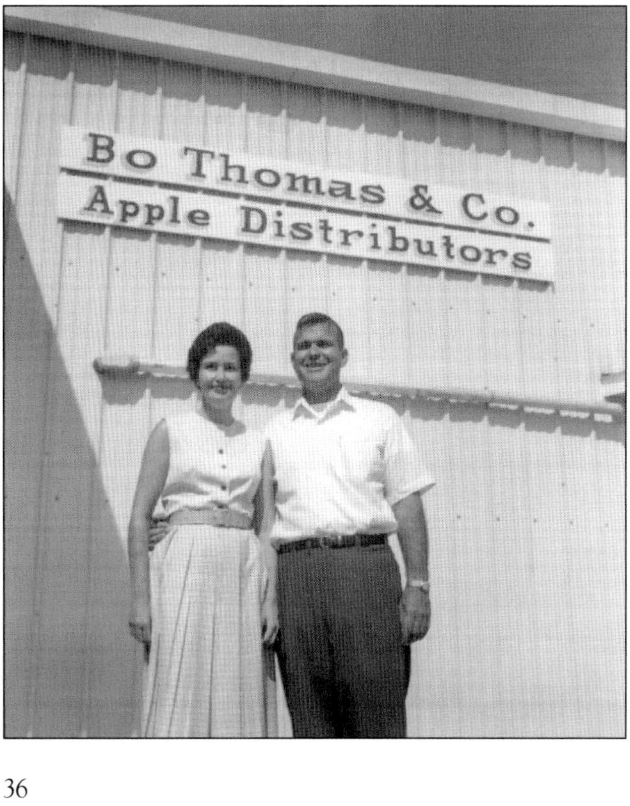

Margaret C. Stonecipher Thomas and her husband, Bo Thomas, pose at their J.R. Thomas Produce Company packing plant on South Church Street. (Courtesy of Margaret Thomas.)

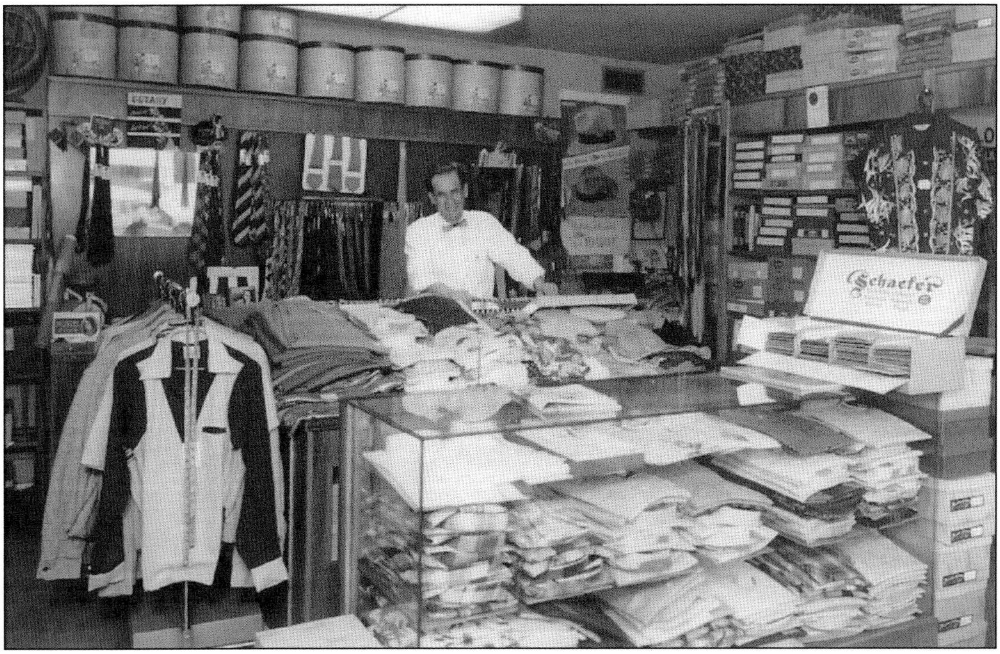

A Hendersonville icon, Max Michel Provda (1918–2009), served as an Army medic in World War II. He married Janet Rosenberg (1922–2017) and joined his father-in-law, Jacob Herbert "Jake" Rosenberg (1871–1957), in his men's clothing store on Main Street next to the Carolina Theatre. In 1957, the store became Mac's Men's Wear, which relocated in 1960 to the east side of Main Street between Fourth and Fifth Avenues. A pioneer in the big-and-tall business in Western North Carolina, Provda retired in 2007. Provda counted among the charter members of Hendersonville's Agudas Israel Synagogue. (Courtesy of Sid Williams.)

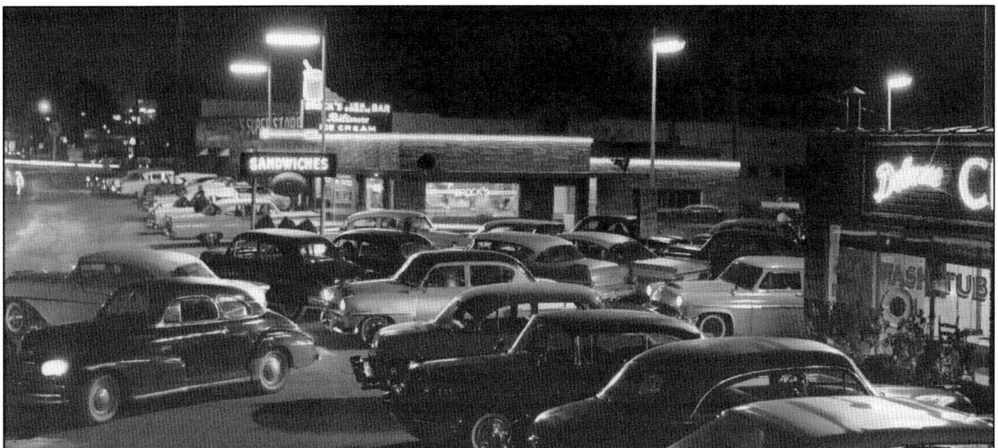

Brock's drive-in stood near the intersection of US 176 and US 25 South, supplying a popular hangout for cruising teenagers from 1949 to 1972, when it burned. William Monroe "Strawberry" Brock (1905–1960) owned the establishment. He owned Chrysler Taxi Service in the 1920s, Strawberry's Place (billiards and lunches) at 306 North Main Street in the 1930s, and Brock's Grocery on the "Busy Bend" of Kanuga Road in the 1940s. Brock's Ice Cream Bar served thick shakes, cherry-lemon Upper 10s, and Big Shot hamburgers and featured an intercom system called the "electro car hop." (Ed Hunnicutt photograph, courtesy of Buddy Brock.)

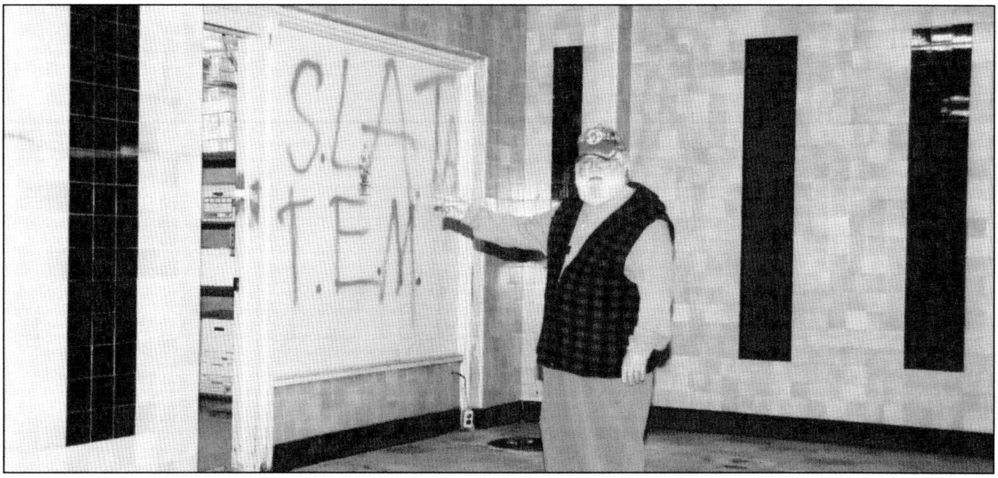

Former *Times-News* columnist Stephen Morrison "Steve" Black (1945–2013) reminisces about good times spent in the Hendersonville Youth Center—the "Teen Canteen." Main Street sported this underground arcade, accessed through the sidewalk near the northwest corner of Fourth Avenue and Main Street. Occupants included Tom's Barbershop, Blue Bonnet Beauty Shoppe, a shoeshine parlor, and in the early 1940s, a gentlemen's establishment known as the Eagle's Club. The Teen Canteen occupied the space from 1948 to 1957, with amenities including billiards, Ping-Pong, a jukebox, and a dance floor. Ollie Lee (1906–1998) and Sally Heilig Jones (1930–1985) attended its snack bar. The Teen Canteen moved into a pavilion at Boyd Park in 1958. (Photograph by the author.)

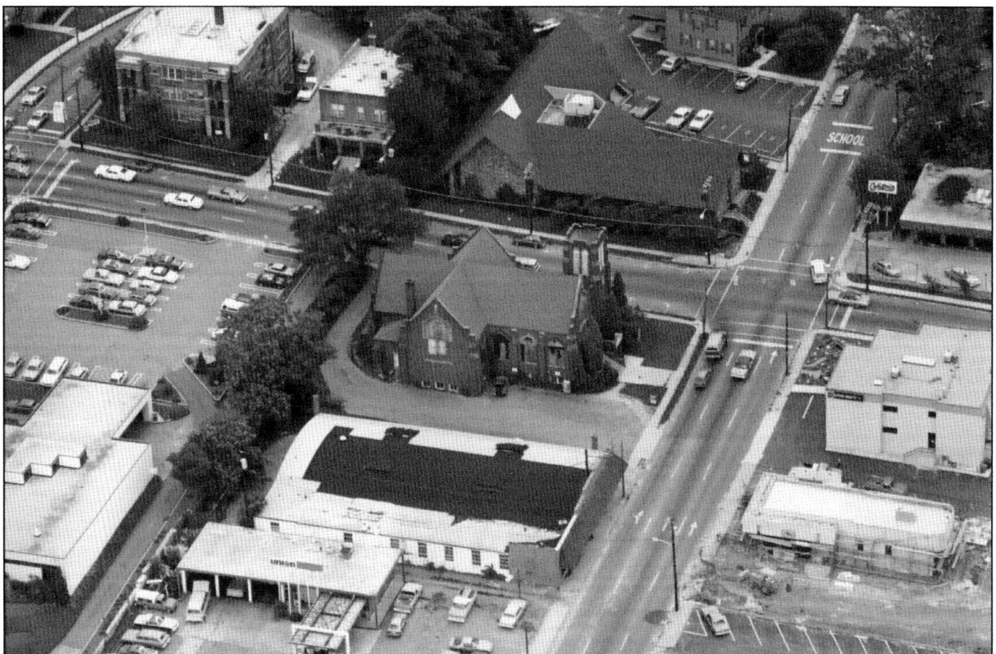

The former Grace Lutheran Church is in the center of this 1992 aerial photograph. Established in 1916, the sanctuary has been occupied since 2006 by the Reformation Presbyterian Church. The rock-faced Immaculate Conception Church, pictured at the top center, has been replaced with a brick-veneered sanctuary. (Courtesy of Reformation Presbyterian Church.)

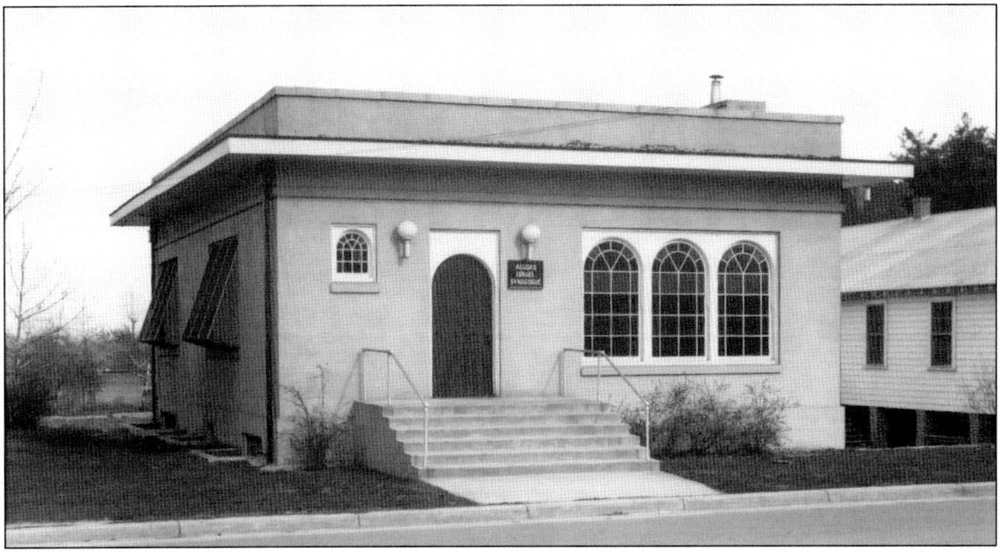

Established in 1922, the Agudas Israel congregation met in members' homes before acquiring the Home Electric Company building—pictured here on King Street—in 1925. By 2002, a new synagogue had been completed in Laurel Park. (Courtesy of Agudas Israel Congregation and Dr. Jack Frisch.)

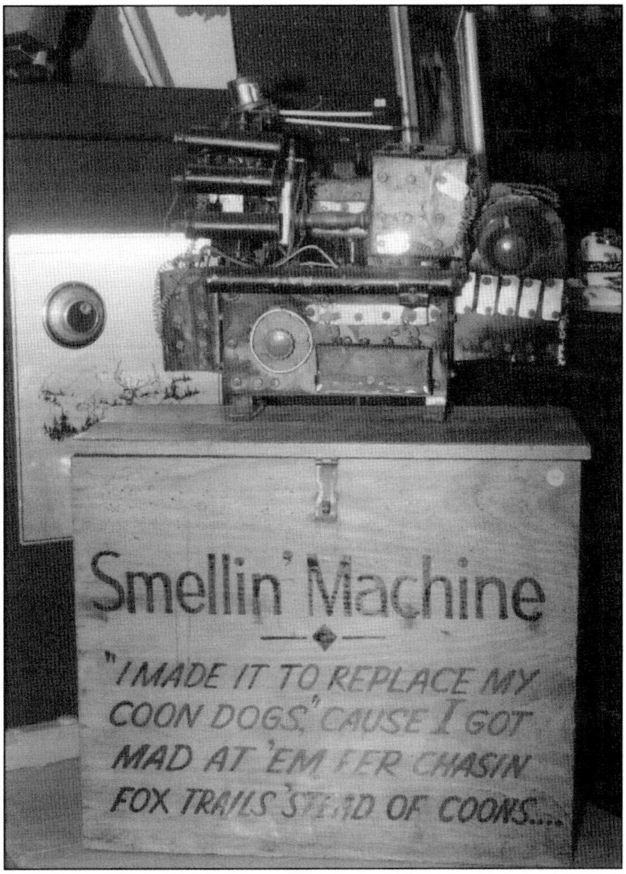

Luther W. Shipman (1890–1959) of Henderson County invented the Smellin' Machine in 1940. The contraption purportedly sniffed out wild game. Shipman said of it, "I made it to replace my coon dogs, 'cause I got mad at 'em fer chasin' fox trails 'stead of coons." (Courtesy of Jean Pace.)

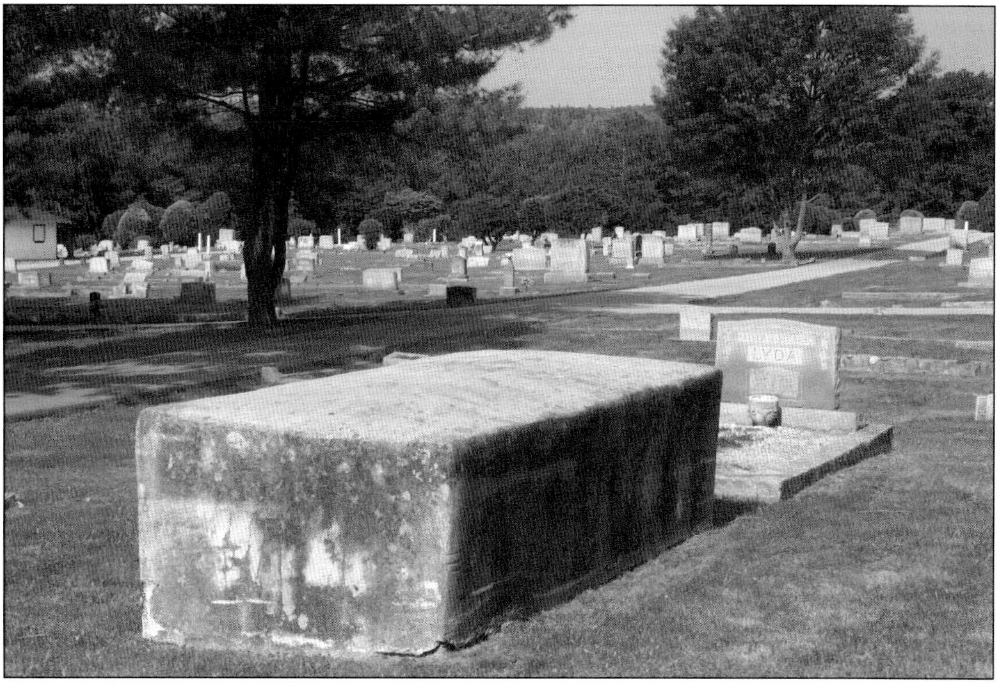

Seeking a cure for tuberculosis, Leila Maud Davidson Hansell (1861–1915) traveled from Thomasville, Georgia, to Hendersonville for treatment. Before she succumbed to the disease 18 months later, Hansell appealed to be buried where the sun would shine perpetually upon her. Her husband arranged for her interment in an aboveground vault at Oakdale Cemetery, with the lid removed from the casket and glass prisms installed in the top of the tomb. Townsfolk nicknamed the corpse the "Sunshine Lady." Officials later overlaid the tomb with concrete. (Photograph by the author.)

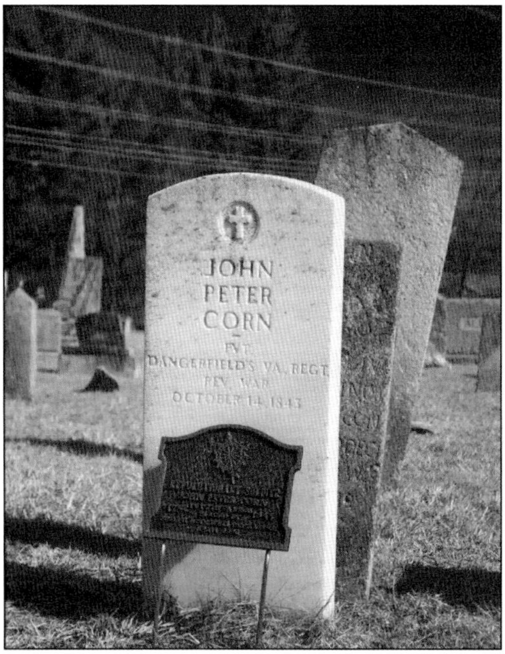

The grave of Revolutionary War veteran John Peter Corn (1752–1844) can be found at Ebenezer Baptist Church Cemetery. One of the region's earliest pioneers, Corn settled in the Green River community in 1793 when it fell within Buncombe County. By 1830, Corn moved his family to the Clear Creek section. (Photograph by the author.)

Two

Movers and Shapers
A Multiplicity of Personalities and Disciplines

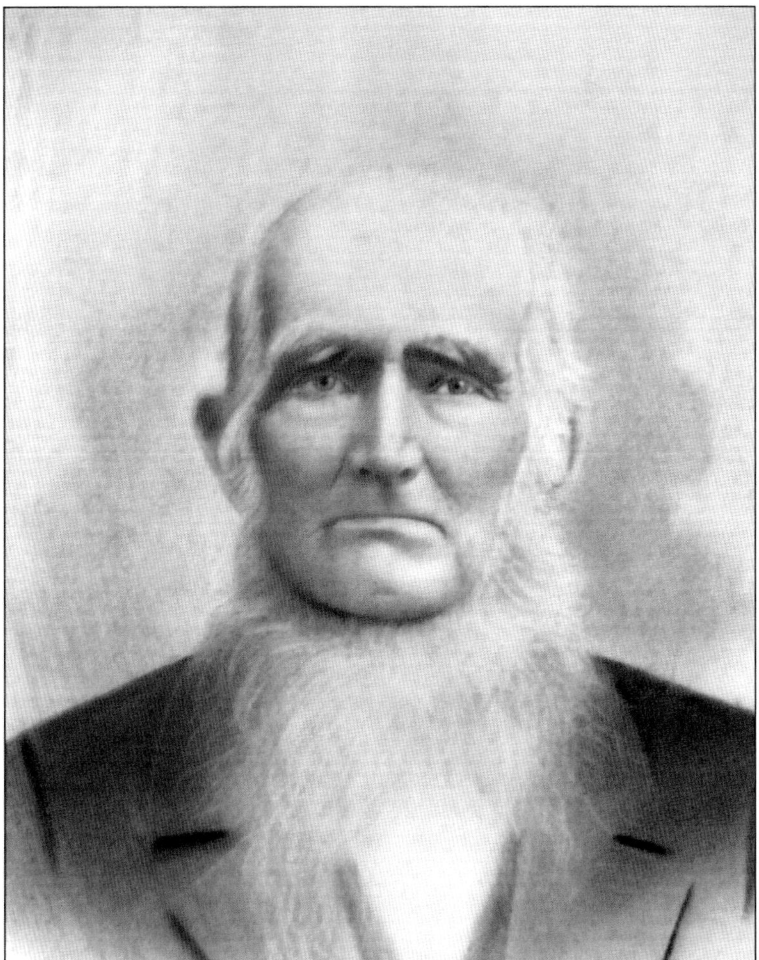

Solomon Jones (1802–1899), known as the "road builder," dug out early roads into the mountains with the assistance of horses, oxen, and men. History credits Jones for the Green River and Flat Rock Turnpikes, Cashiers Valley Road, and sections of present-day US Highways 64 and 25. Legends suggest that pathfinder Jones's instruments included his keen eye, wisdom, and judgment—and a sow named Sue. (Courtesy of Daphne Hedden.)

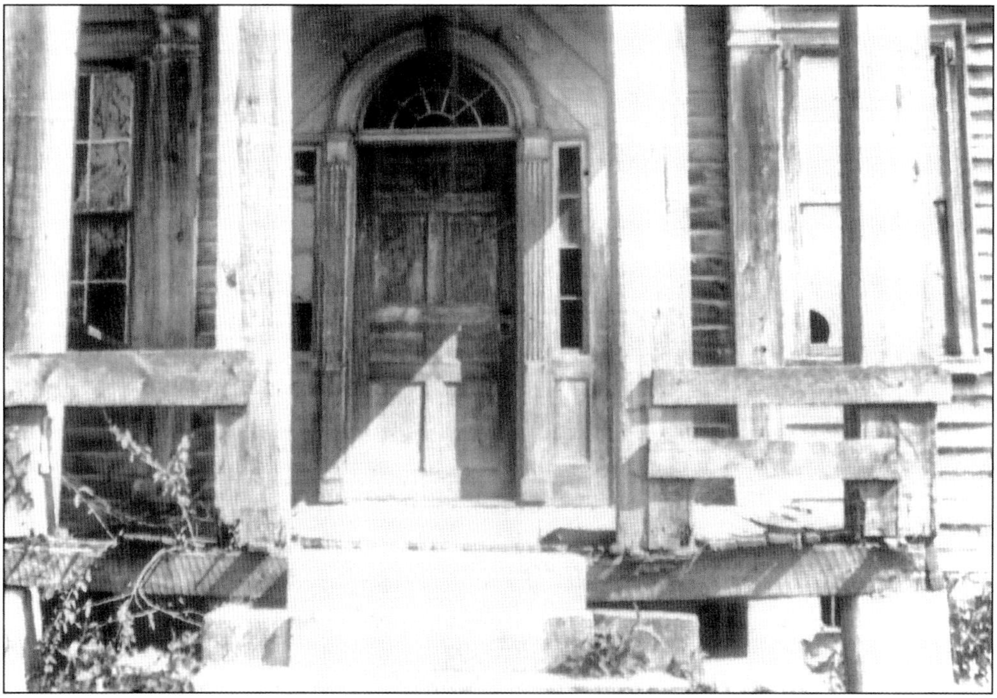

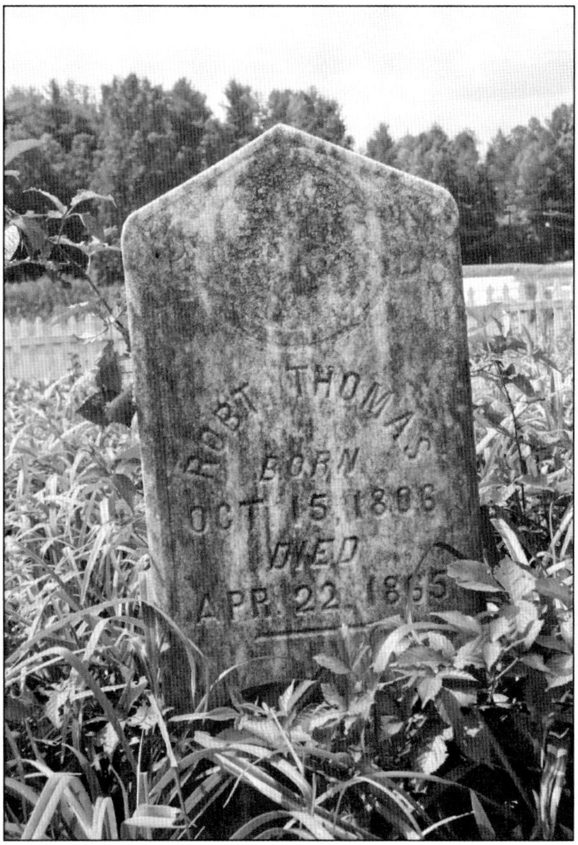

The Reverend Samuel Edney (1765–1844) covered Methodist circuits in Eastern and Western North Carolina and Eastern Tennessee. Samuel and his brother Asa (1772–1842) were the namesakes of Edneyville. The long-since razed home pictured here belonged to one of Samuel's sons, James Madison Edney (1814–1866). William Baxter Coston (1839–1910) later owned the home. (Courtesy of Doris Banning Marlowe.)

The grave of Robert Thomas (1806–1865) can be found in the Fletcher-Thomas Cemetery in the Pleasant Grove section of Etowah. Thomas served as Henderson County's first sheriff from 1839 to 1844. He was also a member and chairman of the Henderson County Court of Pleas and Quarter Sessions. (Photograph by the author.)

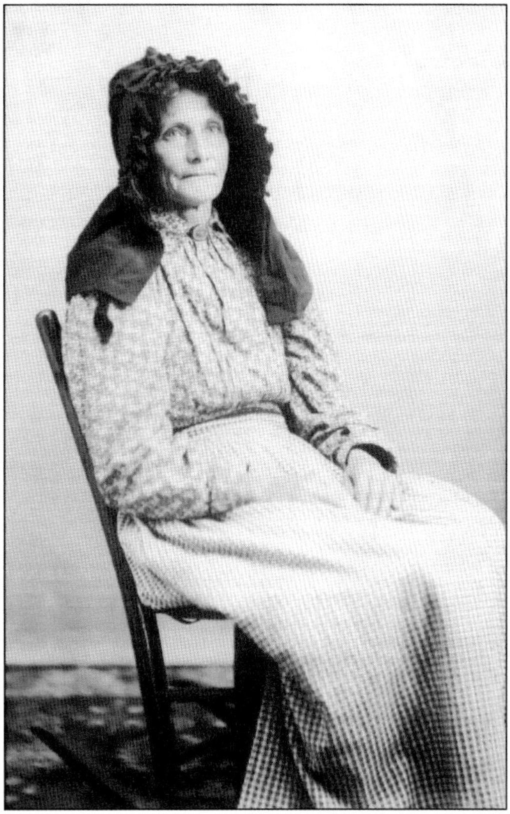

Mary Jane "Dr. Polly" King Justice (1819–1904) married John Hiram Justice (1816–1901) in 1835. The couple had 13 or 14 children and lived in the Dana area. Polly ranked among Henderson County's earliest midwives and medical practitioners. She maintained a keen sense of holistic healing passed down through generations of granny women and Native Americans. Justice was said to have been a licensed physician, but no documentation has surfaced to prove such an accreditation. (Courtesy of Patricia Walker.)

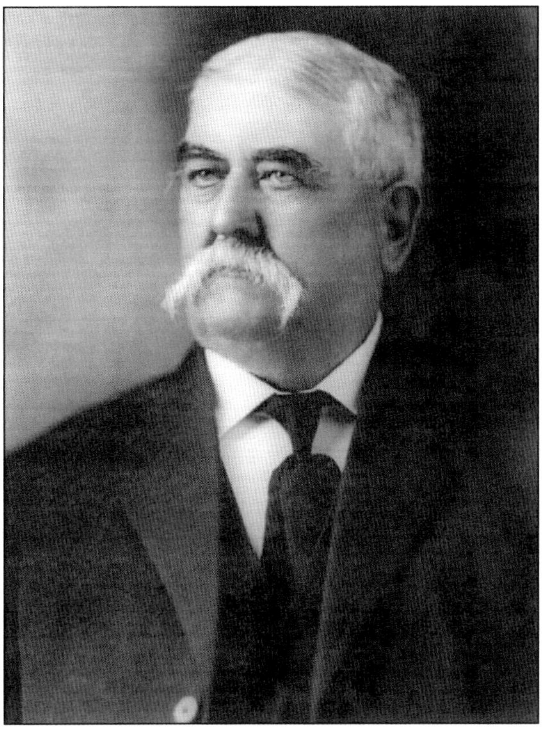

Entrepreneur Capt. Marion Columbus Toms (1843–1917) represented Henderson County in the North Carolina Senate in 1889. He was a lawyer and a Hendersonville city commissioner and owned business concerns including Essowah Orchards on Jump Off Mountain and mineral rights in Green River. He gave land for Hendersonville's first public library, which stood on King Street. (Courtesy of Jim Toms.)

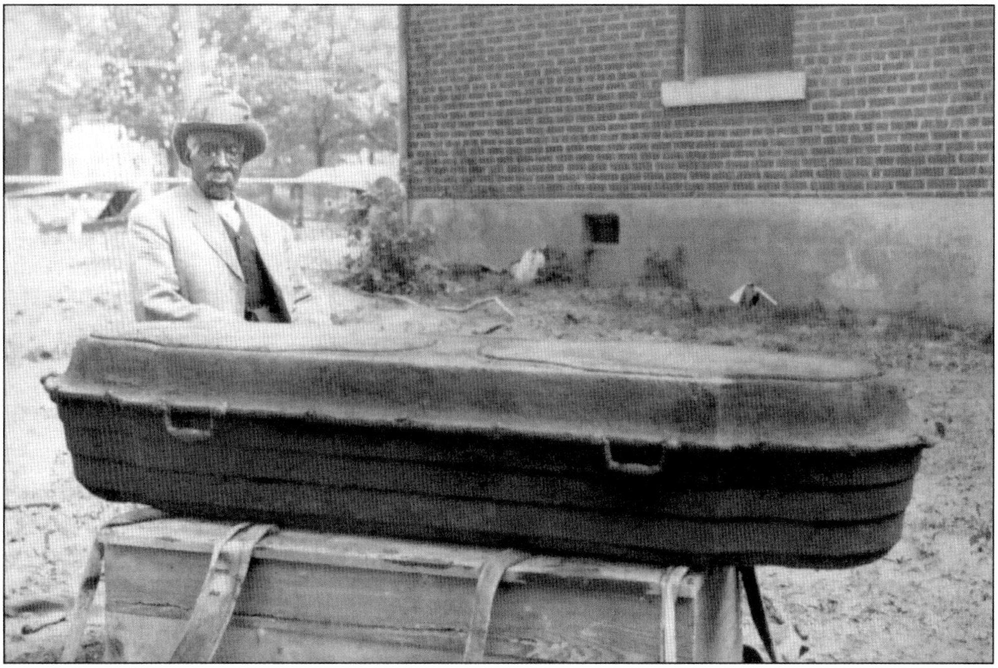

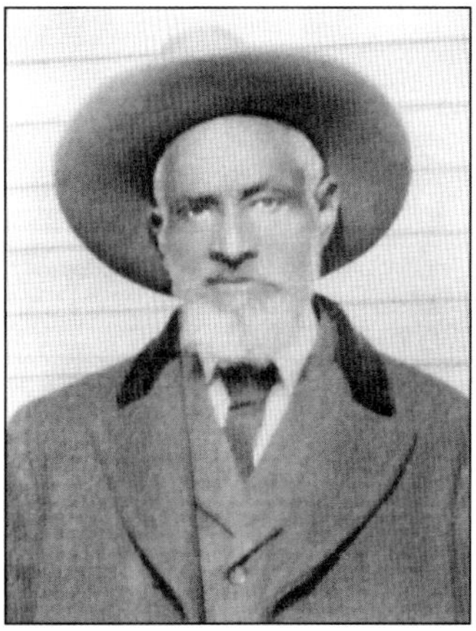

Above, Confederate soldier George Mills (1844–1926) followed his master's son Watt to war. Confederate captain Walter M. "Watt" Bryson (1835–1862) of Company G, 35th North Carolina Regiment, died in the Battle of Sharpsburg (Antietam) on September 17, 1862. Mills, a childhood pal of Bryson's, collected Bryson's body and conveyed it back to Hendersonville. In 1922, officials exhumed Bryson's casket and reinterred it at Oakdale Cemetery. Here, Mills poses with the exhumed casket in the churchyard of the Methodist church. (Courtesy of the Baker-Barber Collection, Community Foundation of Henderson County, Henderson County Public Library.)

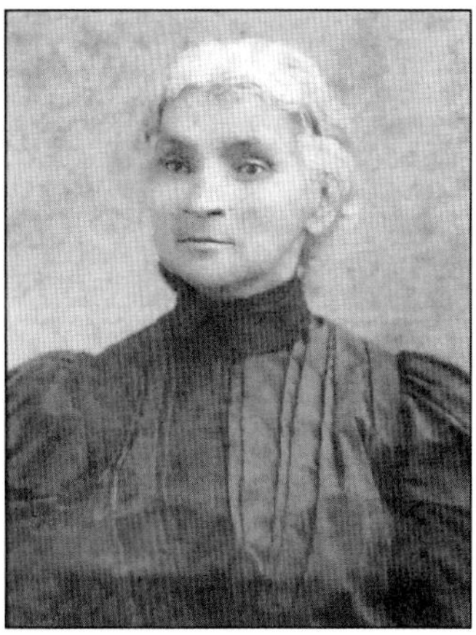

George L. Potts (1844–1926), at left (top), supplied farming and dray services to the King and Trenholm families. He and his wife, Lavinia F. Moultrie Potts (1846–1932), seen at left, had nine children. Born to South Carolina slaves Lawrence and Matilda Potts, George later amassed 132 acres in the Flat Rock and East Flat Rock communities. Lavinia worked as a midwife, seamstress, and baker. She was a daughter of Dr. Mitchell Campbell King (1815–1901) and a slave named Charlotte Moultrie. (Courtesy of E. Hortence Potts.)

Frederick Henderson "Fred" Potts (1885–1975) and his wife, Ethel Kathleen Williams Potts (1896–1993), made their home and raised their two daughters, Frederica and Hortence, in East Flat Rock. Fred, a flautist with an Asheville symphonic group and self-taught horticulturist, was revered for his landscaping prowess and prize azaleas that continue to grace Brook Ledge, the Potts homestead. Fred was a son of George and Lavinia Potts. (Courtesy of E. Hortence Potts.)

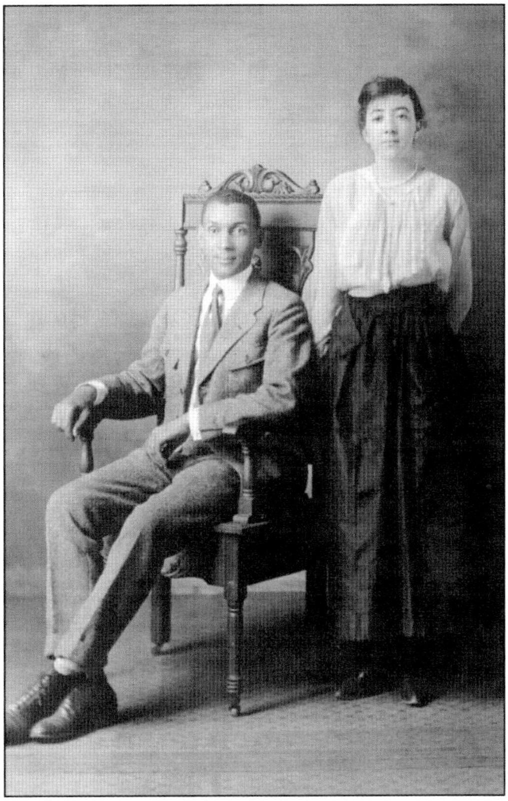

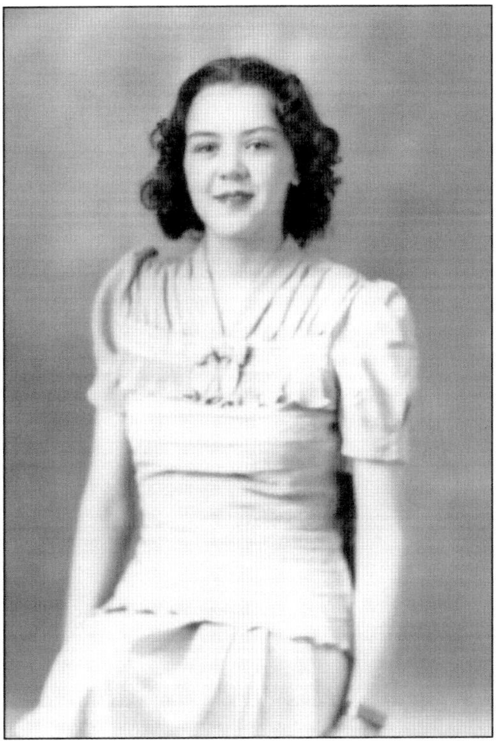

Hortence Potts (born 1926), a daughter of Fred and Ethel Potts, taught home economics in Rutherford County and at West Henderson High School and special education in Henderson County schools. She earned degrees from Bennett College in Greensboro and Western Carolina University in Cullowhee. An Alpha Kappa Alpha sorority member, she was a former volunteer with the Council on Aging and board member of the Dispute Settlement Committee. She involved herself in civic organizations, including the Society of Necessity, which her grandfather George Potts helped found in 1889. (Courtesy of E. Hortence Potts.)

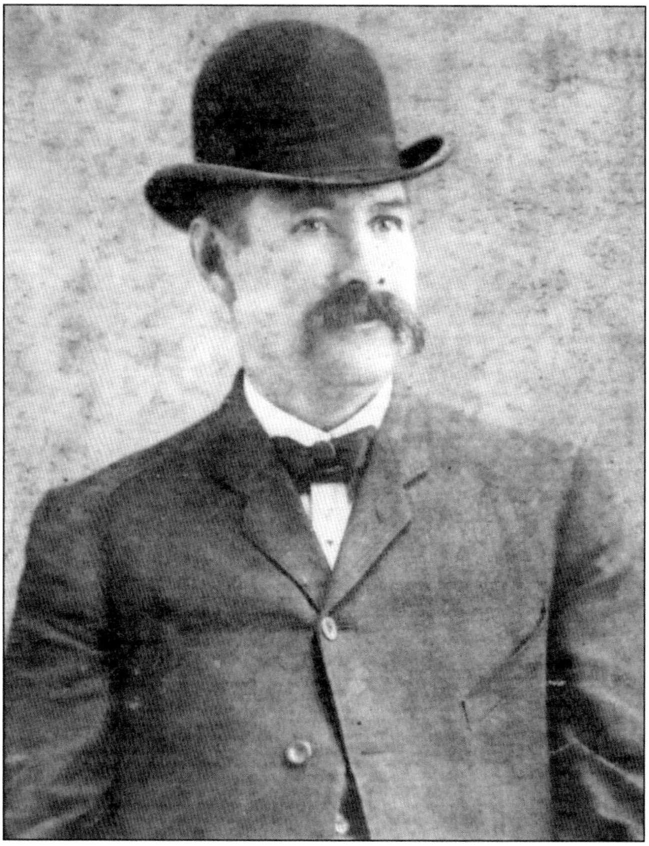

William Franklin Edwards (1848–1921) met and married Martha Elizabeth Gibson (1855–1940) at Fort Mill in 1877. On the couple's journey by stagecoach to their honeymoon in Asheville, the blizzard of 1877 forced them to stop at Hendersonville, where they lodged at Judge C.M. Pace's Globe Hotel. Trapped in Hendersonville for several days, the couple resolved to move here permanently. Edwards would soon become a major contractor and city planner. He opened a hardware store on Main Street and built his home on South Washington Street. (Courtesy of Marcia Mills Kelso.)

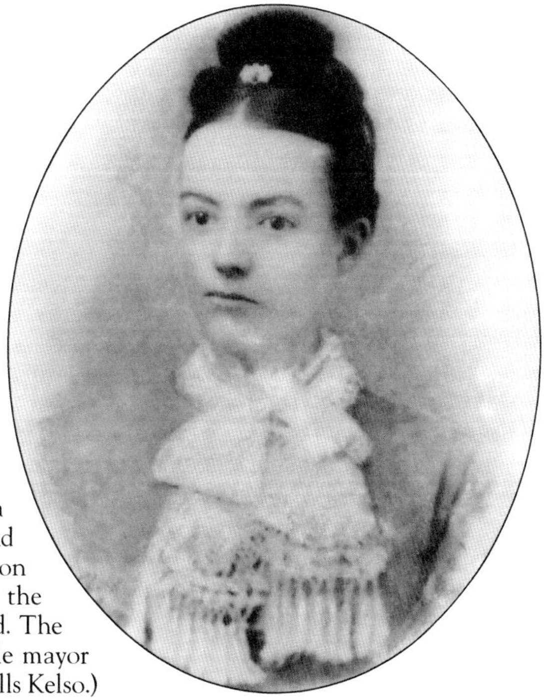

Richard Sharp Smith designed Hendersonville's historic courthouse; W.F. Edwards and his crew built it. Edwards further helped shape the cityscape: his work includes the town's first city hall and opera house, People's National Bank building, and the Park Hill Inn. Edwards's company won the contract to pave Main Street in 1910, the first time the passageway was macadamized. The Edwardses were parents of Hendersonville mayor Albert V. Edwards. (Courtesy of Marcia Mills Kelso.)

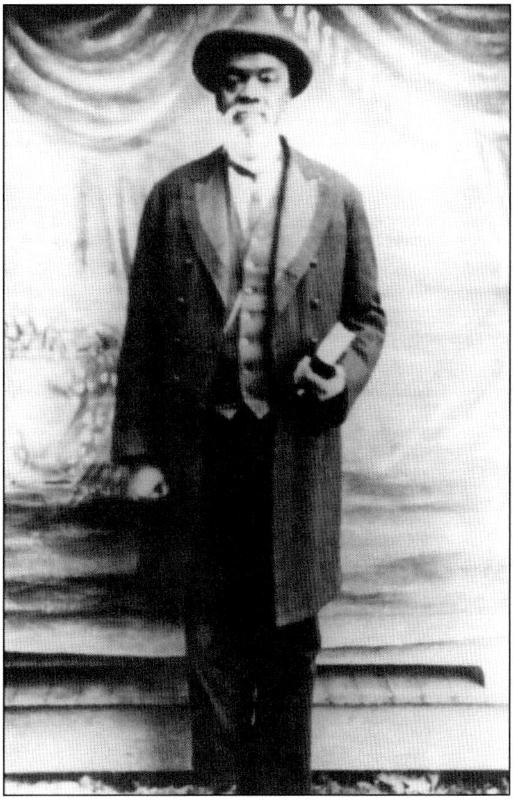

The Reverend John Wesley Logan Jr. (1853–1923) was a later pastor and namesake of Logan's Community Chapel, which began as Shaws Creek African Methodist Episcopal (AME) Zion Church. The oldest black church in Henderson County, it was organized in 1865. The Reverend Logan married Mary Angeline Miller (1860–1939). (Both, courtesy of the Henderson County Genealogical and Historical Society.)

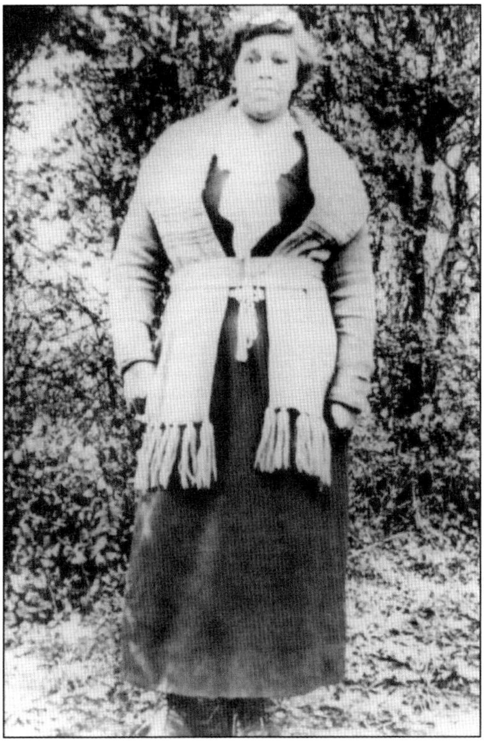

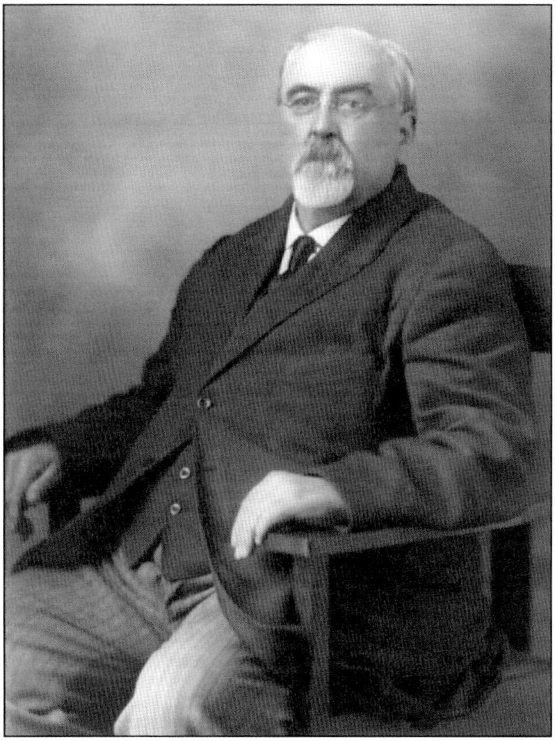

Judge Columbus Mills Pace (1845–1925), a fourth-generation Henderson County native, served in the Confederate army until the surrender of 1865. Following the war, he studied law. Elected clerk of Henderson County Superior Court in 1868, Pace served in this position until his death. Pace married Leona Allen (1849–1929). (Courtesy of the Baker-Barber Collection, Community Foundation of Henderson County, Henderson County Public Library.)

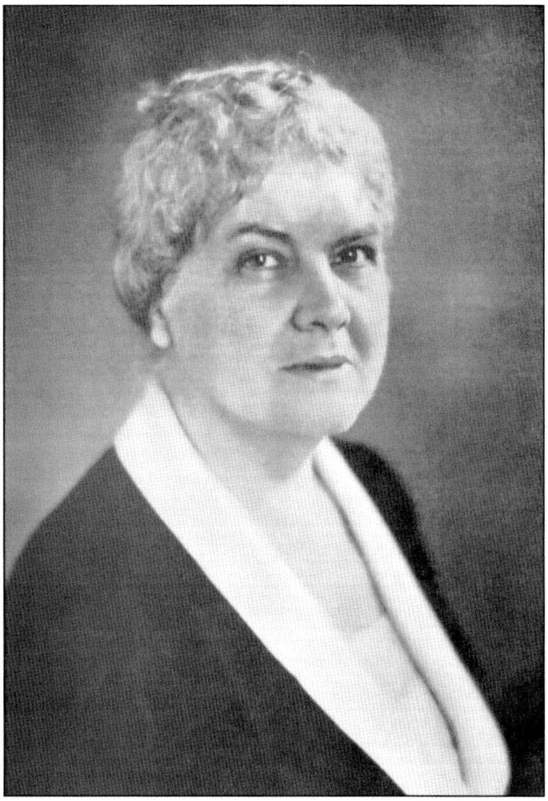

Katherine Cameron "Kate" Shipp (1859–1932) opened Fassifern School for Girls in Hendersonville in 1914, naming the school for the home of Clan Cameron in Fassifern, Scotland. Fassifern, which earned a reputation as one of the South's finest preparatory schools, stood on a hill near the corner of Fleming Street and US 25 North. The institution, later operated by the Reverend Dr. Joseph Ramsey Sevier (1877–1944) and John L. Sevier (1910–2000), closed in 1951. (Courtesy of the estate of Louise H. Bailey.)

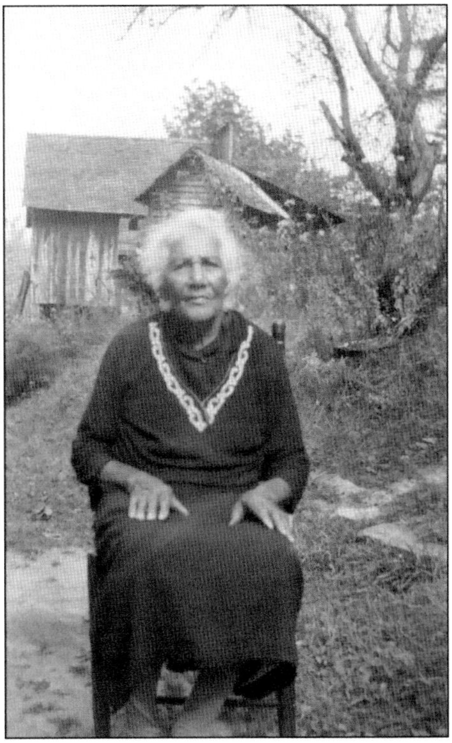

Sallie Samantha Dairty Markley (1854–1959), a Flat Rock and East Flat Rock midwife, delivered hundreds of babies. Her ancestry included African and Cherokee. Sallie married "Honest John" Calhoun Markley, a farrier. Locals knew "Aunt Sallie" also as a storyteller and historian. (Courtesy of Paula Coleman Machen.)

A family of Flat Rock farriers pauses for this photograph at Markley's Blacksmith Shop, which John Markley established around 1870. John Calhoun Markley (1848–1921) and his sons, James Garfield (1881–1932) and James Ripley "Jim" Markley (1887–1965), owned and operated the shop. John also worked as a wheelwright and veterinarian. Pictured from left to right are John Garfield (1911–1997), Jim (John's father), and James Garfield Markley (Jim's brother). The shop was razed in the late 1960s. (Courtesy of the Henderson County Genealogical and Historical Society.)

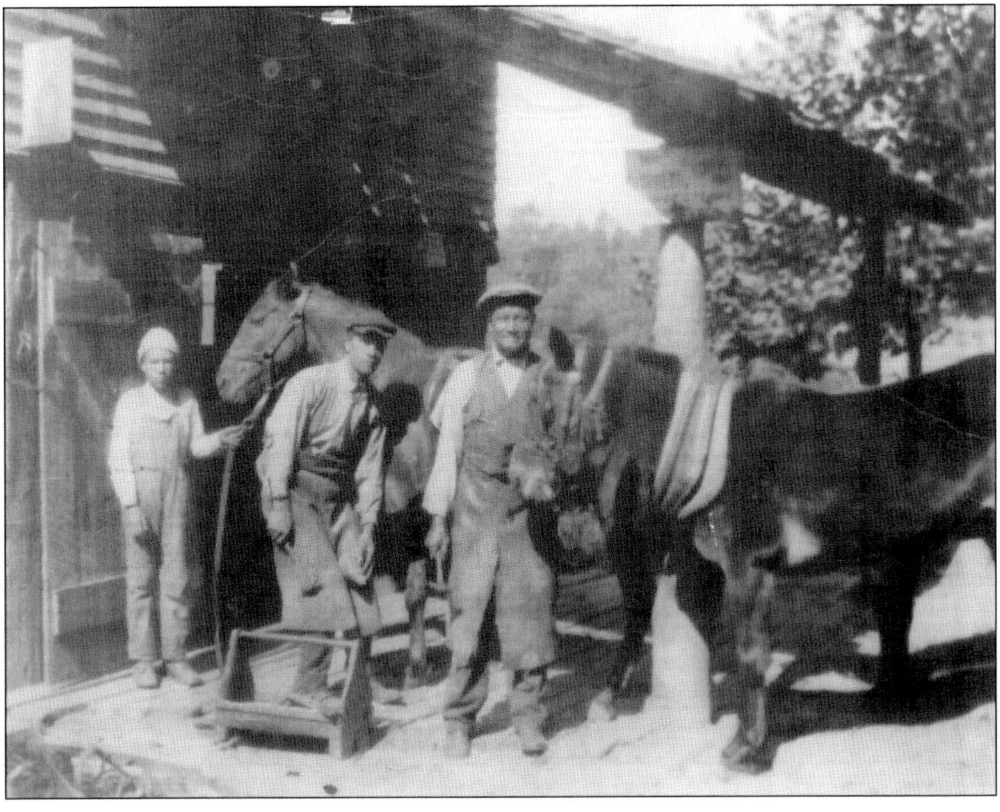

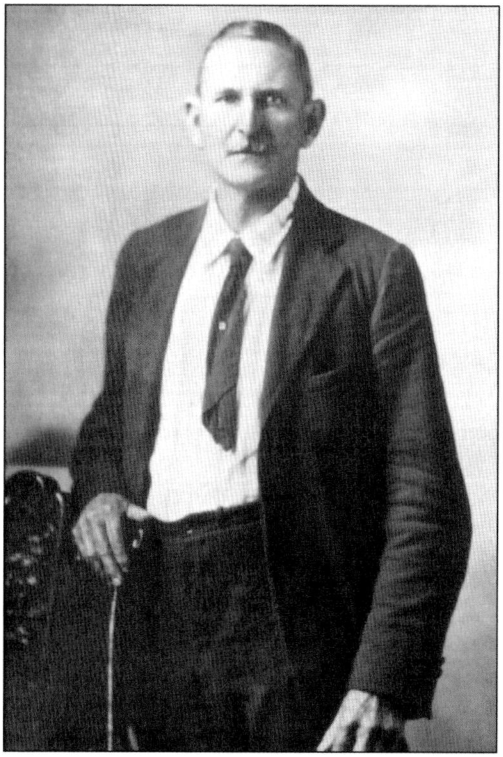

Adam K. Hyder (1860–1932) attended Judson College in Hendersonville. He owned a sawmill in the Big Hungry section of Dana, operated a general store in Upward, served as Henderson County's first superintendent of schools, worked as a cobbler, and hauled produce to South Carolina markets. He built at least three schoolhouses: Adam's Run in Big Hungry (where he taught) and others at Flat Rock and Upward. He also built several houses. (Courtesy of the Henderson County Genealogical and Historical Society.)

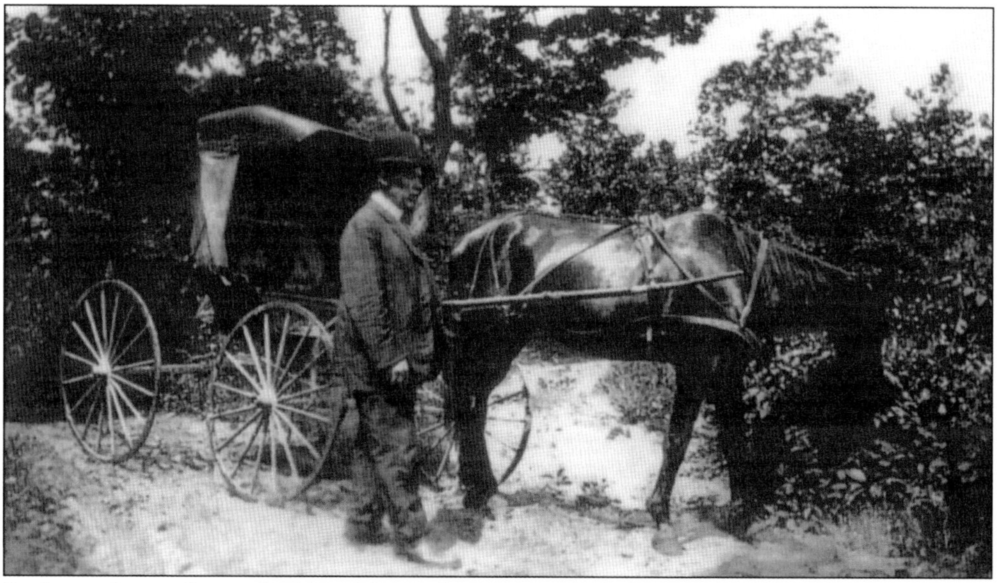

Dr. James Steven Brown (1866–1958), an obstetrician, made house calls in a buggy drawn by his mare Dolly, shown here in 1910. He succeeded the buggy with a Ford Model T, and thereafter with assorted automobiles, some of which he wrecked as he sped to his patients. Brown practiced medicine for 65 years, with his home at times doubling as a pediatric ward. He helped deliver more than 6,500 babies during his illustrious career. In 1948, the American Medical Association awarded a gold medal to Dr. Brown. *Ripley's Believe It or Not* cited Dr. Brown for delivering twins on his 92nd birthday. (Courtesy of Sarah Brown Cannon.)

Milas Monroe "Roe" Shepherd (1867–1929), a pioneer Hendersonville merchant, served as mayor from 1913 to 1915. With his partner Flavius Goodson Hart Sr., Shepherd operated M.M. Shepherd's Dry Goods from Main Street's first building. In 1919, Roe purchased Hart's interest and renamed the business Shepherd Brothers Furniture and Undertakers. His brother Thomas (1875–1940) operated the undertaking business. Four years later, Roe bought the merchandise interest of Thomas. Roe moved to a brick-veneered store, completed in 1847, on the east side of Main Street between Second and Third Avenues. M.M. Shepherd sold everything from shoes and general merchandise to furniture and caskets. He married Susan Patton (1882–1967). (Courtesy of the Henderson County Genealogical and Historical Society.)

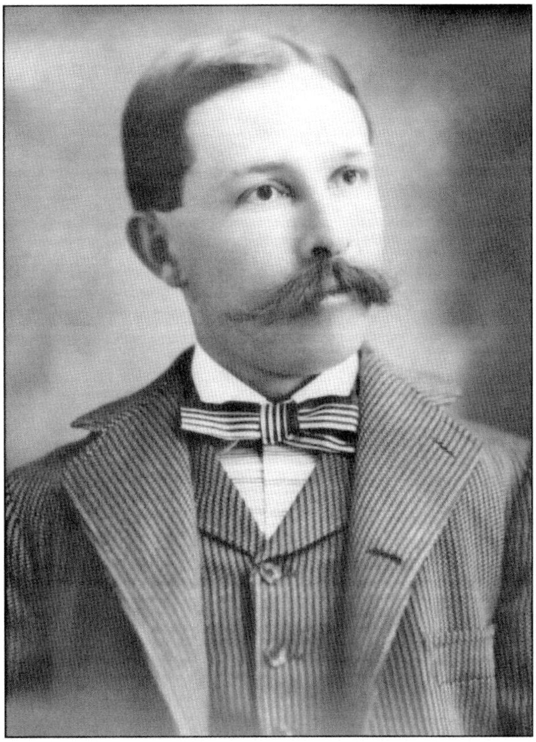

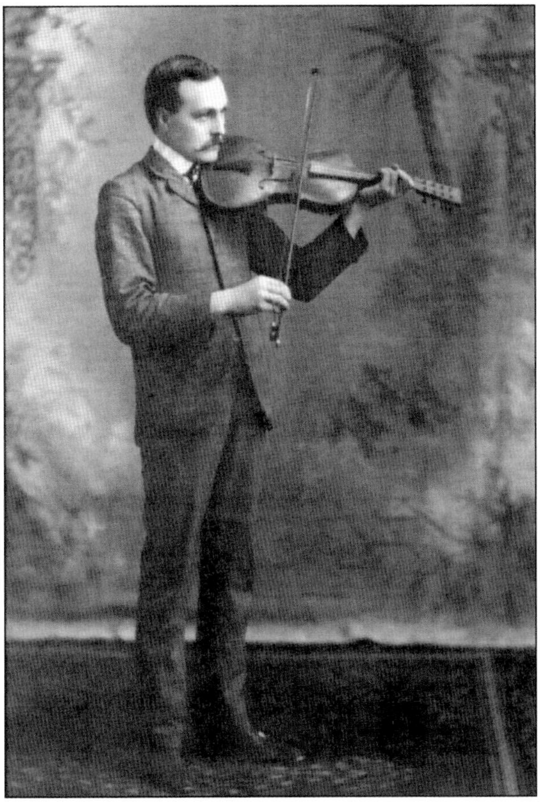

Thomas Dulus Stepp (1878–1966), a Renaissance man, attended Judson College, co-owned Laureldale Cannery, served as a Henderson County commissioner (1927–1930), helped bring electricity and paved roads to Dana, and became a master miller. Dulus married Anna Margaret Pace Pittillo (1884–1960) in 1910. (Courtesy of Carolyn Justus.)

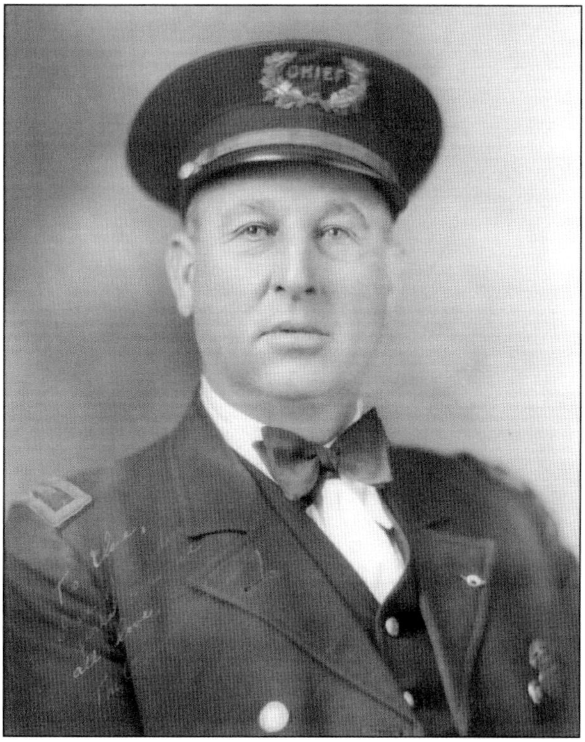

Otis Vernon Powers (1886–1940), Hendersonville's longest-serving chief of police (1915–1940), served also as fire chief and head of the city's street and sanitation departments. (Courtesy of the Henderson County Genealogical and Historical Society.)

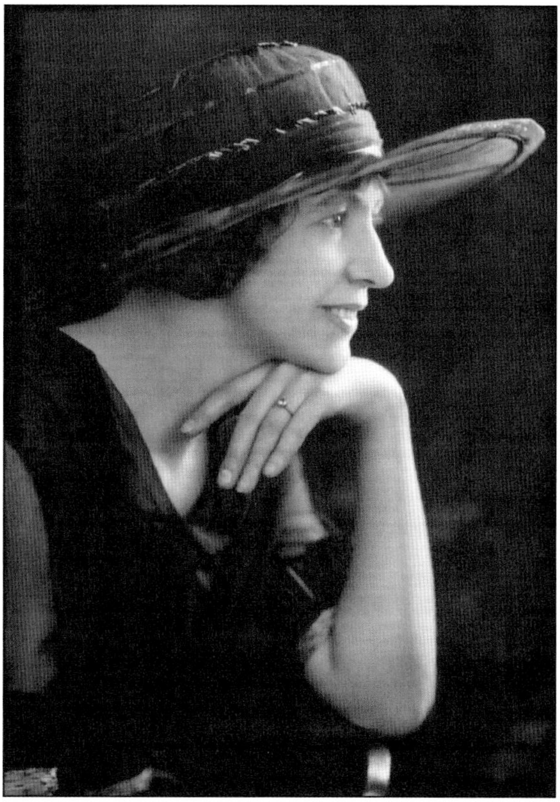

Jennie Bowen (1890–1976) learned haute couture and operated a successful fashion house in Hendersonville. She expanded her Main Street business, Land O' Sky Fashions, moving it into her newly purchased hotel on Church Street, which she renamed the Hotel Bowen. She also owned Bowen Apartments on Fifth Avenue West. Bowen, a philanthropist, involved herself in many civic causes. She was a granddaughter of the Reverend Nelson Bowen—an educator, minister, president of Judson College, and publisher of the Baptist publications *Carolina Baptist* and *Cottage Visitor.* (Courtesy of Patsy Pryor.)

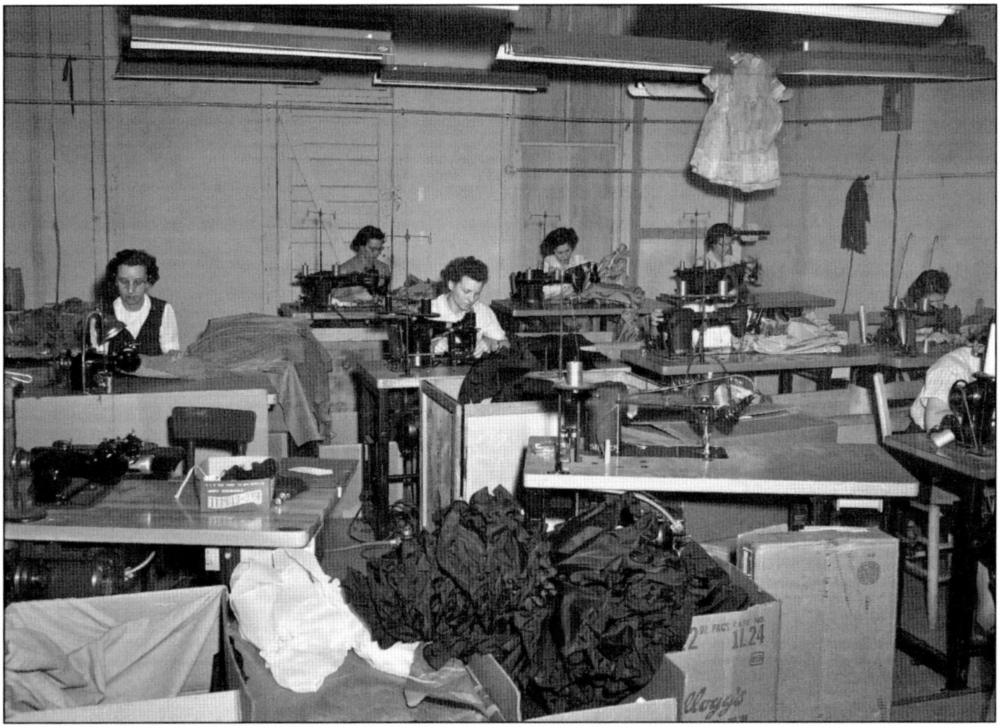

Business partners Ruth Waddill Combs (1917–1984) and Daisy Rice Bartlett Sample (1908–1981) opened a design-and-sewing business in Sample's Hendersonville home in 1950. Before long, Ruth's Originals Corporation grossed multiple millions in international sales. The company maintained manufacturing plants in Brevard and Forest City and showrooms in several cities around the country and employed more than 400 people. The company, which specialized in high-end children's clothing, moved into the Ripley/Huggins building at Main Street and First Avenue West, pictured here, in 1953. The business relocated to Stoney Mountain Road (1956) and finally to Francis Road (1973). Absorba Incorporated of France bought the company in 1977. (Courtesy of the Henderson County Genealogical and Historical Society.)

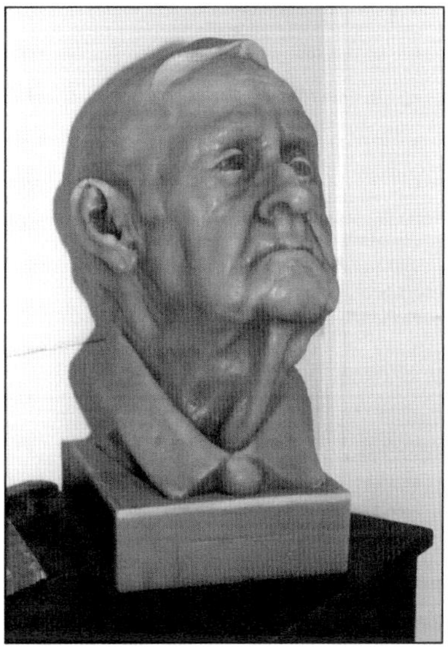

This wax bust of Frank Lockwood FitzSimons Sr. (1897–1980) served as a mold for the bronze casting currently on display in the Henderson County Public Library. Best remembered as a raconteur, WHKP radio personality, and author of the three-volume series *From the Banks of the Oklawaha*, FitzSimons also served as a register of deeds, a schoolteacher, a coach, a farmer, and a banker. (Photograph by the author.)

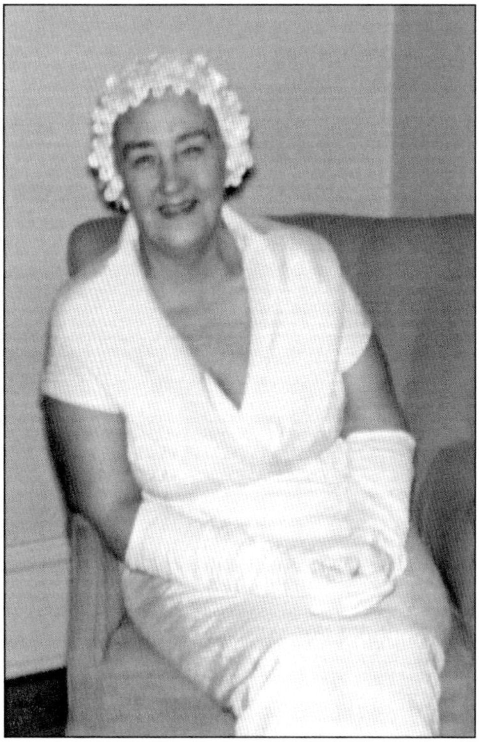

Margaret Catherine "Kate" Dotson (1901–1971) began playing the organ at Hendersonville First United Methodist Church from 1927 and celebrated 30 years there in 1957. Dotson taught voice and keyboards to young musical hopefuls in a studio above her father's harness shop on North Main Street in the building currently housing Mezzaluna restaurant. She remained single and continued to play for her church until suffering a heart attack. (Courtesy of Mary Elizabeth Blair McLeod.)

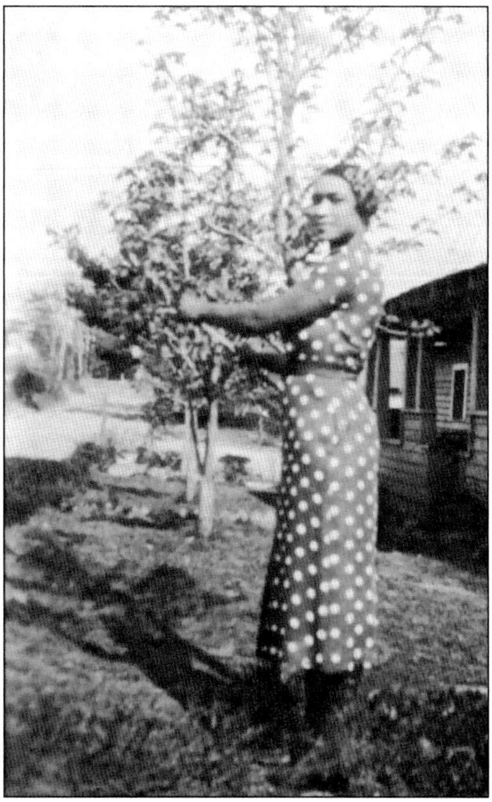

Alberta Jowers Mooney (1907–1992), the first African American registered nurse at Patton Memorial Hospital, started *Mountain News*, the only black newspaper ever published in Henderson County. She also founded the first black Girl Scout troop in Hendersonville and sponsored a black baseball team in the 1920s. Jowers opened a beauty salon at 719 Maple Street—Hendersonville's first beauty shop, not counting those operated from private homes. (Courtesy of Dorothy Means.)

From 1948 to 1960, Elizabeth G. Rogers (born 1917) taught at Flat Rock High School, which in 1960 was absorbed into the newly formed East Henderson High School. She next taught at East Henderson High School until her retirement in 1979. Rogers celebrated her 100th birthday in September 2017. (Courtesy of Jo Ann Fain.)

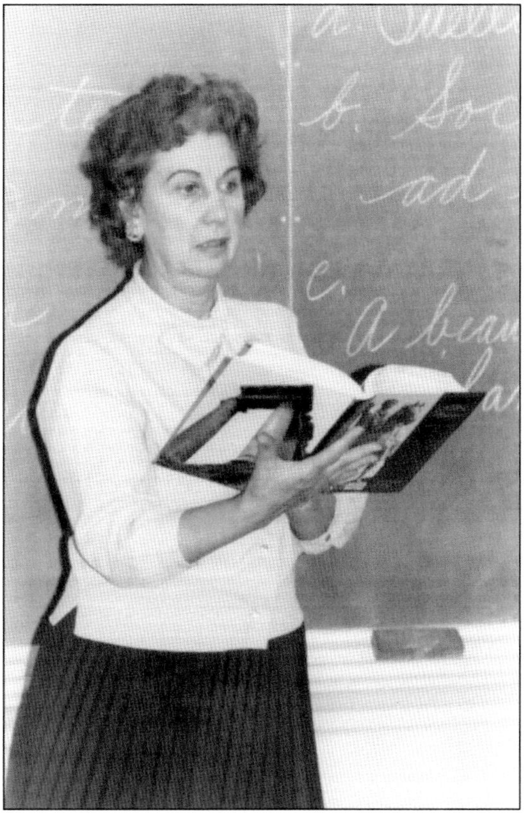

Roy "Bush" Laughter (1927–2013) was a revered storyteller, pipe fitter, and charter member of the Valley Hill Fire Department. (Courtesy of Tammy Laughter Manley.)

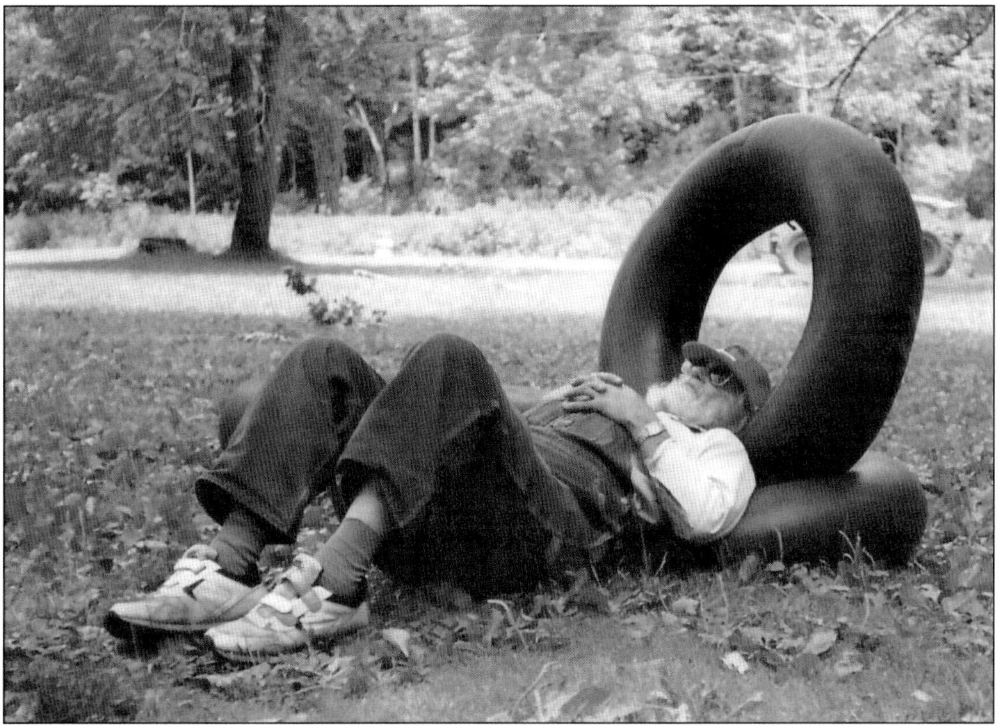

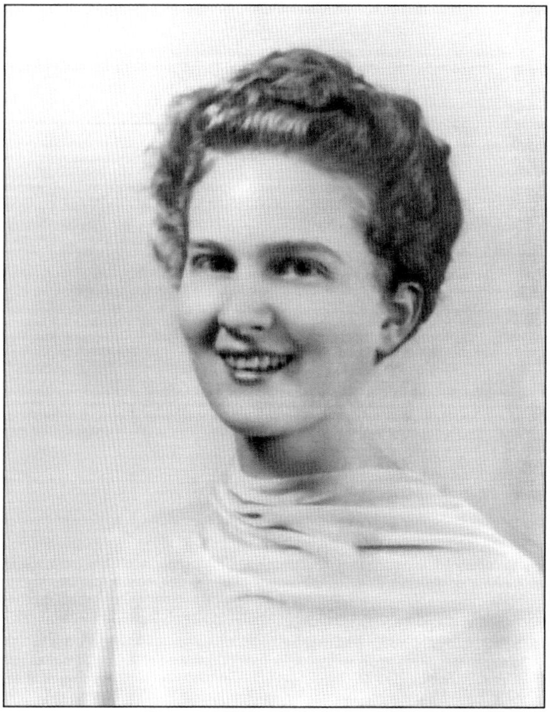

Louisa "Louise" King Howe (1915–2009) married Dr. Joseph Peden Bailey (1917–1986), a World War II veteran and Henderson County physician. The couple had three sons: Joseph Jr., William, and Robert. Louise taught in Edgefield, South Carolina, and was a member of the National League of American Pen Women, a trustee of Historic Flat Rock, and an author, historian, storyteller, and newspaper columnist. (Both, courtesy of Joseph P. Bailey Jr.)

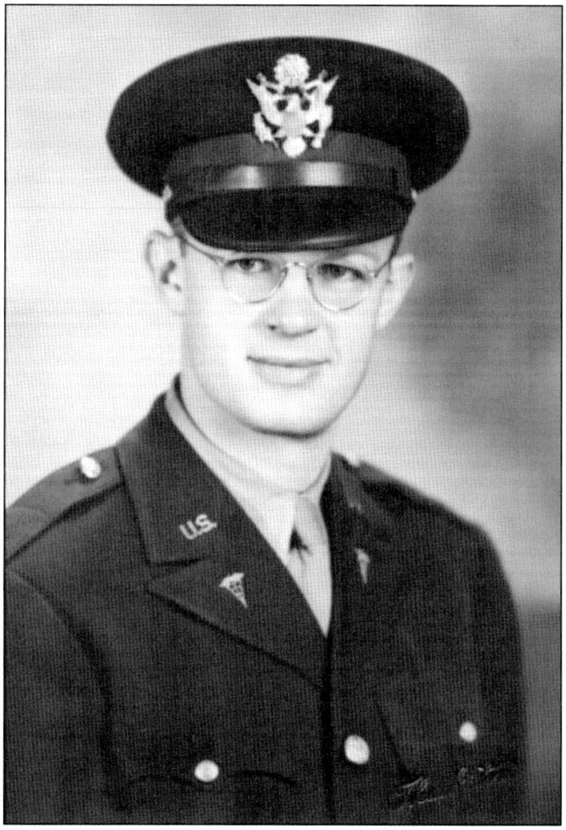

Known as "Old Doc Howe," Dr. William Bell White Howe III (1881–1948) of Charleston and Flat Rock worked as a country doctor. He began his practice with a horse and buggy and then a motorcycle, later employing his Ford Model T and Buick touring car to make house calls. Doc Howe first married Theodosia Marie Hart, later married Elizabeth Anderson Glasgow (1900–1974), and was the father of Jennie Louise Howe (Merrill) (1913–2013), Louise King Howe (Bailey), W.B.W. Howe IV (1928–2003), and Joseph Glasgow Howe (1930–2005). (Courtesy of the estate of Louise H. Bailey.)

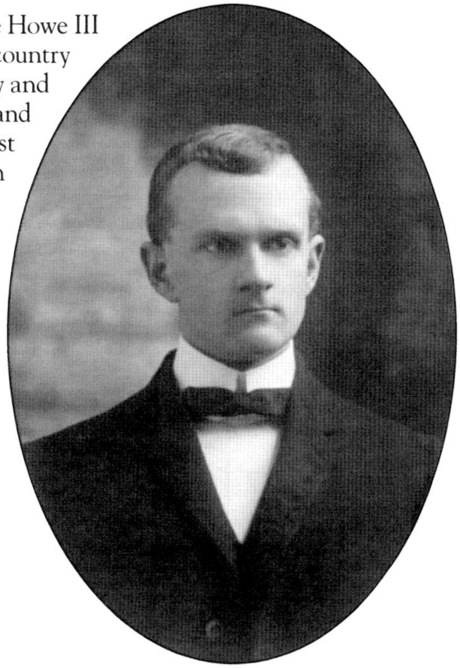

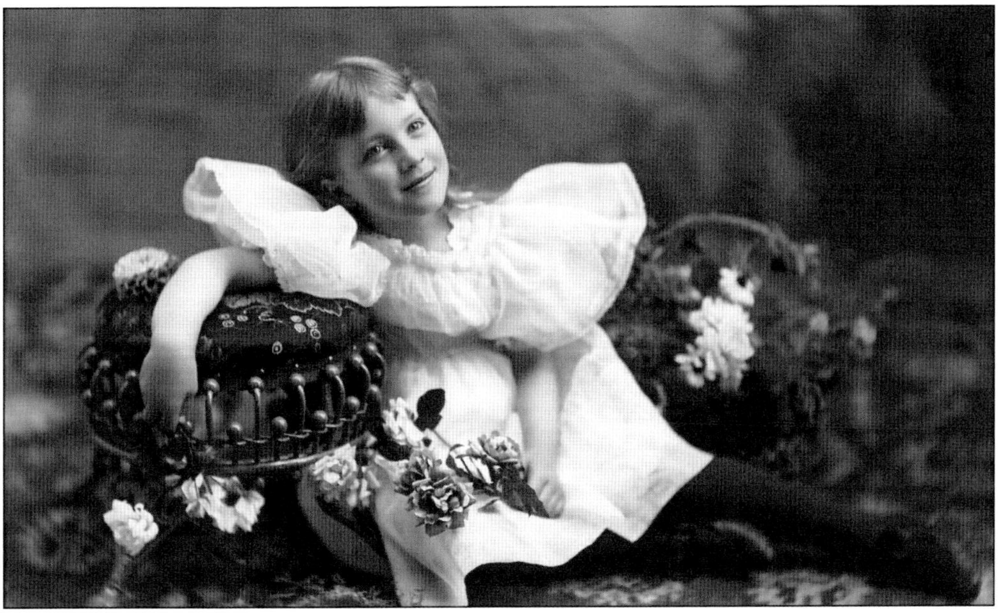

Theodosia "Theo" Marie Hart (1891–1984) was a daughter of Flavius Goodson "Flave" Hart Sr. (1852–1940) and Susan K. Allen Hart (1854–1948) and a granddaughter of Dr. Thomas Alexander Allen (1824–1914), Hendersonville's first mayor. Flave owned a produce-shipping company. Theo married Dr. W.B.W. Howe III in 1911. The couple had two daughters, Jennie Louise Merrill and Louise King Howe Bailey. After the Howes divorced, Theo married John Archer Speight (1894–1975), a pharmacist who owned Speight's Cut Rate Drug Store at 112 South Main Street. Theo taught music, performed on radio programs, and sold goods from the Curb Market. The Speights had a daughter, Jane Sue Speight Suttles (1925–2008). (Courtesy of the Baker-Barber Collection, Community Foundation of Henderson County, Henderson County Public Library.)

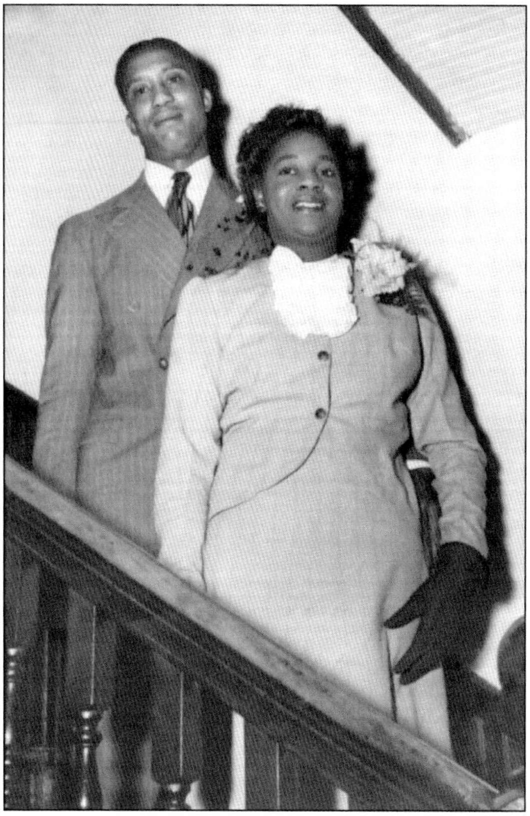

Alexander (1917–1986) and Sarah Louise Gash Pilgrim (1925–2004) posed for this portrait on their wedding day, September 15, 1948. Alexander worked with the family business, Pilgrim's Funeral Home. (Courtesy of Melinda Pilgrim Lowrance.)

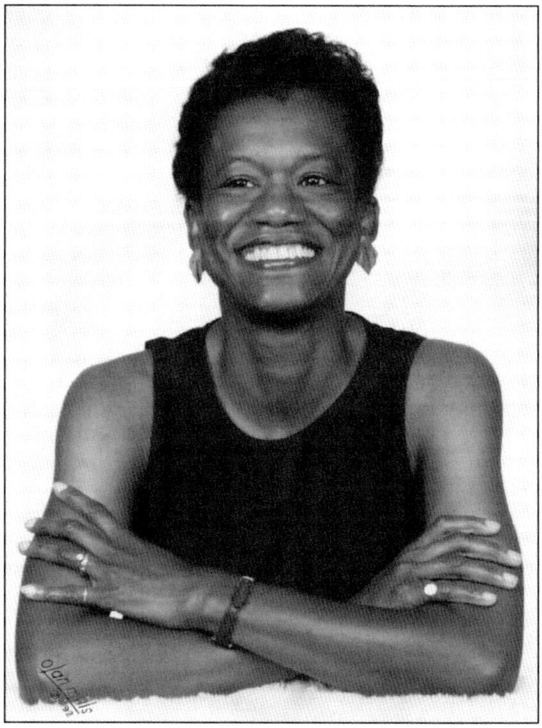

One of four daughters of Alexander and Sarah Pilgrim, Melinda Pilgrim Lowrance (born 1951) owns Mophead Cleaning Services in Hendersonville and serves as president of the local chapter of the NAACP. (Olan Mills photograph, courtesy of Melinda Pilgrim Lowrance.)

The Reverend Harold Lloyd McKinnish (1933–2013), known as the "Baptist Bishop of Henderson County," pastored several churches, including Ebenezer, Fletcher, Fruitland, Liberty, Refuge, and Tuxedo. (Courtesy of Lois McKinnish.)

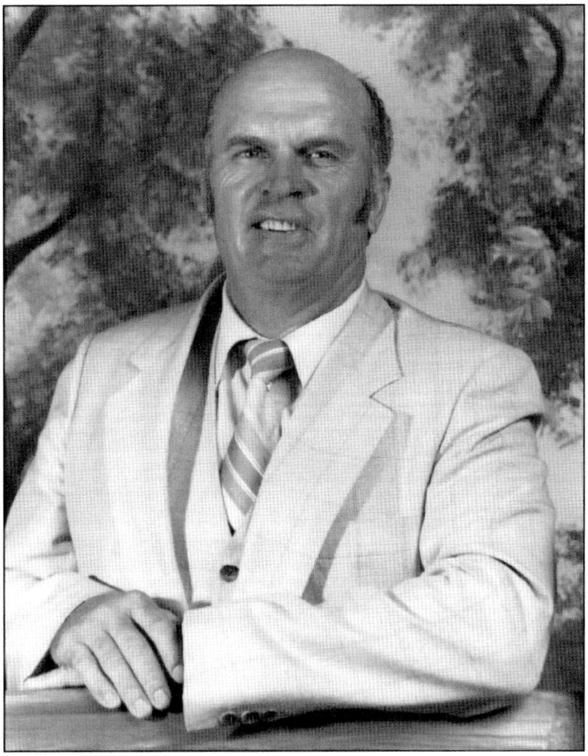

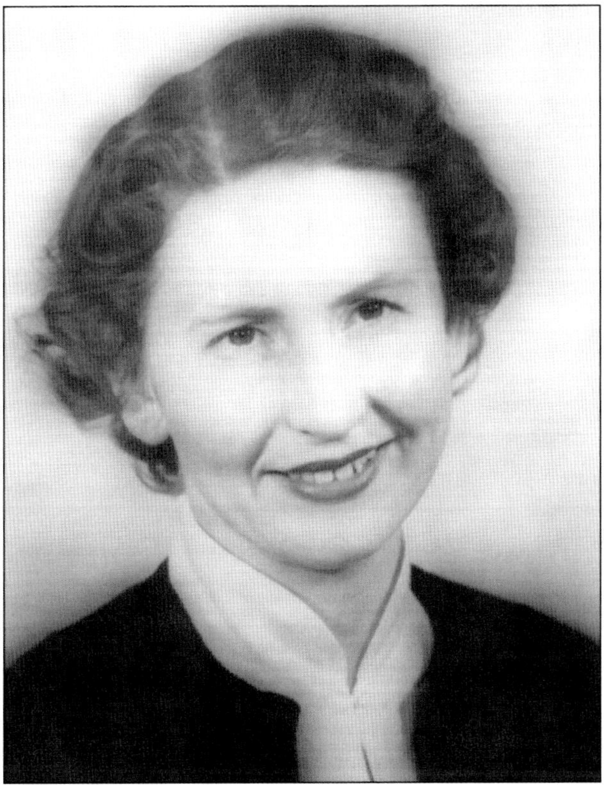

Margaret Ann Hunsinger Davidson (1929–2012), an Edneyville native, taught home economics at Flat Rock and East Henderson High Schools. Davidson owned and operated her parents' lodging facilities, Hunsingers' Cottages, and worked as a tireless leader of the Edneyville Grange. She conceived of and carried through the building of the Edneyville Community Center and kept the farm-centered organization alive when many of its sister clubs in rural communities faded into history. (Ed Hunnicutt photograph, author's collection.)

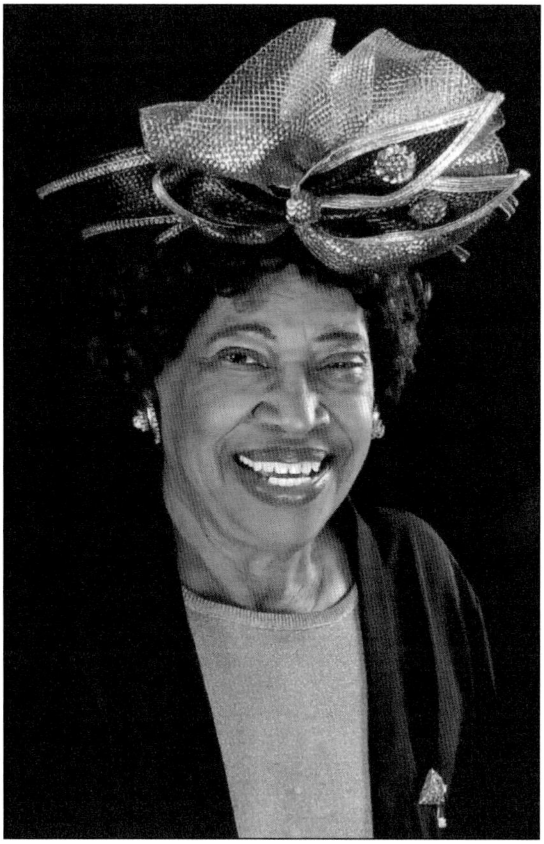

Beloved educator Hannah Logan Edwards (1929–2017), a native of Etowah and resident of East Flat Rock, was born to Clingman Manuel Logan (1881–1972) and Bertha Smith Logan (1882–1965). Hannah married James L. Edwards (1917–1987). She taught at Ninth Avenue School and Hendersonville High School, served as a member of numerous community organizations, and was an active member of St. Paul Tabernacle AME Zion Church. (Photograph by the author.)

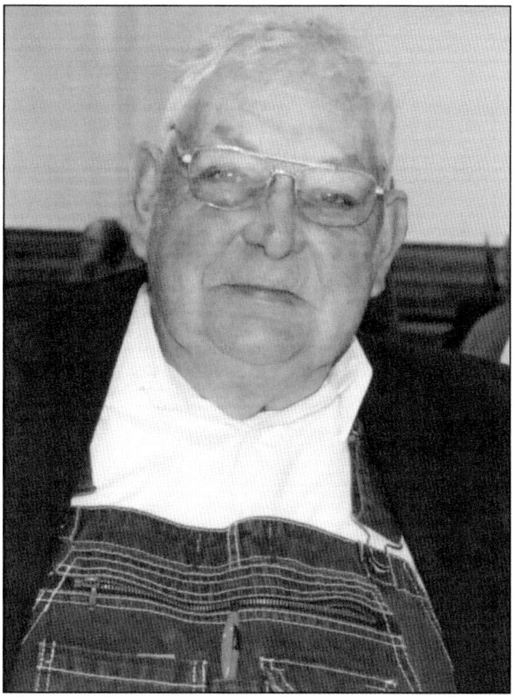

Theron Larnce Maybin Sr. (1943–2017) was known as the "Mayor of Green River." A Vietnam veteran and descendant of Matthew Maybin (1756–1840), one of Henderson County's earliest settlers, Theron was celebrated for his prizewinning produce and his mentorship in the field of agriculture. (Photograph by the author.)

Three

Central Henderson County

Laurel Park, Big Willow, Pleasant Grove, Shaws Creek, Horse Shoe, Etowah, Dana, and Upward

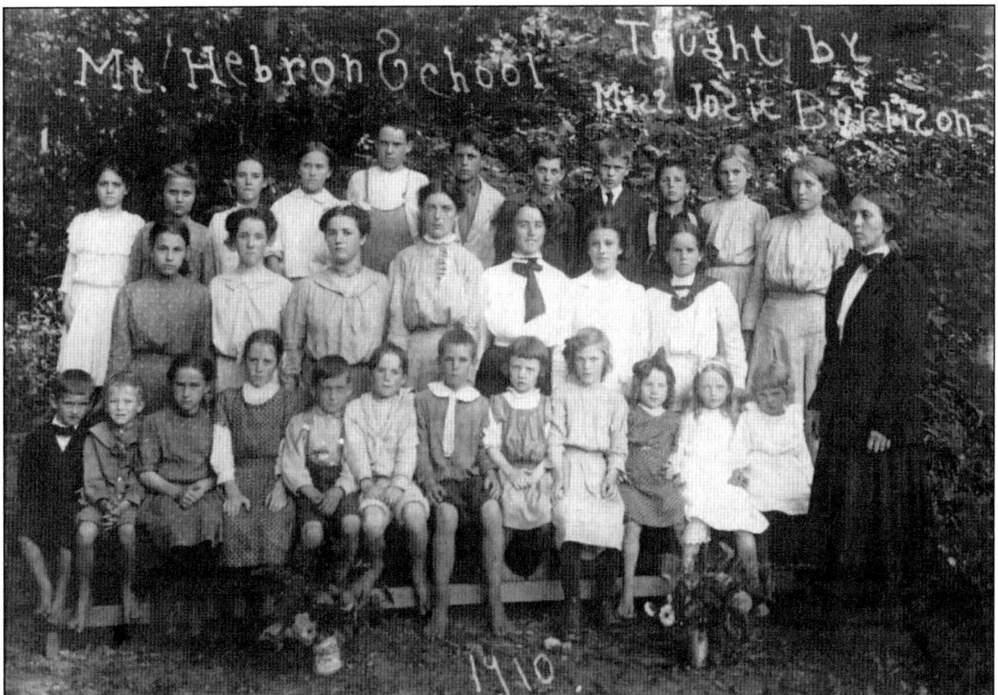

Posing for this 1910 photograph of Mount Hebron School at Jones Gap, are, from left to right, (first row) George Leslie, George Justus, Louise Nelson, Bonnie Jones, John Leslie, Virgil Jones, Weldon Blythe, Reba Orr, Julia Belle Leslie, Maude Jones, Lillie Summey (Barnette), and Mary Ann Leslie; (second row) Della Nelson, Dosha Jones, Effie Jones, Bessie Leslie, Daisy Jones, Mary Justus, and Bertha Blythe; (third row) Edith Justus, Maude Middleton, Ethel Orr, Dee Middleton, Coy Orr, Howard Wright, Albert Leslie, Hobson Justus, Yancy Revis, Annie Leslie, Jane Leslie, and teacher Josephine "Josie" Burleson (Brigman) (1884–1963). (Courtesy of Ella Corn Surrette.)

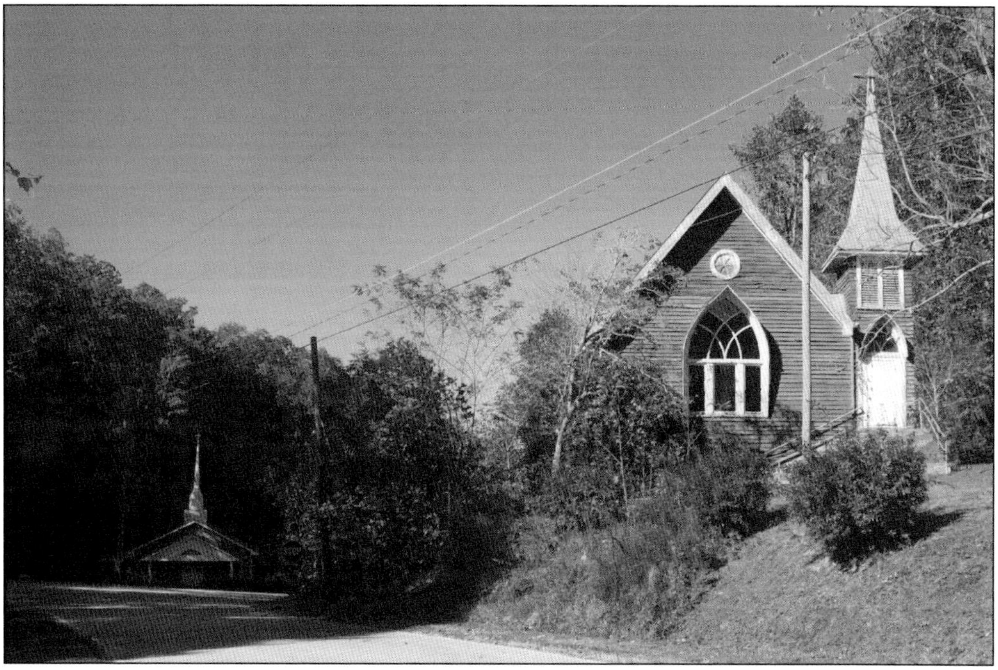

Charter members assigned the name Mount Crystal to the church they constituted from Shaws Creek Baptist Church and organized a fellowship in 1892 on Jump Off Mountain. In February 1912, Capt. M.C. Toms and his son Charles French Toms (1872–1937) gave $1,000 toward relocating the church. Congregants hauled the structure in sections by horse and wagon to its present site in 1913. Suggesting Jones Gap as the new church name, Hicks Jones conferred a half acre near the Mount Hebron schoolhouse for the relocated sanctuary, since known as Jones Gap Baptist Church. In 1995, the fellowship began construction of a new brick sanctuary across the road; it was completed and dedicated in 1998. (Photograph by the author.)

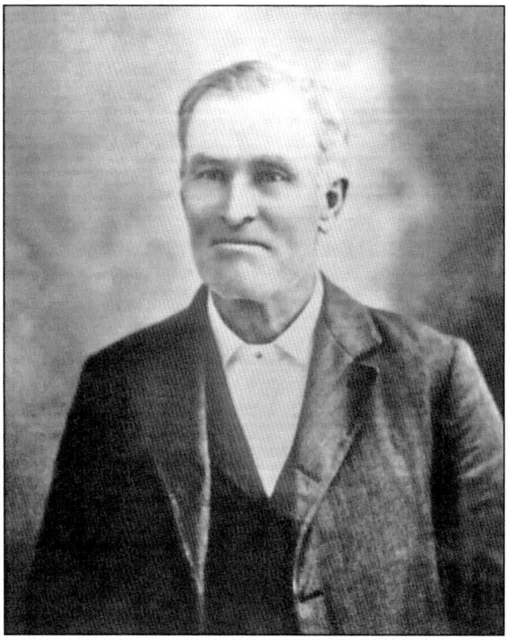

Hicks Jones (1841–1922), son of Solomon Jones, gave the land for Jones Gap Baptist Church. (Courtesy of Don McCarson.)

John Finlay (1819–1901), the namesake of Finley Cove, owned acreage below Solomon Jones's land on Mount Hebron. Finlay amassed more than 500 acres on the mountainside stretching to Valley Hill. Between 1879 and 1885, Jones and Finlay were embroiled in a civil suit concerning the construction of a road from Hendersonville to Mount Hebron. (Courtesy of Robert Justus.)

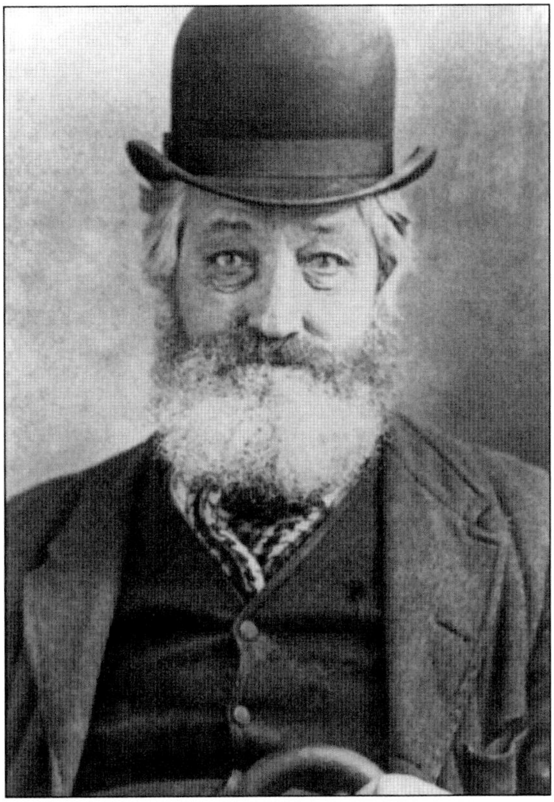

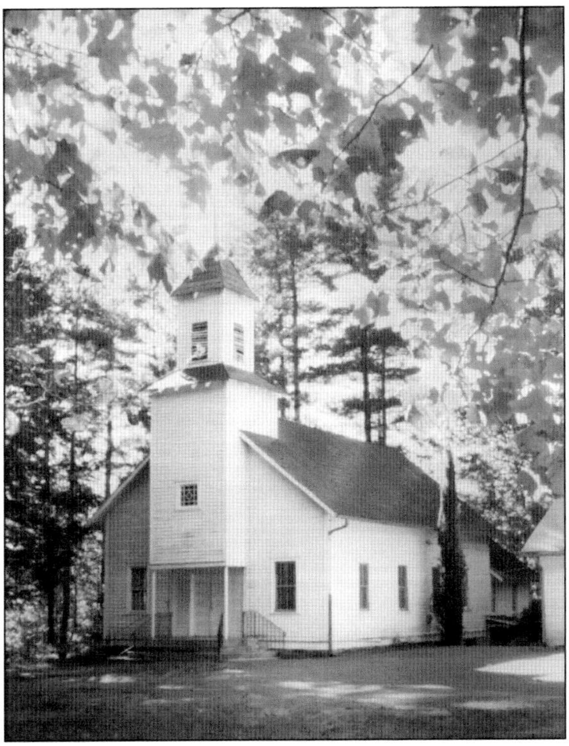

Members established Beulah Baptist Church in 1815 in the Pleasant Grove section of Etowah. (Courtesy of the Henderson County Genealogical and Historical Society.)

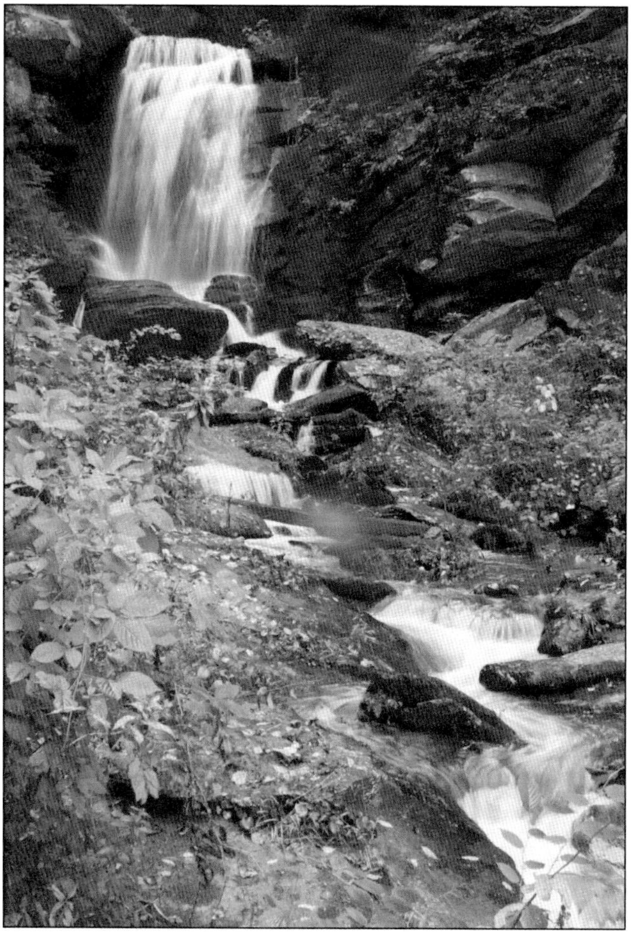

Seven Falls flows near an area once known as the Follies in Pleasant Grove where moonshine could be exchanged for money during Prohibition. (Photograph by the author.)

In the 1890s, William Alexander Smith (1858–1922) began developing Laurel Park as a recreational area with Crystal Spring as its focal point. Visitors flocked to the foot of the mountain to picnic and sip purportedly healthful water from this spring. A latticed shed initially covered the site, but by 1910, the structure had been replaced with an arch of native stone. Visitors could also stroll nearby Cupid's Path, bordered by thickets of rhododendron and laurel, on their trek to nearby Horseshoe Spring and Rainbow Lake. (C.H. Oak Collection, courtesy of the Henderson County Genealogical and Historical Society.)

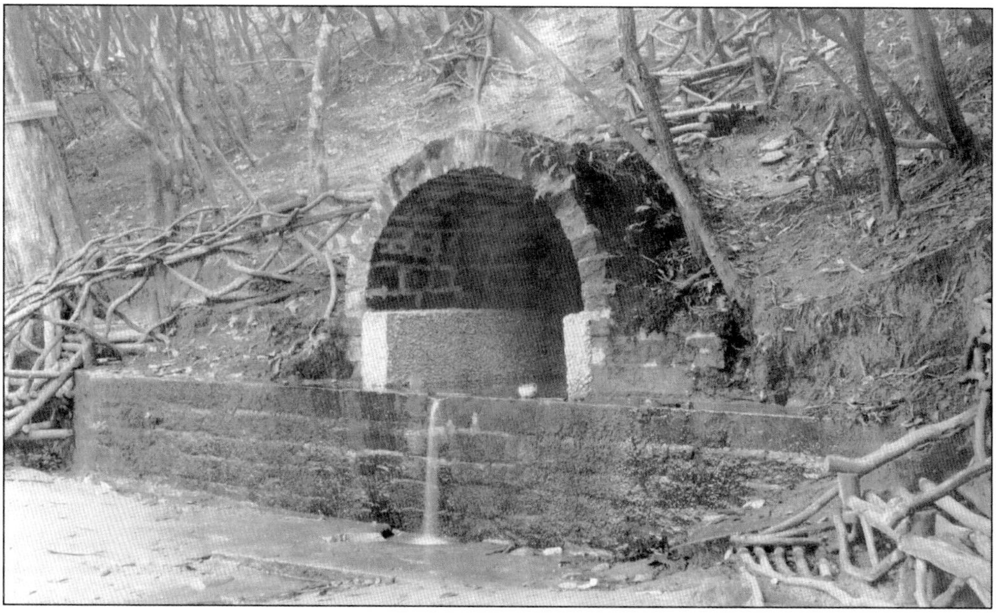

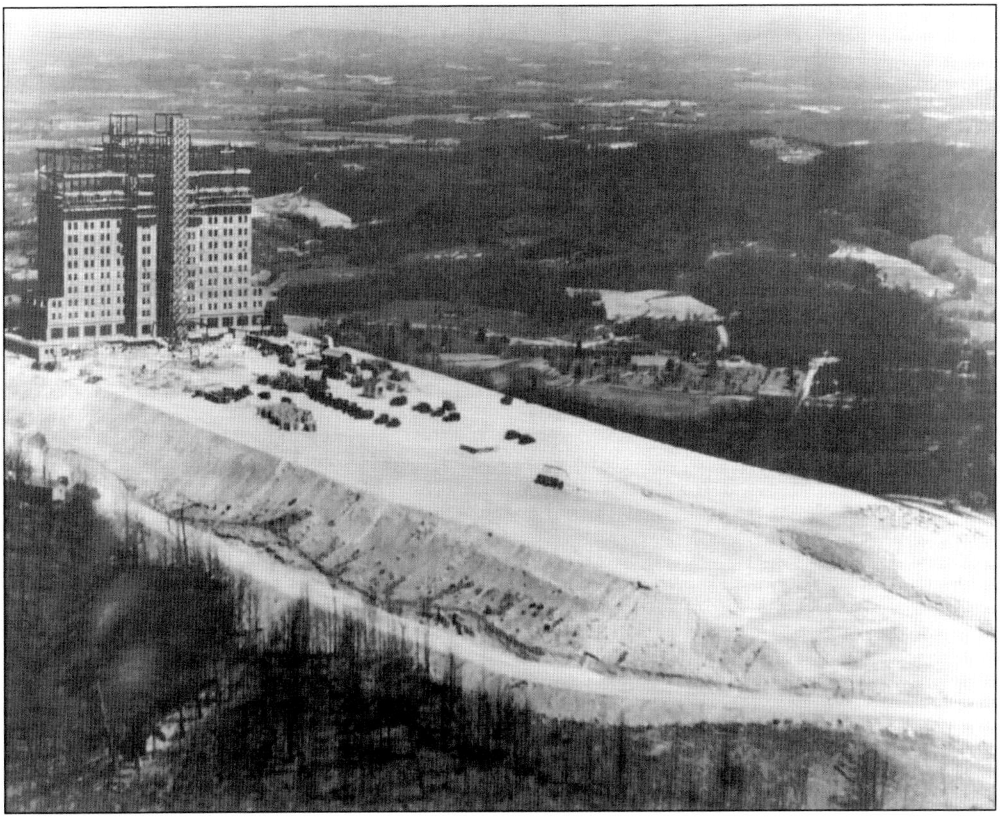

By 1926, the 15-story Fleetwood Hotel neared completion at the summit of Jump Off Mountain. The ill-fated development included a grand plaza and 101 acres of home sites. Developments leading to the stock market crash of 1929 spelled failure for the opulent skyscraper atop the mountain in Laurel Park Estates. (Courtesy of Jim Toms.)

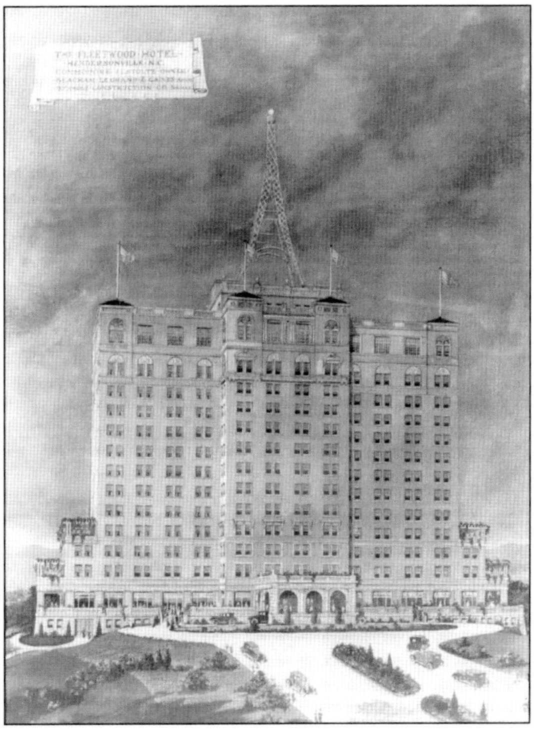

This architect's sketch of the Fleetwood Hotel portrays an intended radio tower on its roof. Faltering land speculation in Florida together with the 1926 hurricane doomed such projects as the Fleetwood. The nearly completed hotel, the brainchild of J. Perry Stoltz (1870–1945) of New York and Miami Beach, was razed in 1937 and sold for scrap. Stoltz also owned a Fleetwood Hotel in Miami Beach and had intended to build yet another in Atlanta. (Courtesy of Jim Toms.)

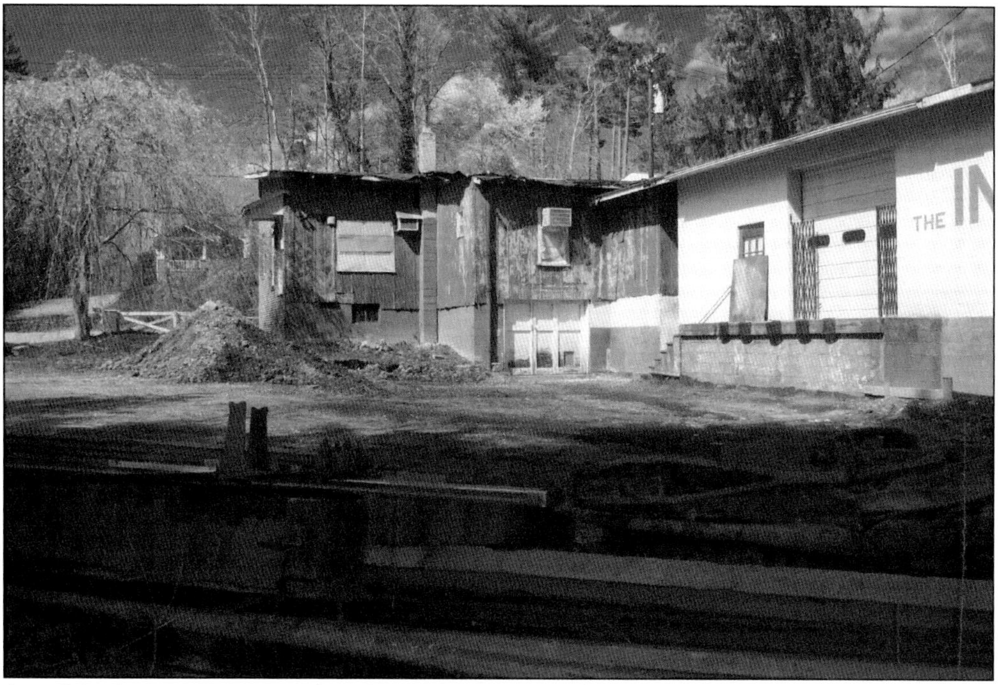

A coal-fired steam-generating plant for powering street rails stood at this site on Fifth Avenue West near Wash Creek Drive. The building later housed INdoors (formerly Raynor Garage Doors) and Richardson's Fuel and Supply Company (coal, oil, and paint). The plant powered Laurel Park's Swiss incline railway and the Dummy Line train in its latter days. (Photograph by the author.)

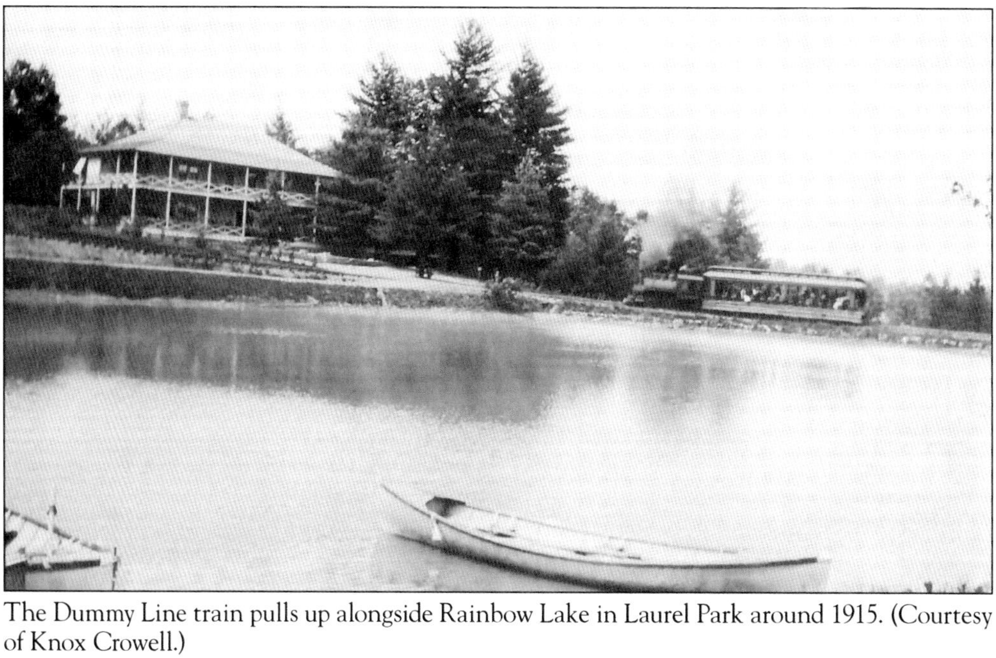

The Dummy Line train pulls up alongside Rainbow Lake in Laurel Park around 1915. (Courtesy of Knox Crowell.)

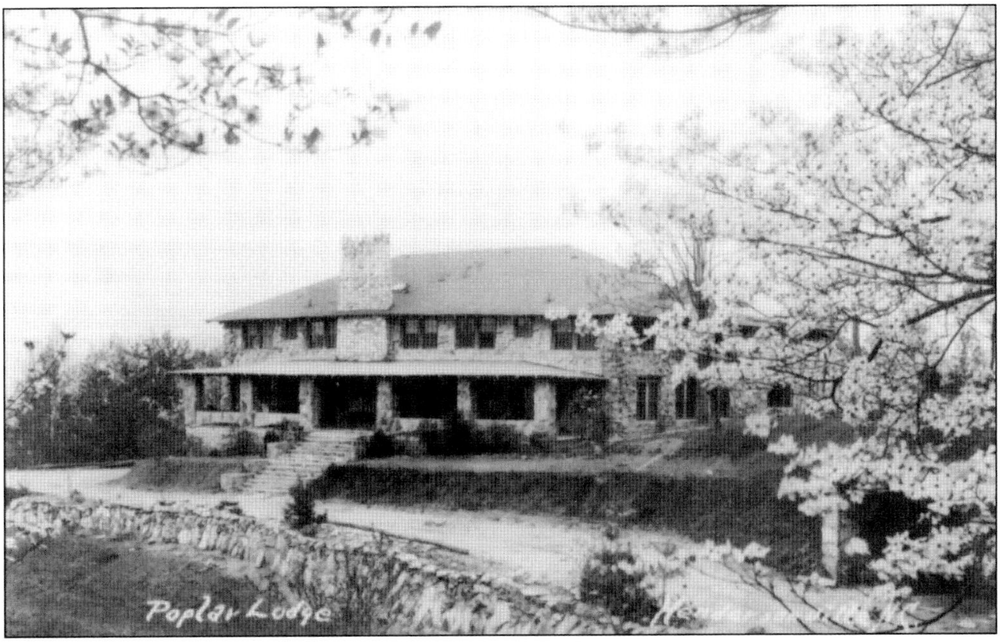

Built in 1919 as a hunting lodge alongside Hebron Road in Laurel Park, Poplar Lodge featured 10 guest rooms and a clubby dining room with a rock fireplace and walls of chinked logs. Accounts suggest that early owners of this lodge benefitted financially during the Prohibition years. (Courtesy of Knox Crowell)

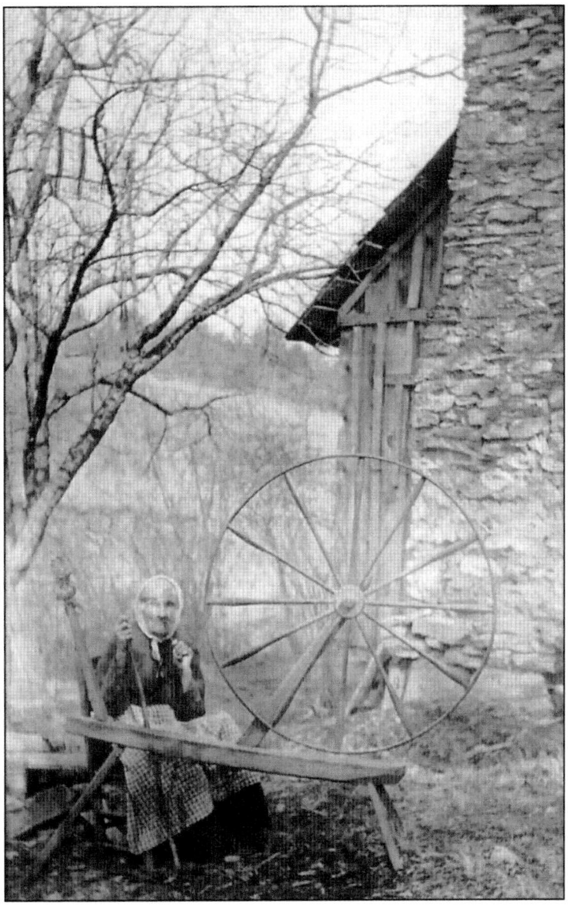

When author Roland Funk Holloway (1898–1978) traveled as a young man through Henderson County in 1913, he met Mary Ann Belcher (1826–1918). When Holloway asked if he could take her photograph with her spinning wheel, she said, "I reckon 'bout five hundred people done tuk mah pitcher with that, but I guess onc't more won't do no harm." The photograph appears in Holloway's book, *Five Months in the Old North State*, published in Chicago in 1914. The photograph later appeared on souvenir postcards. Belcher lived on Willow Road and in Lenox Park. She was buried at Mud Creek Baptist Church Cemetery with—according to her obituary—her hands clutching her Bible. (Courtesy of Knox Crowell.)

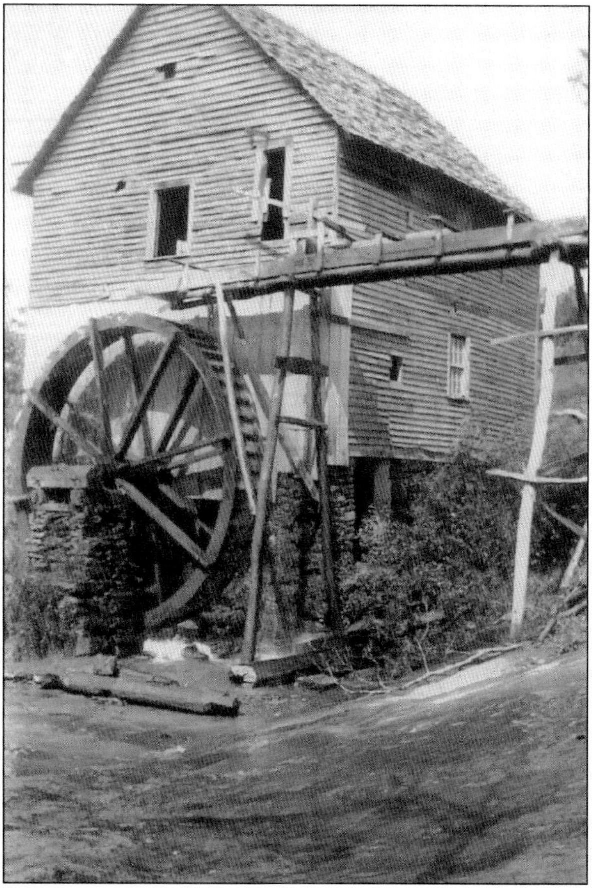

A repurposed gristmill stands in the sector known as Big Willow. Frank L. FitzSimons and other raconteurs dubbed this the "haunted mill," spinning yarns of an eerie glow and specters of an Indian and a miller. Jesse Pritchard Huggins Sr. (1892–1976) purchased the property from James A. Brock (1856–1933) in 1932. The structure later housed an art studio and café and currently serves as a residence. (Courtesy of Barbara Hudson.)

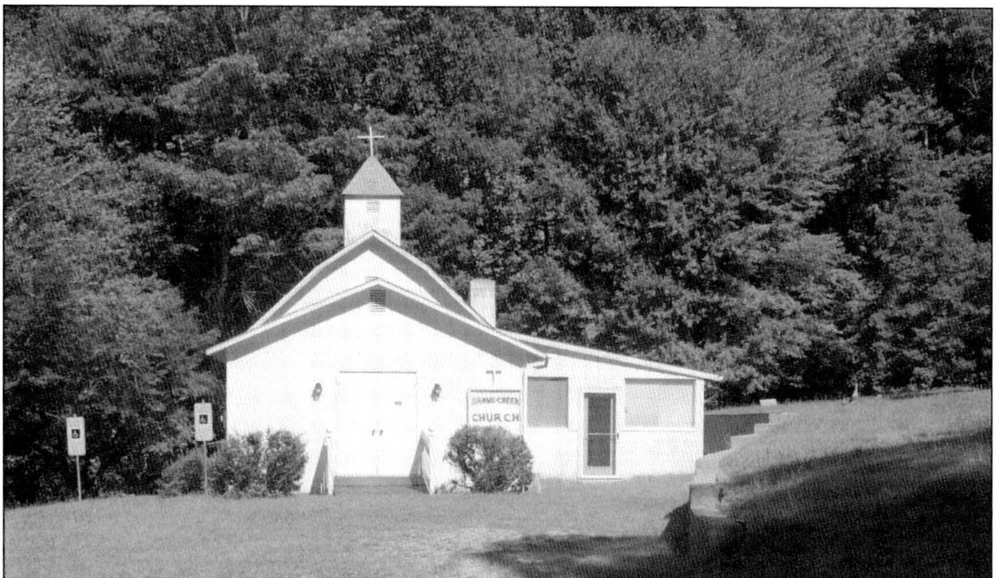

Shaws Creek AME Zion Church, Henderson County's first black church, was established in 1865. Members first held services under a brush arbor. (Photograph by the author.)

Martha Childs Pryor poses with an egg basket used by her parents, Robert B. (1918–1999) and Alice Jane Turner Childs (1920–2004), at their farm. Samuel James Childs (1874–1962) bought 200 acres in 1923 and operated Brightwater Farms, a dairy operation and New Hampshire chicken ranch alongside the Brevard Highway. The Brightwater Heights subdivision grew from the Childs family's resort, Brightwaters Cottages. (Photograph by the author.)

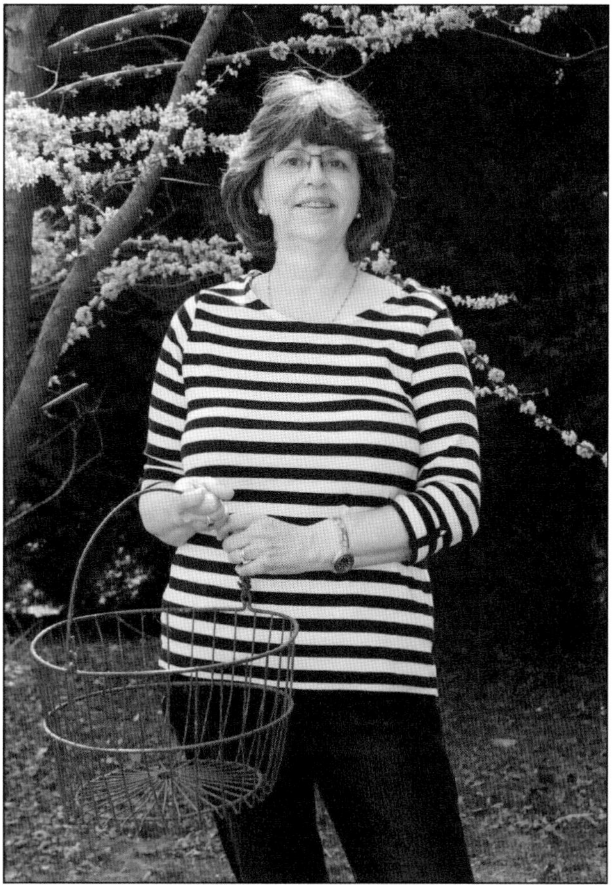

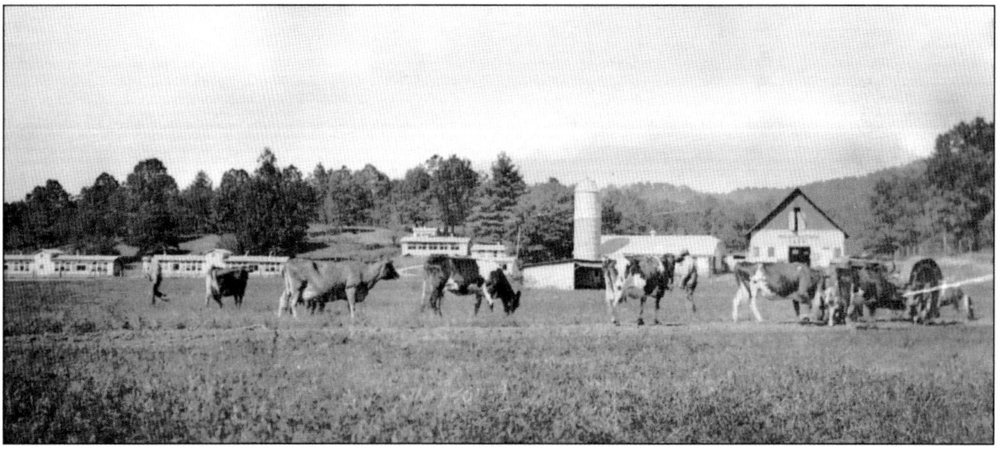

Guernsey and Holstein cattle graze at Brightwater Farms. The large buildings in the left background housed chickens. Samuel Childs raised thousands of prizewinning poultry, 100 sheep, and a herd of goats. In 1933, Childs bought another 200 acres across the highway on a southern slope of Long John Mountain. The Childses converted the former Yale schoolhouse into a lodge and erected a stone guesthouse to supplement their 25 guest cottages. After the Childses sold the poultry operation in 1964, Bradley Gladiolus Farm of Mills River leased the land. (Courtesy of the Childs family.)

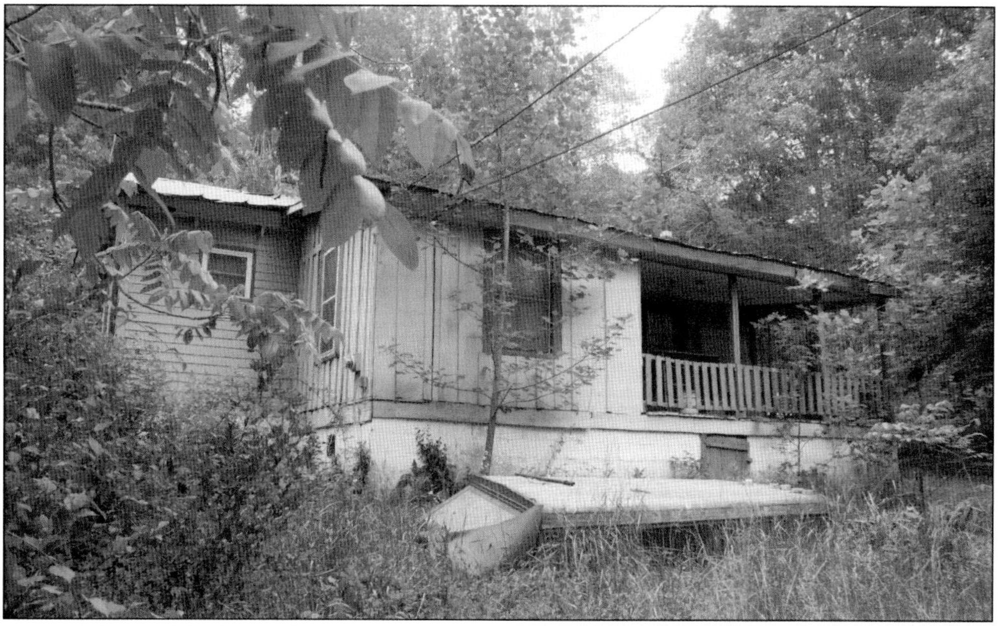

John W. Dausuel (1866–1935) taught at Shaws Creek Colored School, also called the "Dausuel School," pictured here. Artie T. Washington Lynch (1910–2009) and his wife, Lola Ledbetter Lynch (1913–1992), later lived in this converted schoolhouse. (Photograph by the author.)

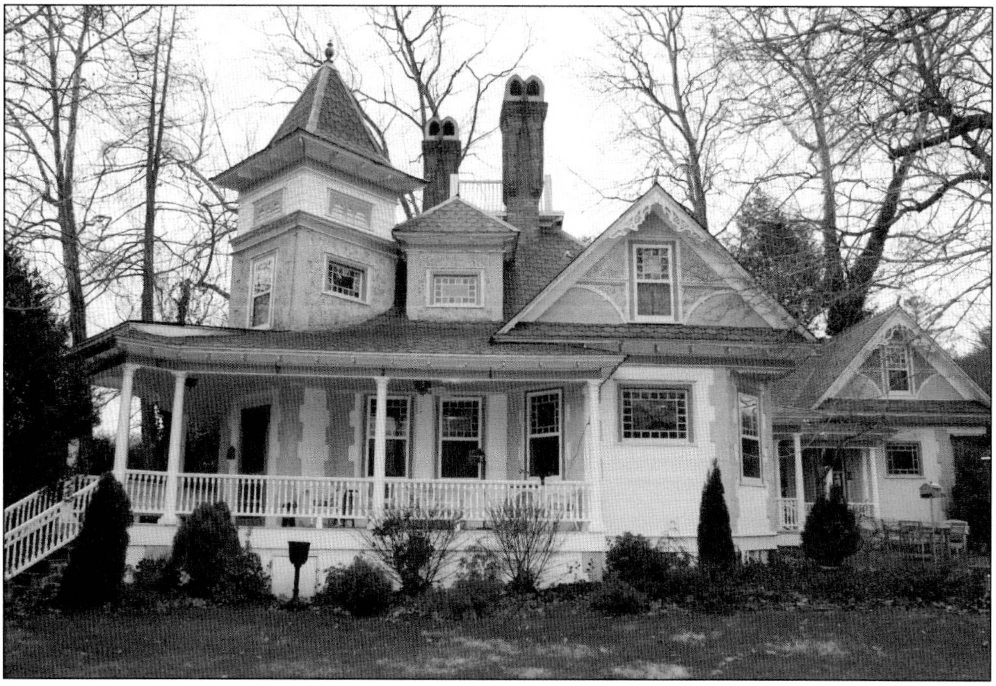

This pebble-dashed, Queen Anne–style home was built in 1891 at Horse Shoe for David Norman Davenport (1856–1925). His son David Laxton Davenport (1911–1986) and David Laxton's wife, Margaret Anderson Davenport (1914–1994), next lived in the home, which later served as a parsonage for Horse Shoe First Baptist Church. The Davenports owned a general store across the road from their home near Banner Farm Road. (Photograph by the author.)

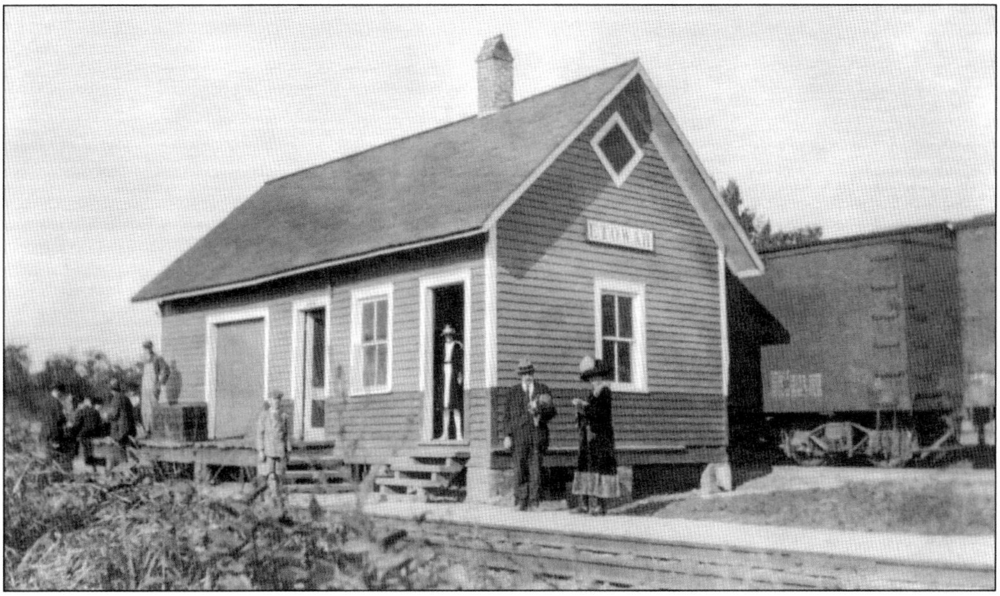

The depot at Etowah was built in 1895 by the Hendersonville and Brevard Railway Telephone & Telegraph Company. The railway station also housed the Etowah Post Office from 1924 to 1962. Pearl Gillie Gash (1883–1971), station agent (1916–1948) and postmaster (1914–1948), stands in the doorway. (Courtesy of Argyle Wells Gash and etowahncheritage.org.)

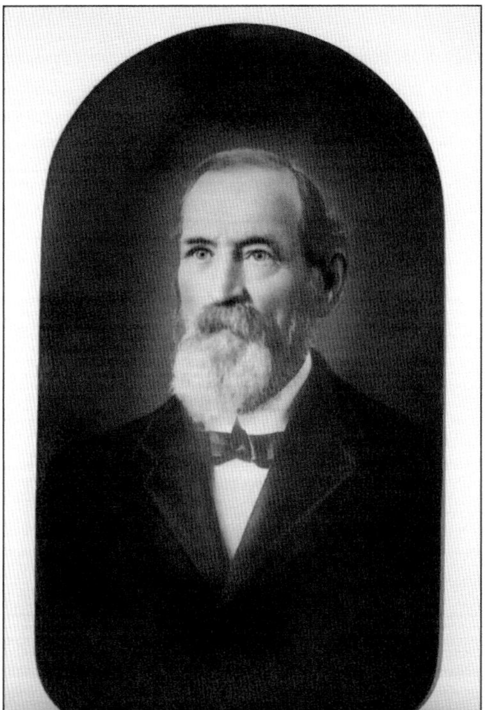

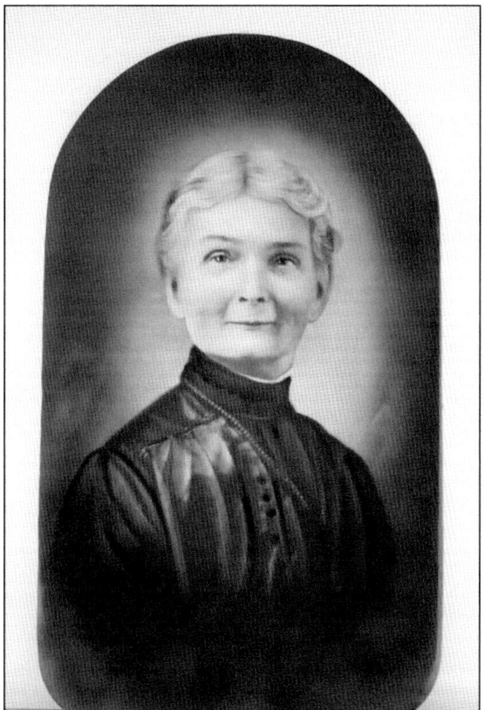

Joseph Leander Gash (1833–1916) gave the land for a railroad station in Etowah and served as station agent. He married Margaret Indiana Stewart (1850–1922). (Both, courtesy of Argyle Wells Gash and etowahncheritage.org.)

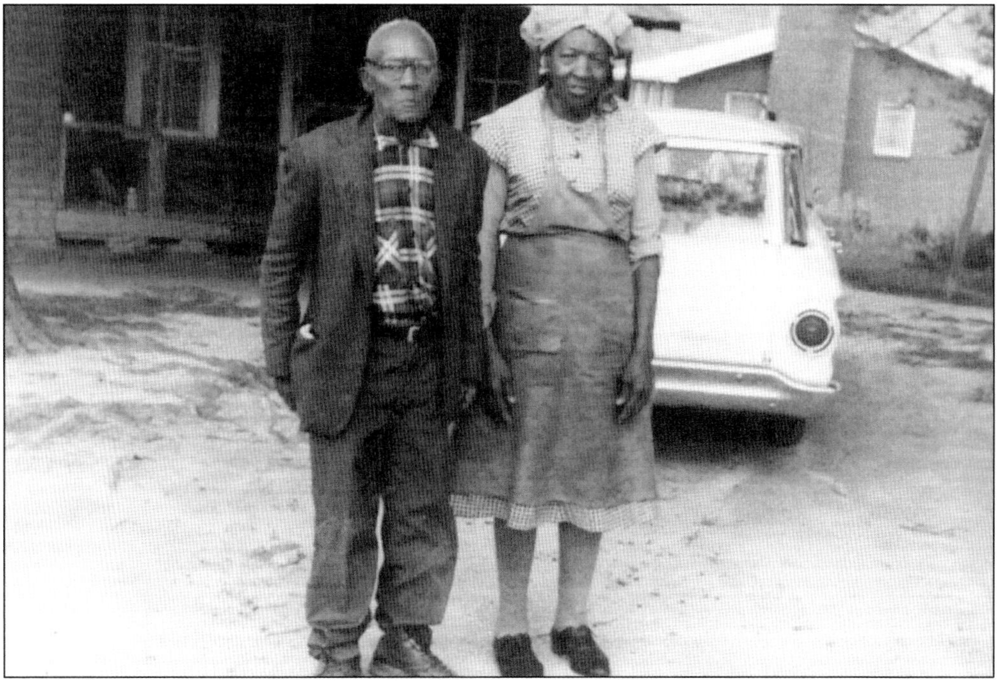

Willie "Babe" (1882–1968) and Anna Fredrick "Anner" Wright (1887–1979) lived on Brickyard Road in Etowah for 40 years. Babe worked as a farmhand for railroad man Wilson Avery Morgan (1891–1981) for 30 years. (Courtesy of Barbara Willis.)

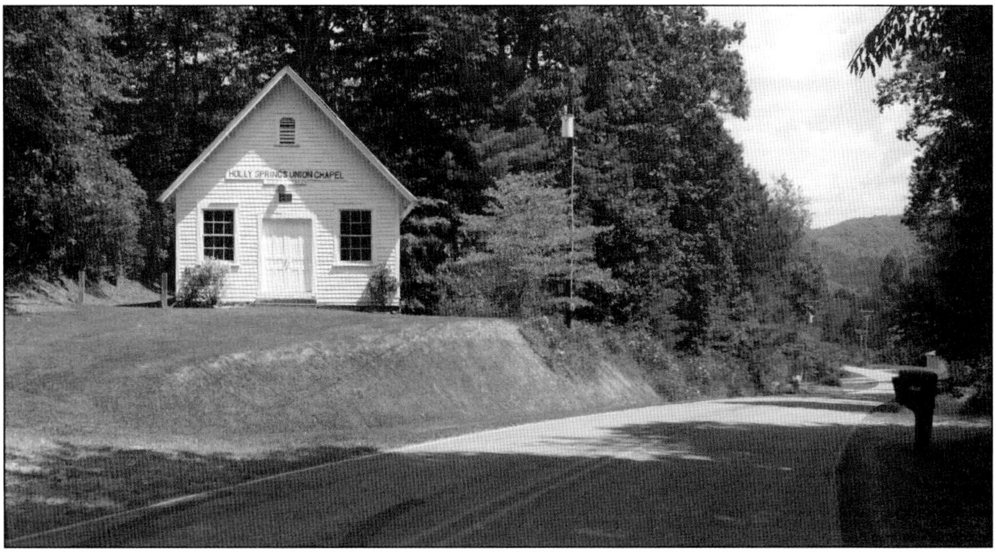

The Holly Springs union chapel and schoolhouse, established in 1878, stands on land deeded by the Reverend John Franklin Woodfin (1830–1914) and Emily Hood Woodfin (1846–1922) in the Holly Springs community between Etowah and Mills River. The structure pictured here replaced another that burned in 1900. Local students attended school here until they transferred to Mills River School in 1924. Church members worshiped in the building through 1957. (Photograph by the author.)

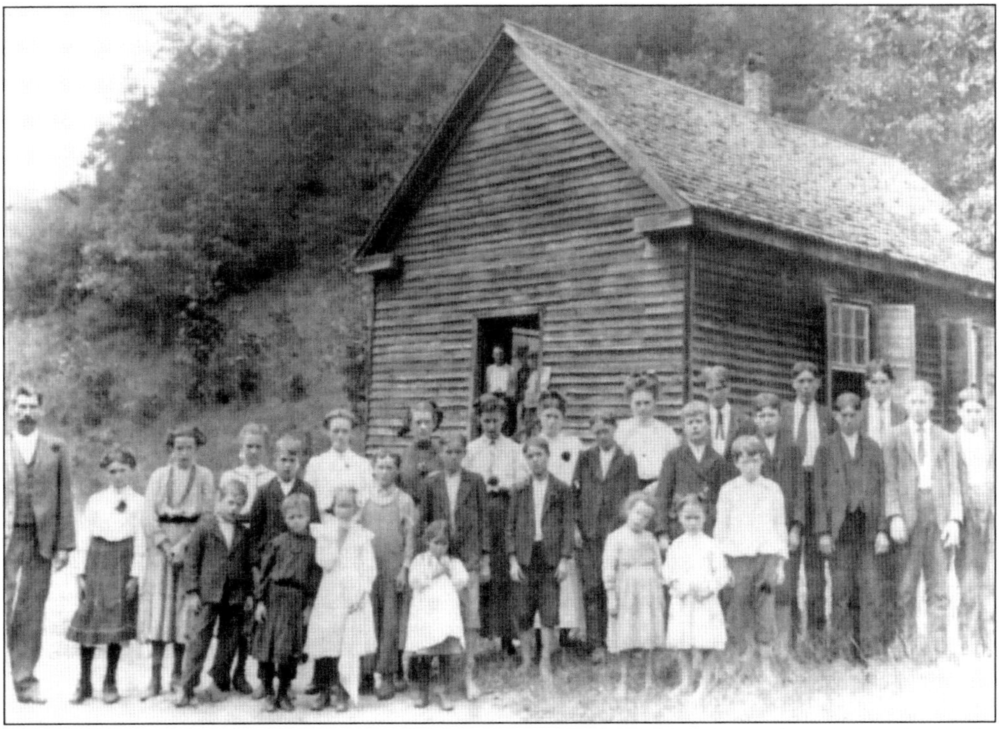

Frank Clark (1870–1958) poses with his students at Adam's Run School in the early 1900s. This was the last one-teacher school in the county. Adam K. Hyder and William Scott Young (1858–1940) also taught at this schoolhouse in the Big Hungry section. Hyder built the school. (Courtesy of the Henderson County Genealogical and Historical Society.)

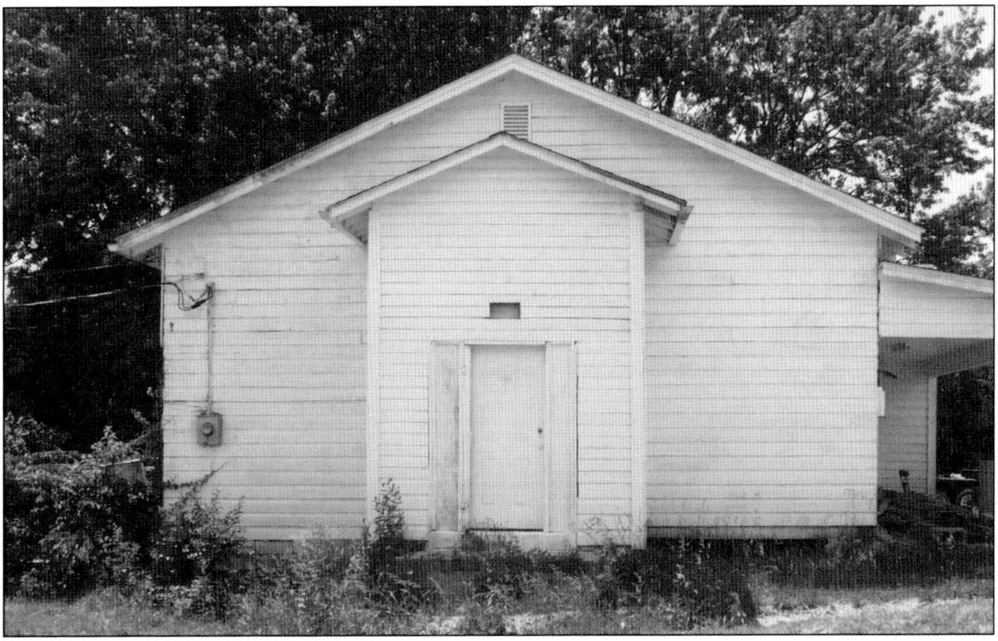

This early sanctuary of Upward Baptist Church (founded 1943) was later repurposed as a general store and gasoline station. (Photograph by the author.)

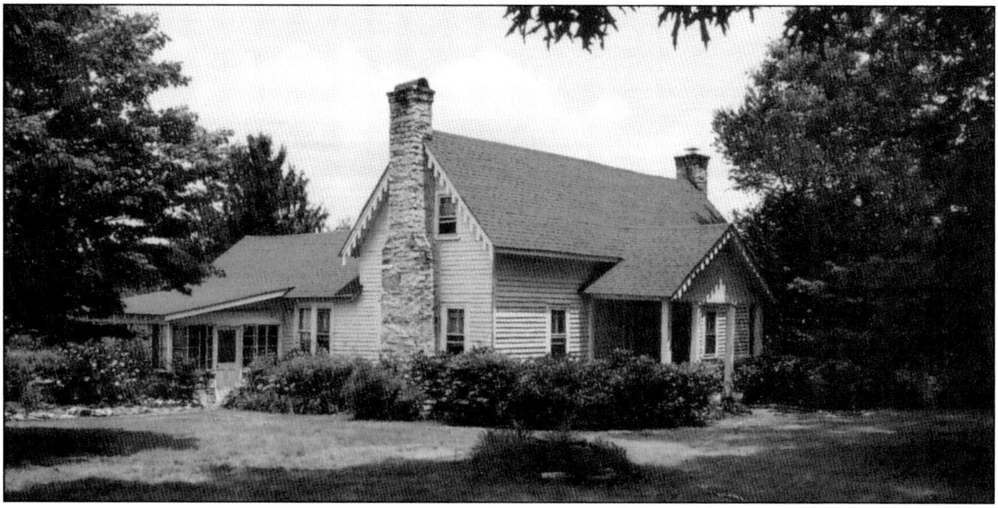

Golden Glow farmhouse, built by James Lemuel Hood (1809–1884), was later home to Frank L. FitzSimons Sr. for more than 50 years. FitzSimons, best remembered as a storyteller, author, and radio personality, operated a dairy and orchard on this 150-acre property in Dana. (Photograph by the author.)

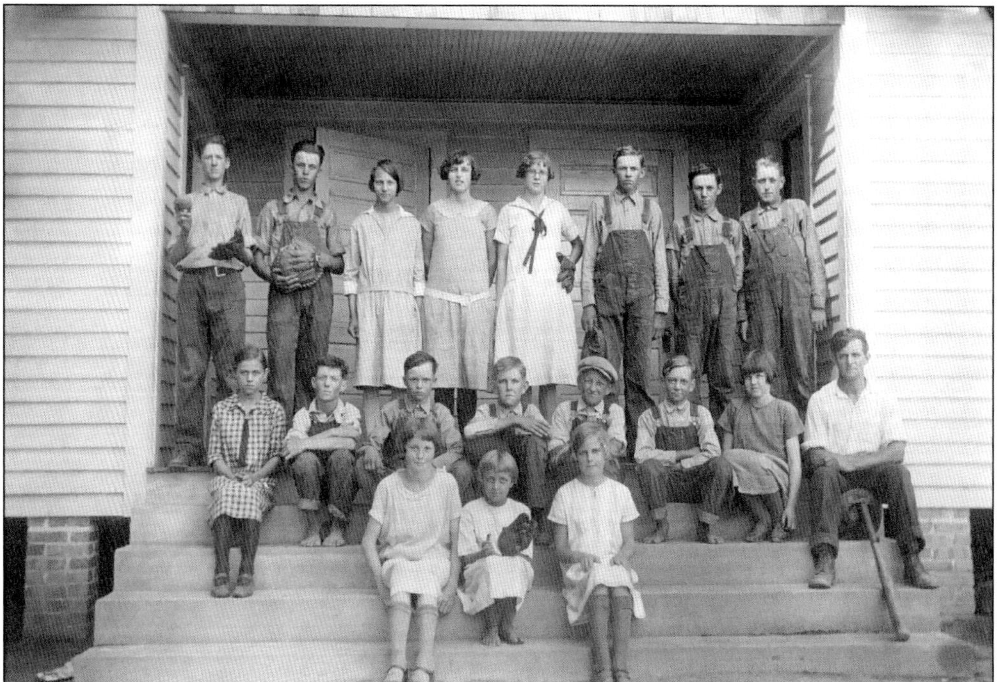

This photograph of Mount Vernon School at Dana during the 1924–1925 school year features, from left to right, (first row) Bernice Corn (Owenby), Millie Pace (Henderson), and Ruth Henderson; (second row) Ora Mabel Crosby, Edison Pace, Clarence Hill, Leroy Henderson, Glover Pace, Ector Capps, Annabelle Pace, and teacher/coach Frank Lockwood FitzSimons Sr.; (third row) William "Bill" Pace, Curtis Hill, Ethel Capps, Clara Newman, Leva Corn, Emmet Capps, Elmer Capps, and Carl Pace Sr. Students nicknamed the school "Dry Hill" because its well frequently ran dry. (Courtesy of Christy Corn.)

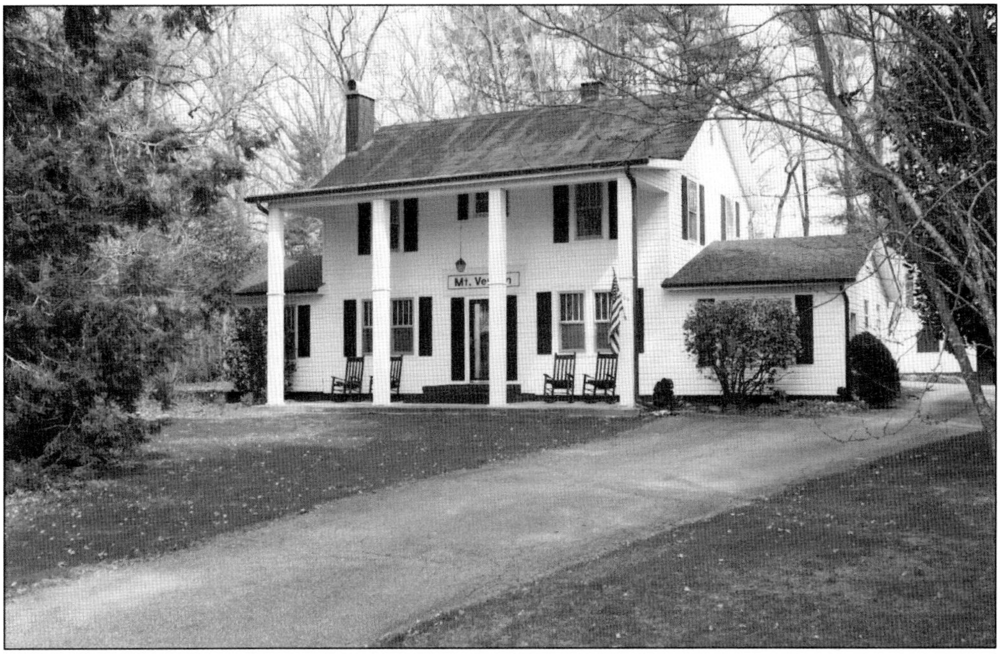

John Henry Capps (1880–1976) gave the land for the Mount Vernon School, which replaced the Hood School. When Henderson County schools consolidated in 1928 and Mount Vernon's students transferred to Dana Elementary School, the land reverted to the Capps family. John's son Ector Capps (1911–1997) dismantled the schoolhouse and built this foursquare home from the repurposed materials a few yards from where the school once stood. Rod and Christy Corn currently own the home. (Photograph by the author.)

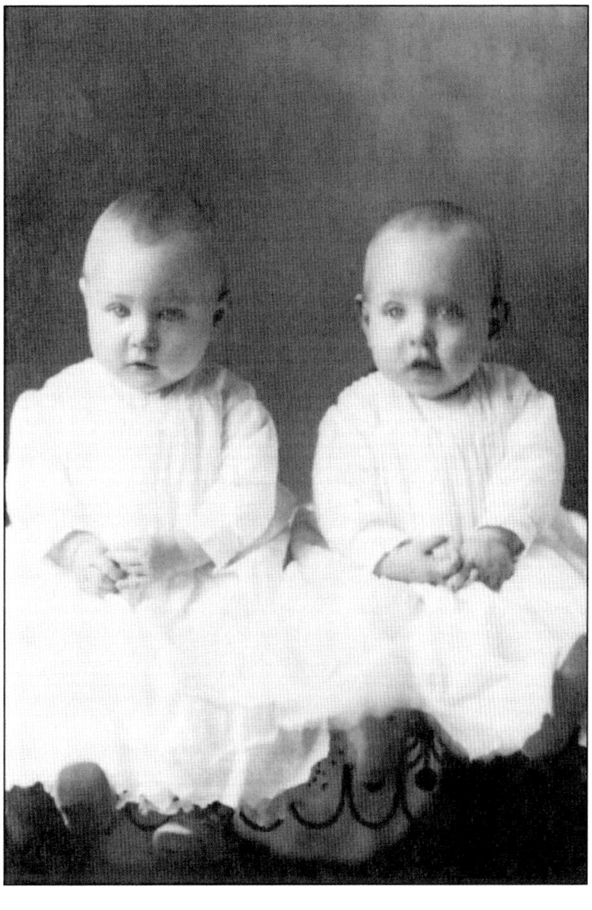

Twins Ector and Ethel Capps, at nine months old, pose for a portrait. (Courtesy of Christy Corn.)

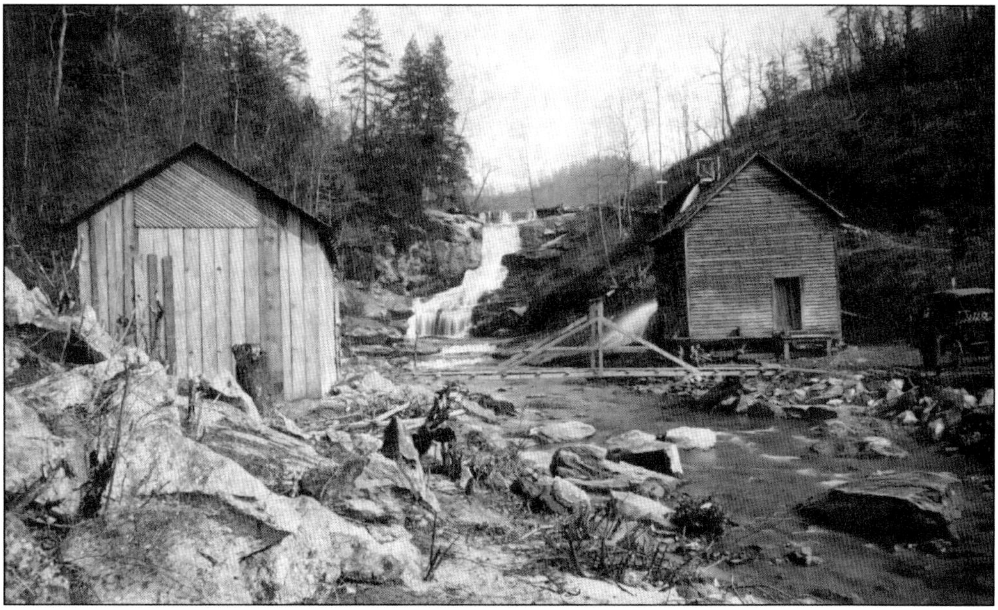

Before Henderson County was formed, John Jones Sr. (1764–1860) constructed a sawmill at this locale, known as Oleeta Falls. Jones also operated one of the first gristmills on the site. Benjamin A. Merrell (1869–1935) later owned and operated the mills. Merrell's wife, Alice Stepp Merrell (1880–1974), served as Oleeta's postmistress until the Merrells moved to nearby Saconon. The 1916 flood washed away the Oleeta buildings. Today, a gated residential community encompasses the falls. (Courtesy of Carolyn Justus.)

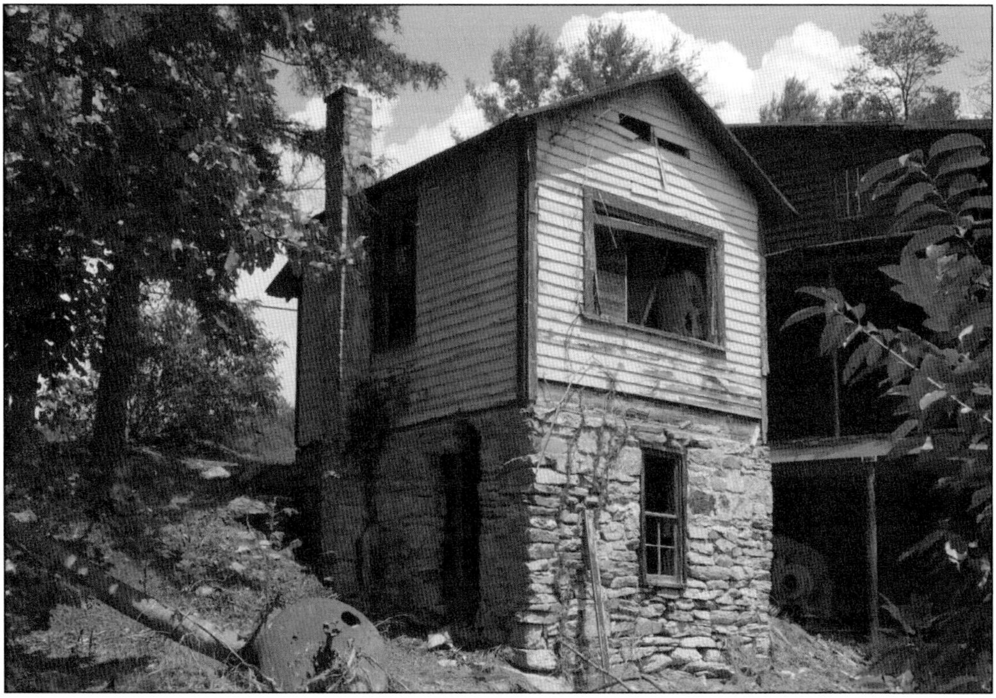

The tiny Saconon Post Office operated above Tumblebug Creek from 1913 to 1923. (Photograph by the author.)

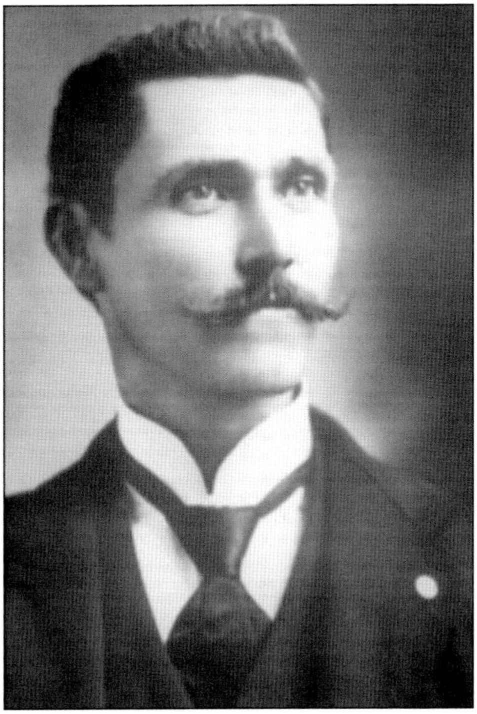

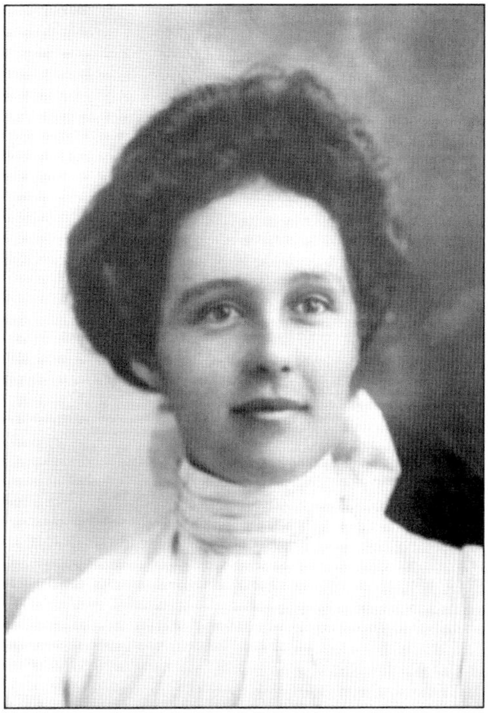

Benjamin A. Merrell moved his milling operation in 1913 from Oleeta downstream to Saconon, alongside the head of Tumblebug Creek, a tributary of the Hungry River. There, he dammed the creek, created a millpond, and built a gristmill. Merrell also moved his post office to this location. Ben's wife, Alice E. Stepp Merrell, served as postmistress from 1913 to 1915, and Ben served as postmaster from 1915 until 1923, when the office closed. In 1933, Merrell traded this property with his brother-in-law Thomas Dulus Stepp. Lowell Alexander Merrell (1907–1982), pictured at right, was a son of Benjamin and Alice Merrell. (Both above, courtesy of the Henderson County Genealogical and Historical Society; right, courtesy of Carolyn Justus.)

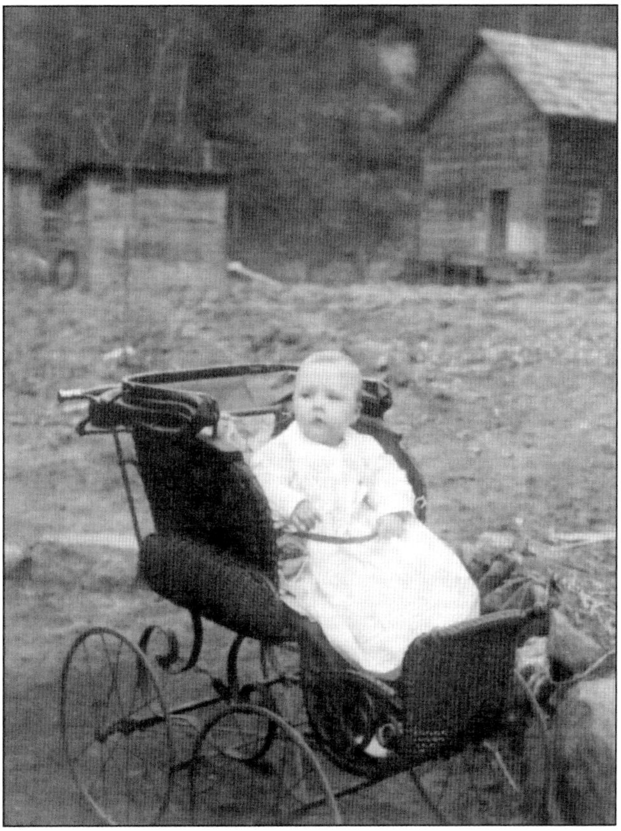

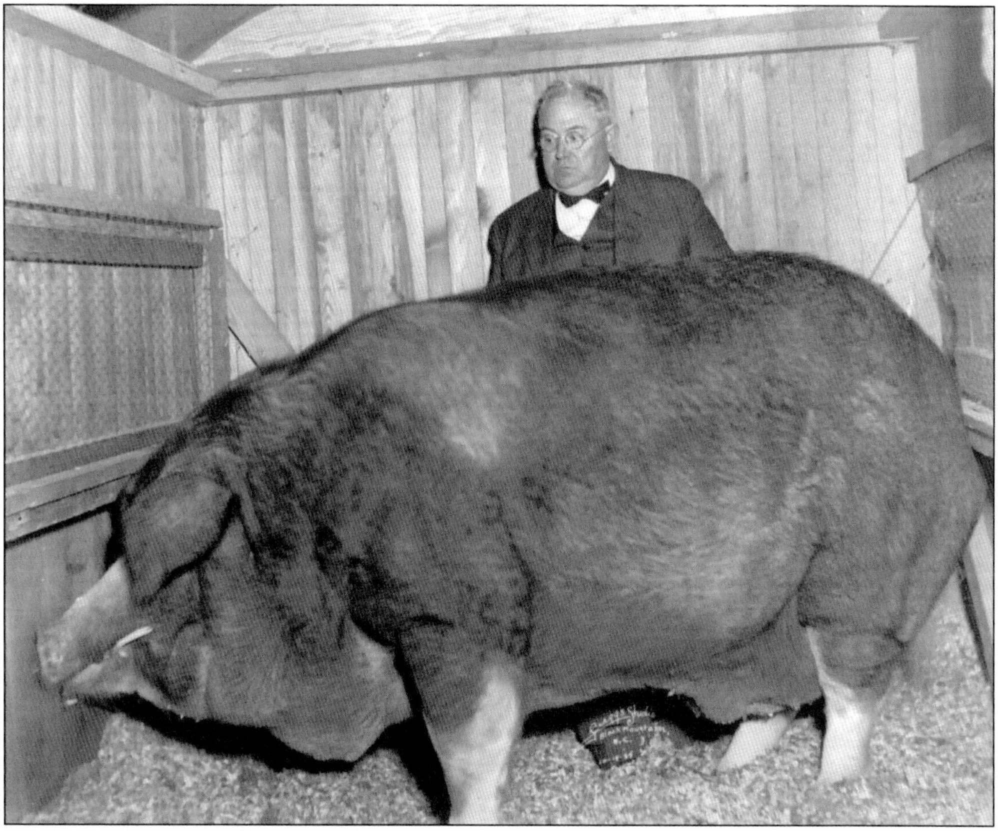

Big Jim was known as the world's largest hog. One of several normal-sized Poland China piglets, he was born in Buncombe County in 1929. When Jim was three years old, Dana resident Henry Clinton Gibbs (1885–1973), pictured here, purchased him from Dulus Stepp. As time wore on, Jim notably outgrew his peers, peaking at 2,415 pounds. Gibbs transported Jim—billed as the "Largest Pile of Pork Living"—to county fairs across the nation, traveling to 43 states. Gibbs retired Big Jim in 1942. Jim died of natural causes at age 15 in 1944. (Courtesy of Roger Henderson.)

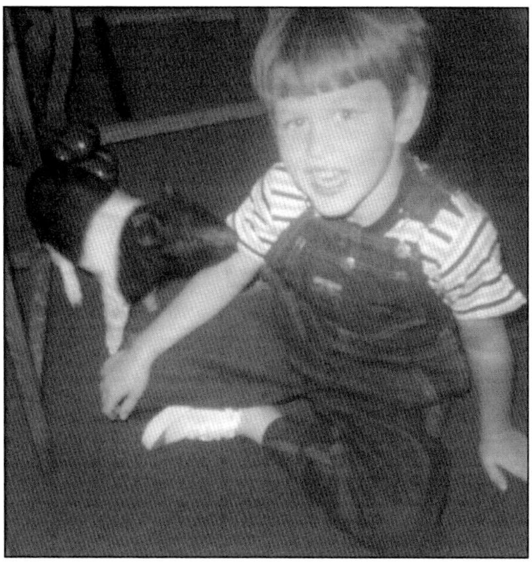

Larry Wayne Stepp Jr. (born 1968) plays with his pet piglet Sunshine Bird in Upward. A love for growing things has kept Larry running the farm originated by his grandfather Clay Clifford Stepp (1928–2012) and continued by his father, Larry Stepp Sr. (born 1947). The family transitioned from apple orchards to greenhouses and berry and asparagus fields. (Courtesy of Gayle Hamilton Stepp.)

Four

North Henderson County

Gerton, Middle Fork, Bat Cave, Mills River, Rugby, Clear Creek, Fruitland, Edneyville, Balfour, Hillgirt, and Fletcher

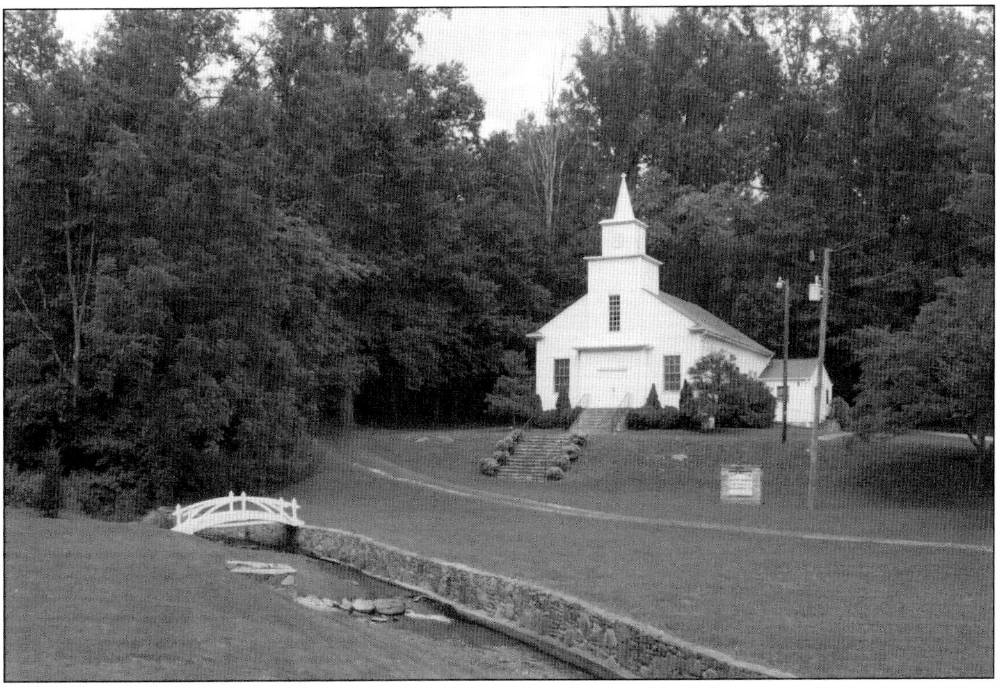

In the shadows of Little Pisgah Mountain, Bearwallow Baptist Church was established in 1868 in Gerton and is the only church in the Gerton community. Early residents named the settlement Pump, but an error in the manufacturing of the postal cancellation stamp resulted in the name Rump. Residents voted to rename the community for a local schoolteacher, Gertrude Freeman, and chose the contraction "Gerton" for the new name. (Photograph by the author.)

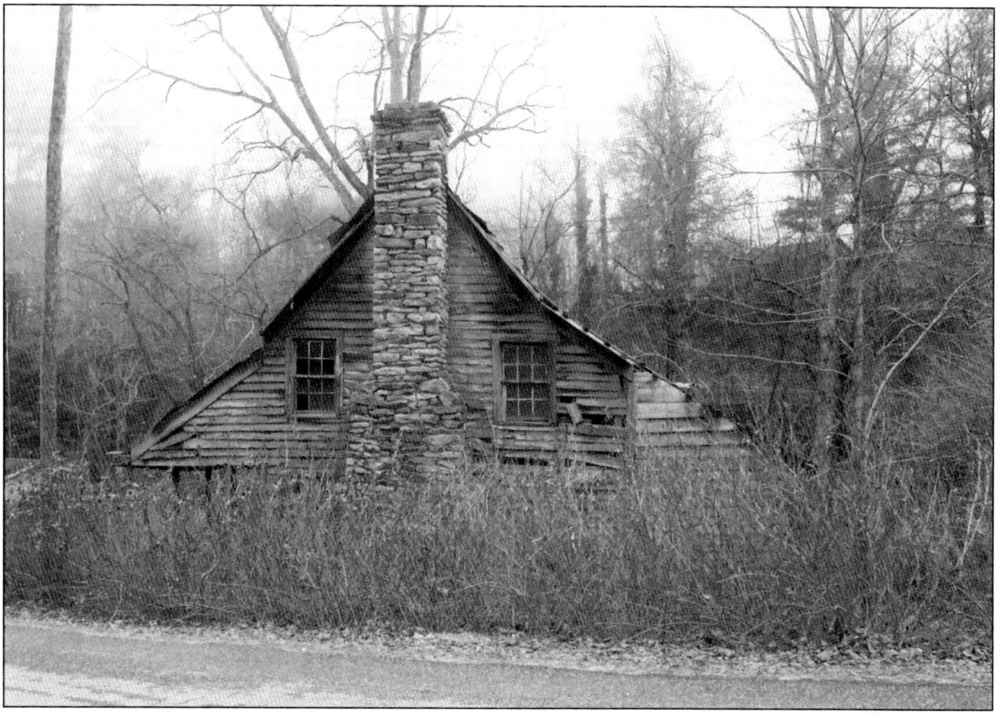

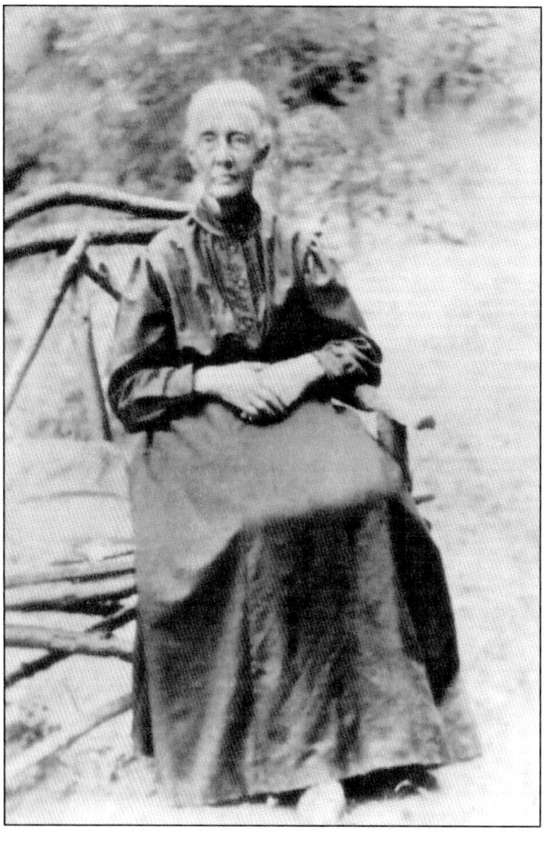

The abandoned home of Civil War veteran Riley Wall (1840–1940) and his wife, Tincy E. Wall (1844–1906), stands in Gerton. The Walls had five children. Their daughter Mary Egiva "Givie" Wall Freeman (1880–1974) grew up in this house, later living in it with her husband, Noble Tildon Freeman (1876–1922). Additional residents included the Reverend Flavius Josephus "Cephus" Huntley (1862–1933) and his wife, Elizabeth Jane Conner Huntley (1861–1952). Cephus preached in and around the Bat Cave community. (Photograph by the author.)

Susan Ann Pryor Huntley (1836–1922) served as a midwife in Rutherford and Buncombe Counties and in the communities of Bat Cave and Middle Fork in Henderson County. Her descendants claimed she never lost a baby or a mother, and she charged $2 for each delivery until a patient's husband suggested that she double her fee. (Courtesy of Marilyn Pryor Horne.)

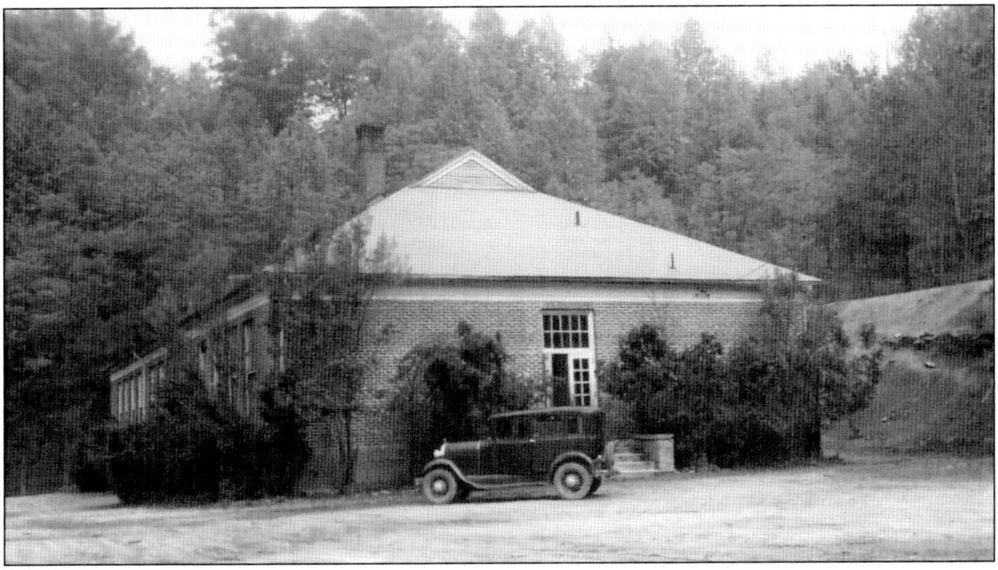

Bat Cave School, designed by Erle G. Stillwell, opened in 1928 with three teachers, seven grades, three classrooms, a library, and an auditorium. The school consolidated with the Little Red Schoolhouse and Hickory and Middle Fork Schools in 1946, after which George F. Bond, MD (1915–1983), and the community of Bat Cave purchased the property at auction to establish Valley Clinic and Hospital. In 1948, Dr. Bond opened a 12-bed clinic in the structure. (Courtesy of the Henderson County Genealogical and Historical Society.)

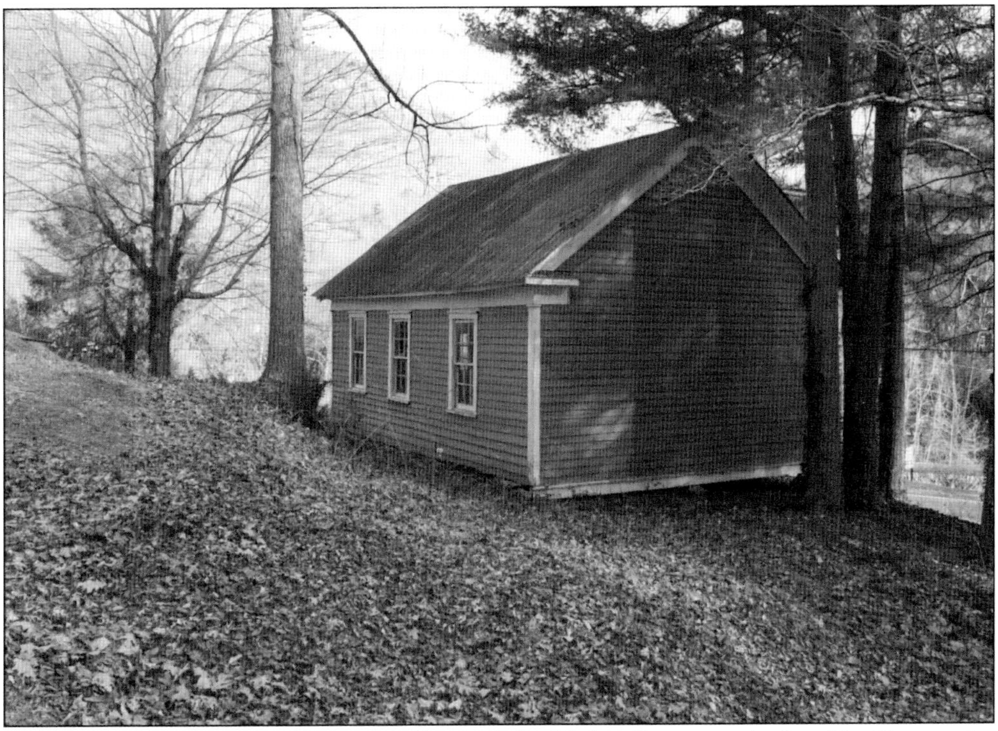

Before this one-room school known as the Little Red Schoolhouse was built at Bat Cave in the early 1900s, youngsters attended classes at Dalton (Reedy Patch). (Photograph by the author.)

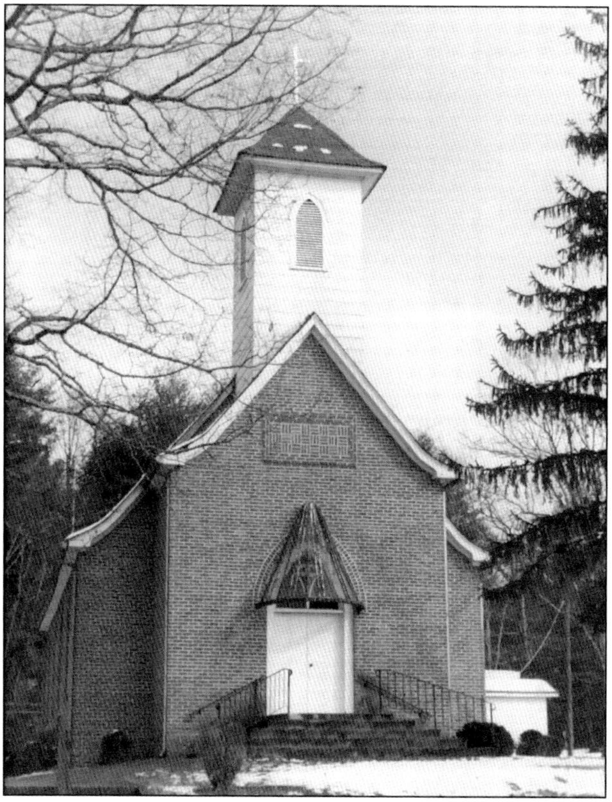

The original French Broad Baptist Church, established before 1792, stood about one mile distant from the sanctuary pictured here in Mills River. A modern church has taken its place. (Courtesy of Sheila Mason and the French Broad Baptist Church.)

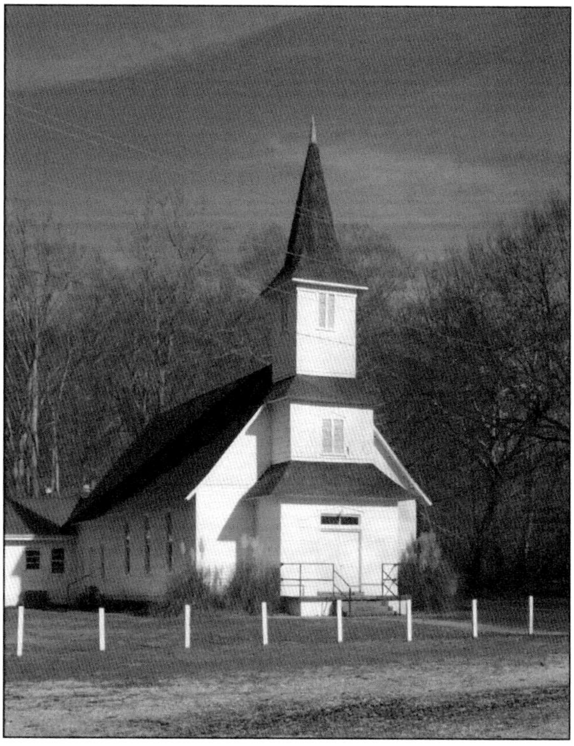

Mills River Baptist Church was named Sycamore Church when established in 1835 on land given by Jesse Rickman (1770–1860). The church stands across the road from the Rickman Cemetery. (Photograph by the author.)

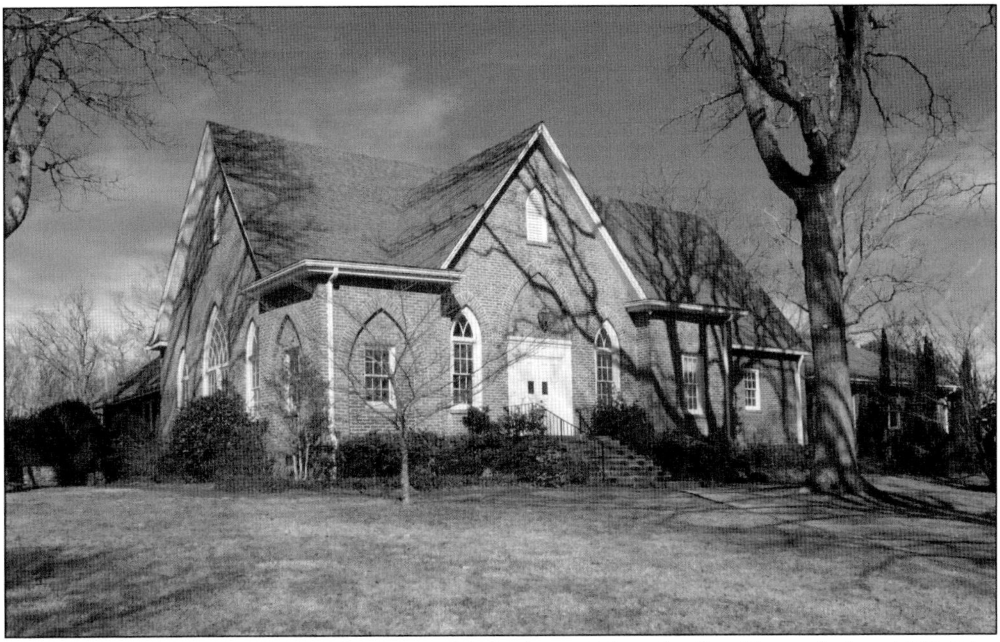

Mills River Presbyterian Church was established in 1798 and officially unified in 1859. The sanctuary pictured here was built in 1908. (Photograph by the author.)

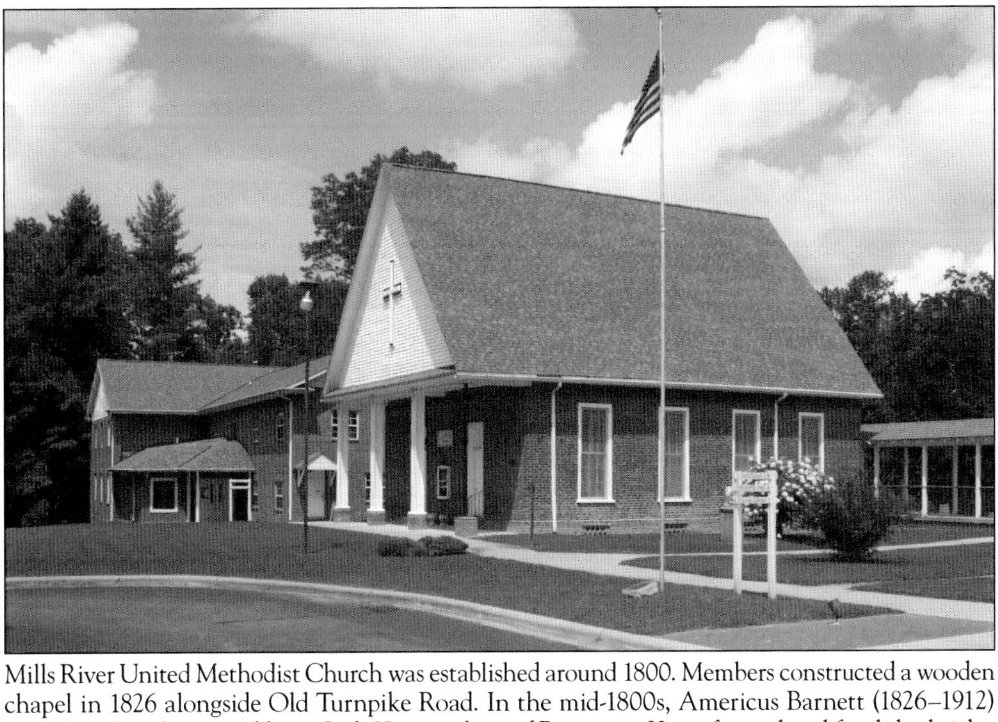

Mills River United Methodist Church was established around 1800. Members constructed a wooden chapel in 1826 alongside Old Turnpike Road. In the mid-1800s, Americus Barnett (1826–1912) built the chapel pictured here. Josh King, a slave of Benjamin King, formed and fired the bricks. (Photograph by the author.)

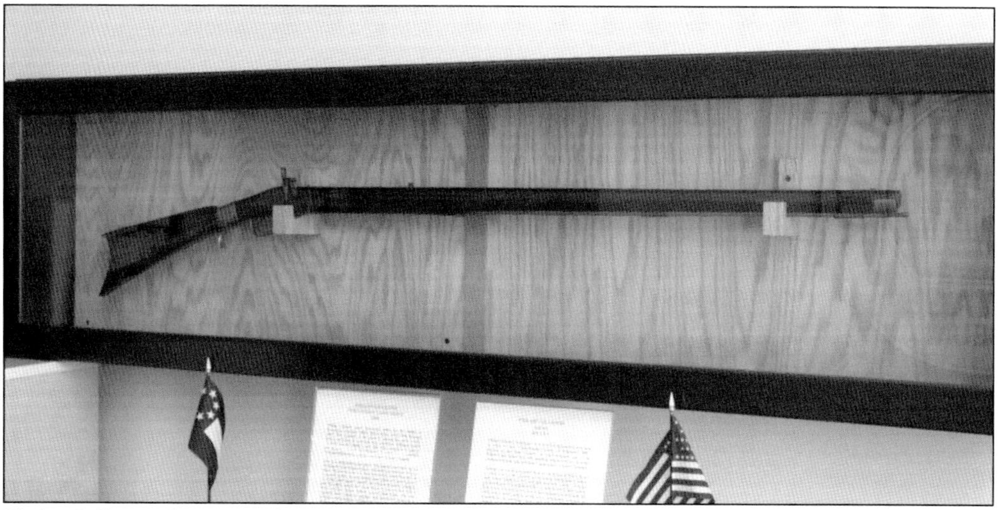

Philip Gillespie (1817–1864) crafted this .34-caliber rifle in 1848 at Mills River in the area known as Forge Mountain. The Gillespies of Mills River were acclaimed gunsmiths in the 19th century. This example of a Gillespie long rifle is among the artifacts displayed at the Henderson County Heritage Museum. (Photograph by the author.)

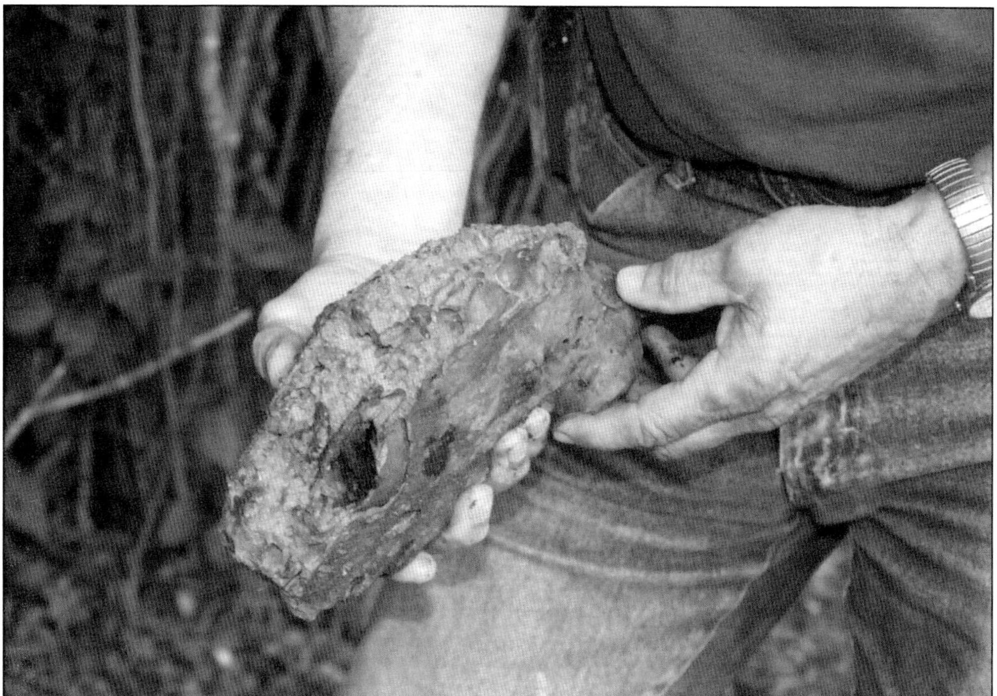

Walter Ray Bryson Jr. displays a chunk of iron slag he scooped from the river at the site of the former Sitton Forge in Mills River. The Sitton Forge supplied iron for the Gillespie long rifles. (Photograph by the author.)

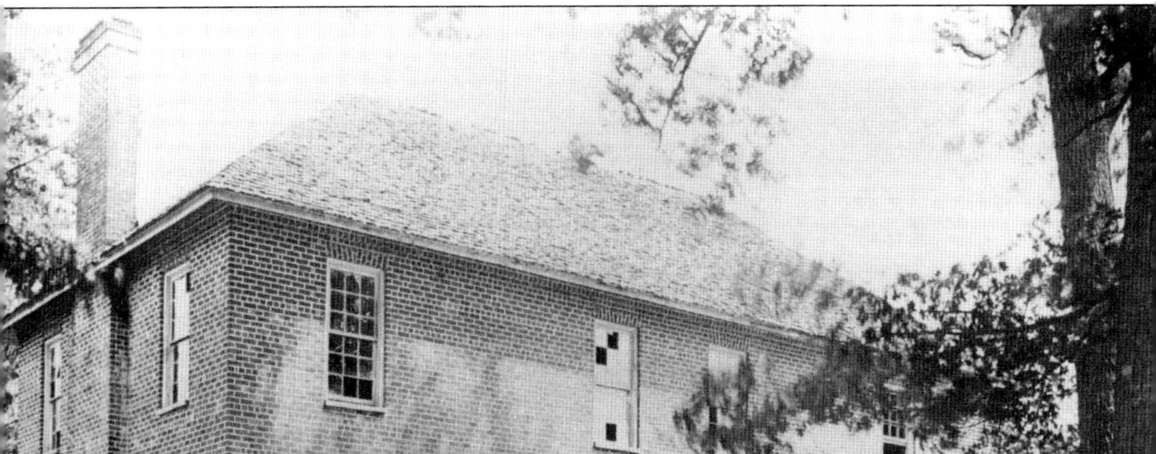

Revolutionary War patriot James Brittain set aside land in 1797 for a school and church in Mills River. Brittain's son Phillip (1787–1849) deeded the land to five trustees in 1829. The school began as a log structure and was later named Mills River Academy, the oldest institution of learning in what became Henderson County and considered the cradle of government and education in the county. Some of the earliest courts of pleas and quarter sessions took place in the building, which was also shared by the Mills River Presbyterian Church until 1908. A two-story, brick-veneered building constructed in the mid-1800s burned in 1921 and was replaced in 1922. This photograph dates from 1907. (Courtesy of Bonnie Heffner Stewart.)

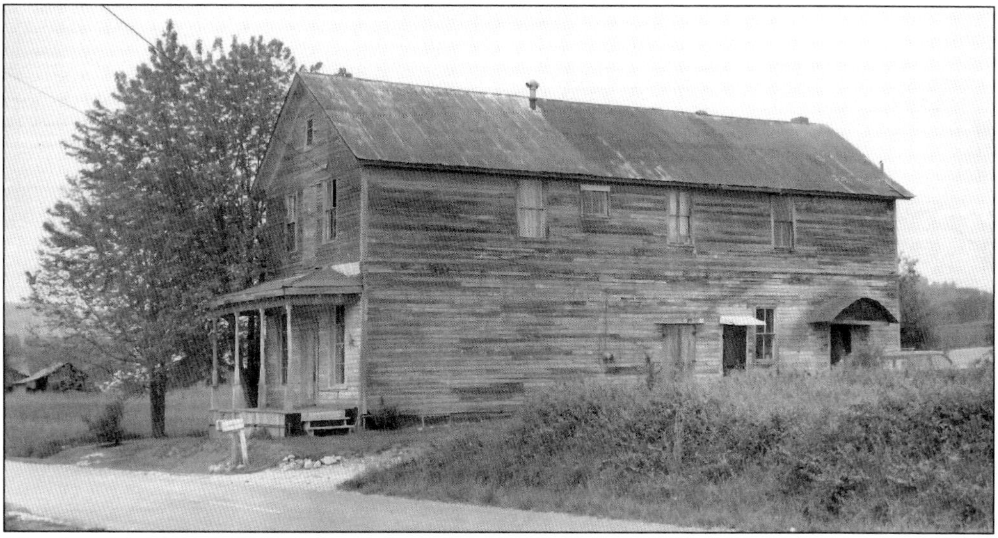

The Angeline Post Office operated from this store building and boardinghouse in Mills River from 1888 to 1904. William Turner Johnson (1817–1889), Thomas Lenoir Johnson (1854–1940), and Jesse Sherrill Rhodes (1850–1912) served as postmasters. (Lucile Stepp Ray photograph, courtesy of the Henderson County Genealogical and Historical Society.)

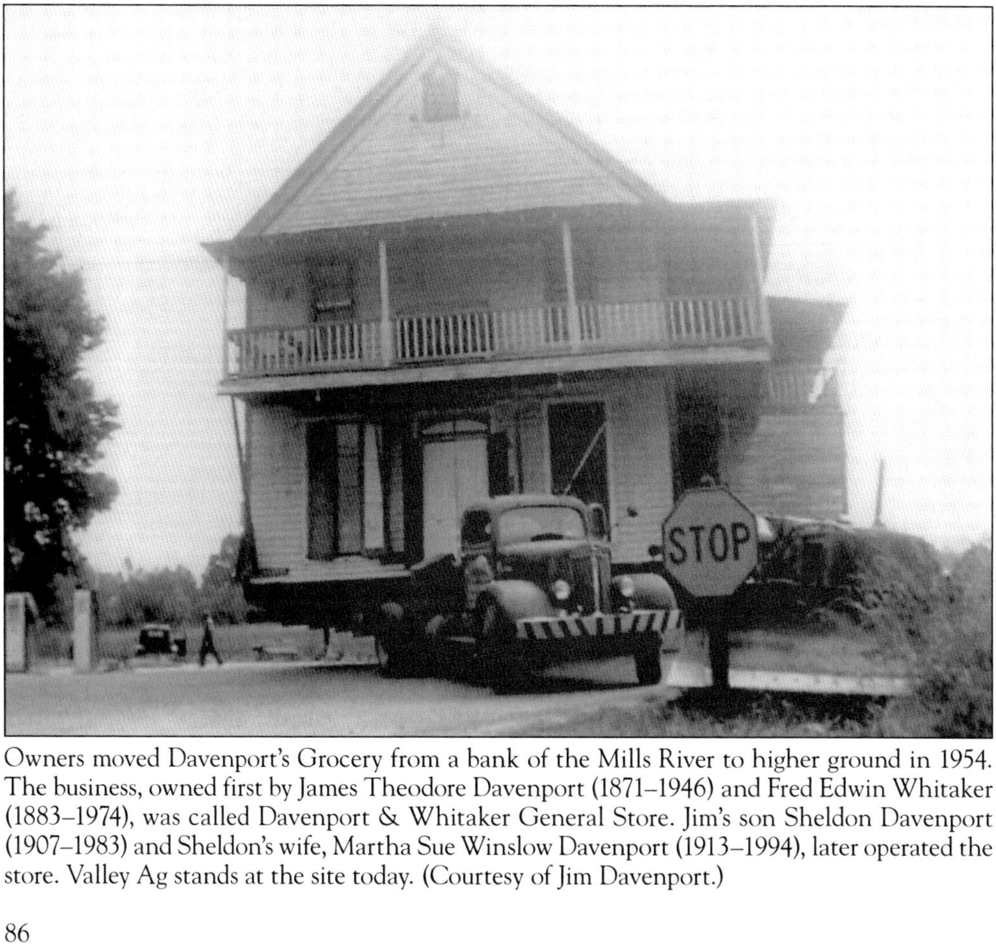

Owners moved Davenport's Grocery from a bank of the Mills River to higher ground in 1954. The business, owned first by James Theodore Davenport (1871–1946) and Fred Edwin Whitaker (1883–1974), was called Davenport & Whitaker General Store. Jim's son Sheldon Davenport (1907–1983) and Sheldon's wife, Martha Sue Winslow Davenport (1913–1994), later operated the store. Valley Ag stands at the site today. (Courtesy of Jim Davenport.)

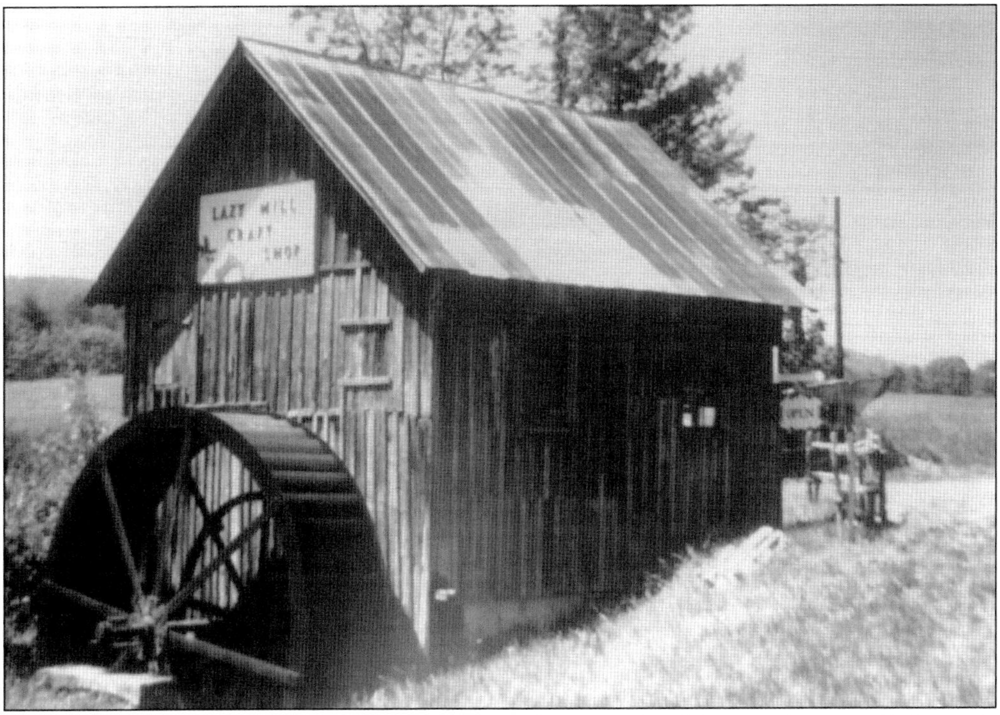

Best remembered as the Hayes Mill, this operation began as Josiah Johnson's gristmill alongside McDowell Creek in Mills River. The mill was rebuilt after suffering major damage in the 1916 flood. Brothers John L. (1851–1933) and Thomas Bradshaw "Tom" Allen (1864–1941) later owned the operation, followed by Lawrence Frederick Hayes Sr. (1893–1966). Operating as a gristmill until 1948, the structure served additional purposes over the years, including a sawmill and a post office named Gypsy. The building was razed in stages as the North Carolina Department of Transportation later widened the road. Its wheel was repurposed for successive uses, including the mill at Forge Valley and then as an attraction at a miniature golf course on the Spartanburg Highway. (Courtesy of the Henderson County Genealogical and Historical Society.)

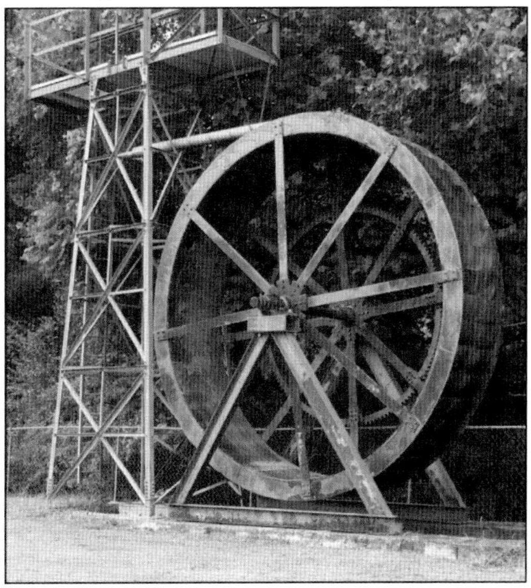

The waterwheel from the Hayes Mill now counts among the many artifacts of the Mountain Home and Farm Museum. (Photograph by the author.)

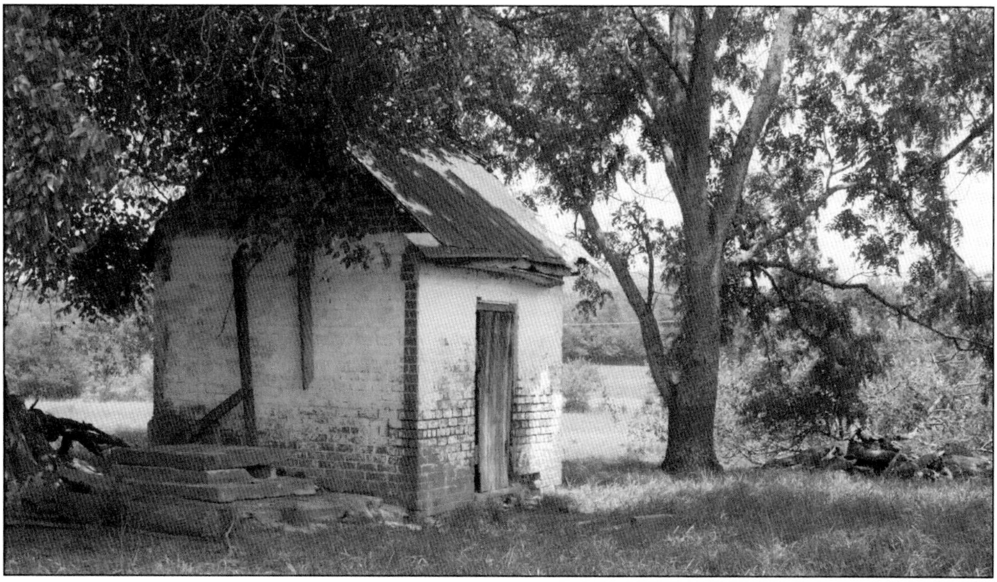

Of the pioneer property of Samuel King (1746–1828) in Mills River, only this structure stands today. Elsie Tate Aiken, a granddaughter of the Jayneses who later owned the farm, remembered her grandmother storing eggs, butter, and milk in this brick springhouse. (Photograph by the author.)

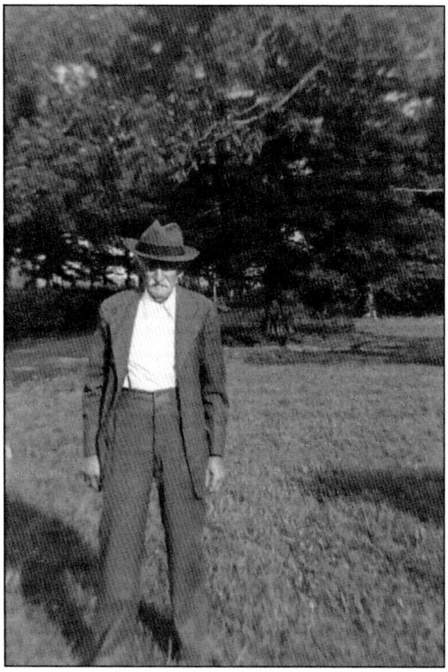

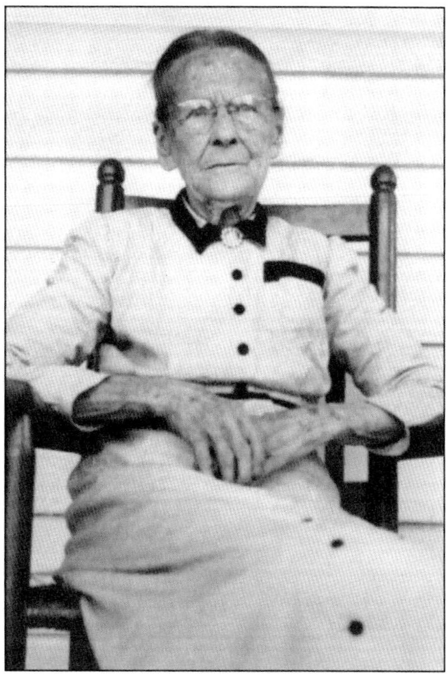

Doc A. Jaynes (1868–1949), his wife, Dora Telitha Tate Jaynes (1874–1960), and their family lived in the old King place, a property owned originally by the Samuel King family and later by families of the names Dufour, Whitt, and Francis. As a child, Doc Jaynes visited Mills River from Haywood County. During his early travels to Henderson County, he fell in love with the old King property and always dreamed of owning it. A Mills River plant of the Asheville Water Authority now encompasses much of the property. (Both, courtesy of Elsie Tate Aiken.)

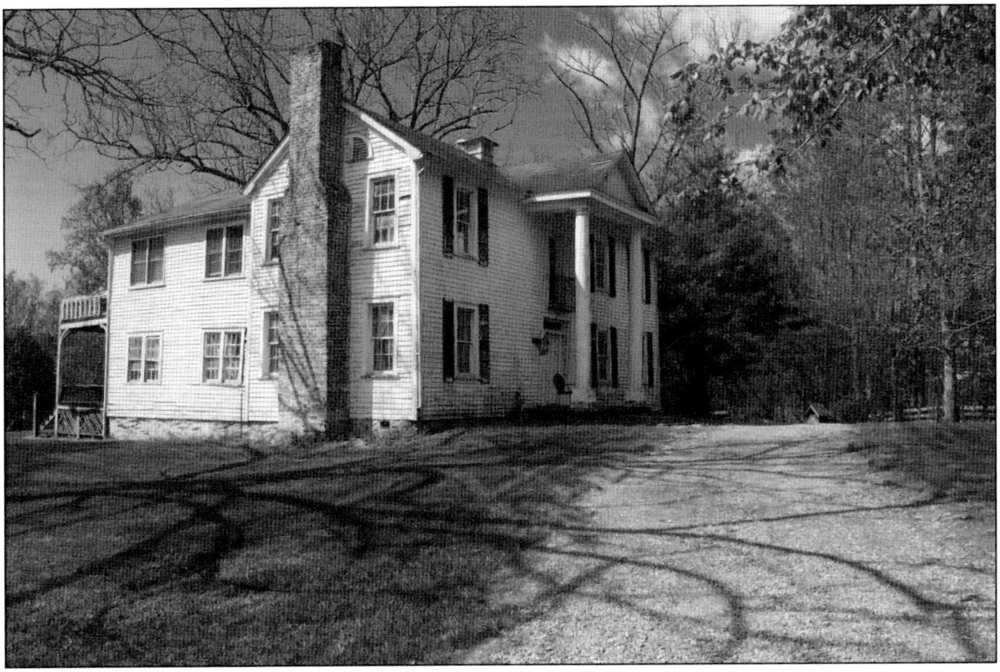

Moses "Mose" Smith (1802–1886) owned land between Banner Farm Road and Kings Bridge in Mills River. Alongside present-day Ladson Road, he built a log home, a dwelling later owned and expanded by Henry Grady (1788–1879) and Laodicea "Leah" King Grady (1796–1829). James Henry Ladson (1852–1929), a factor from Charleston, later bought this property, which has since passed through numerous owners and today stands abandoned. (Photograph by the author.)

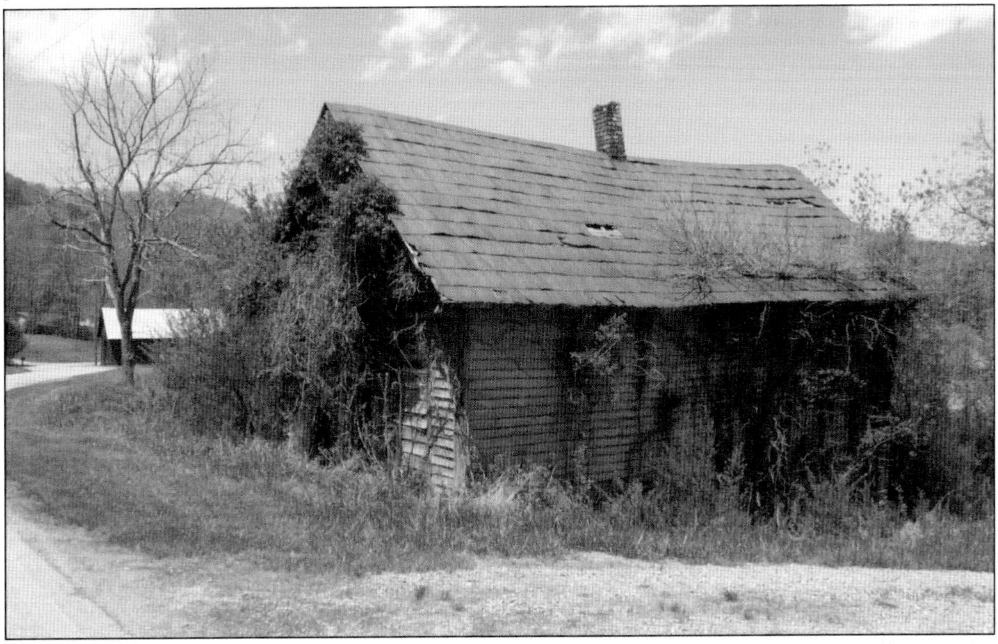

This building alongside Whitaker Road in Mills River served as the Pink Bed Post Office until it closed in 1904. Postmasters included William H. Gillespie, William B. Moore, George M. Brittain, Thomas J. Roberson, John Rickman, and Solomon Whitaker. (Photograph by the author.)

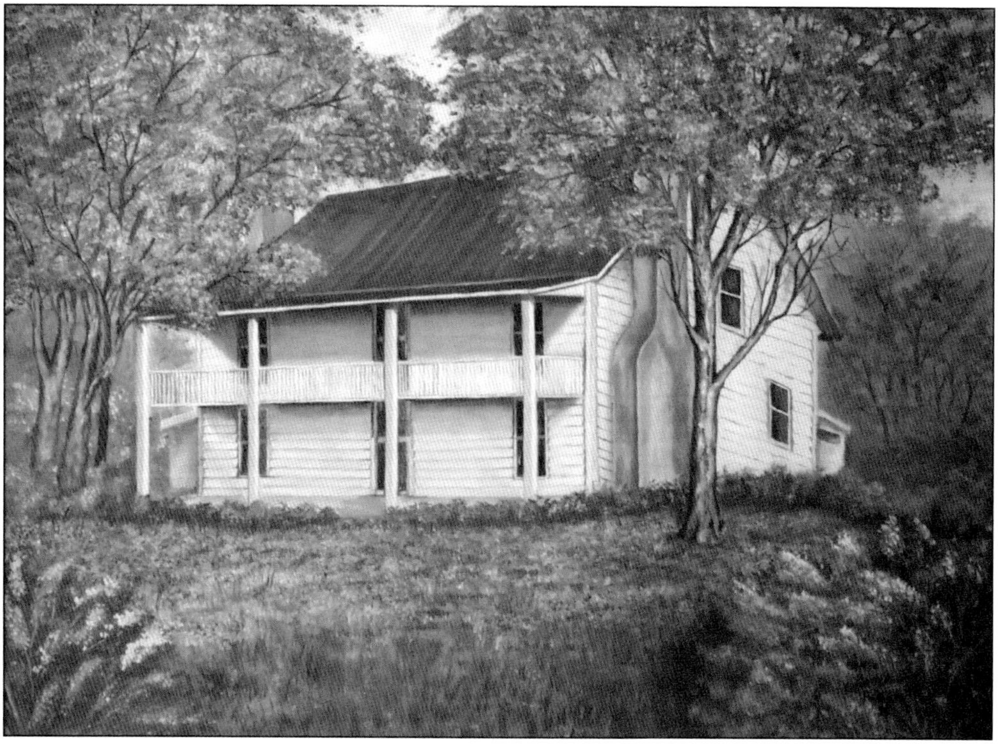

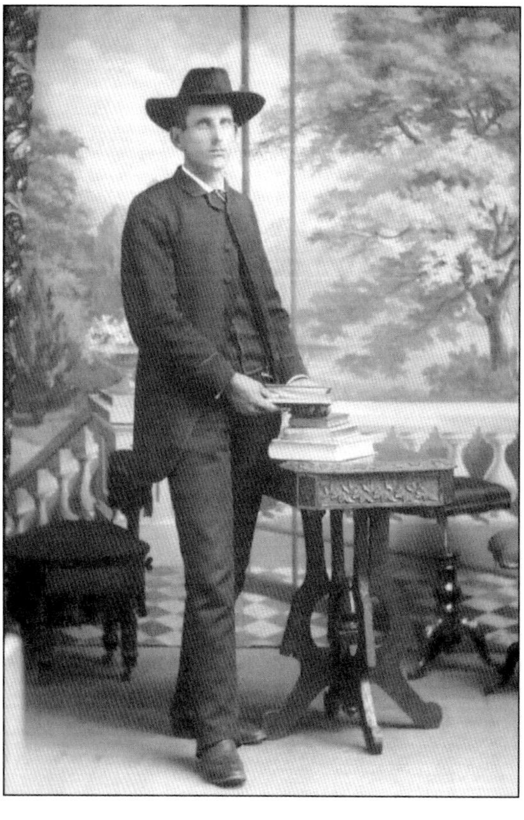

Leander Elburtus Brittain (1820–1900) built this home, one of the oldest standing buildings in Mills River and later home to Brittain's son Montreville Marion "Mont" and his family. Further occupants included Whitakers, Jacksons, and Crawfords. (Painting by Wanda Brittain Frasier.)

Montreville Marion Brittain (1859–1927) descended from the first Brittains to enter what became Henderson County. (Courtesy of Stella Faye Lance Edney.)

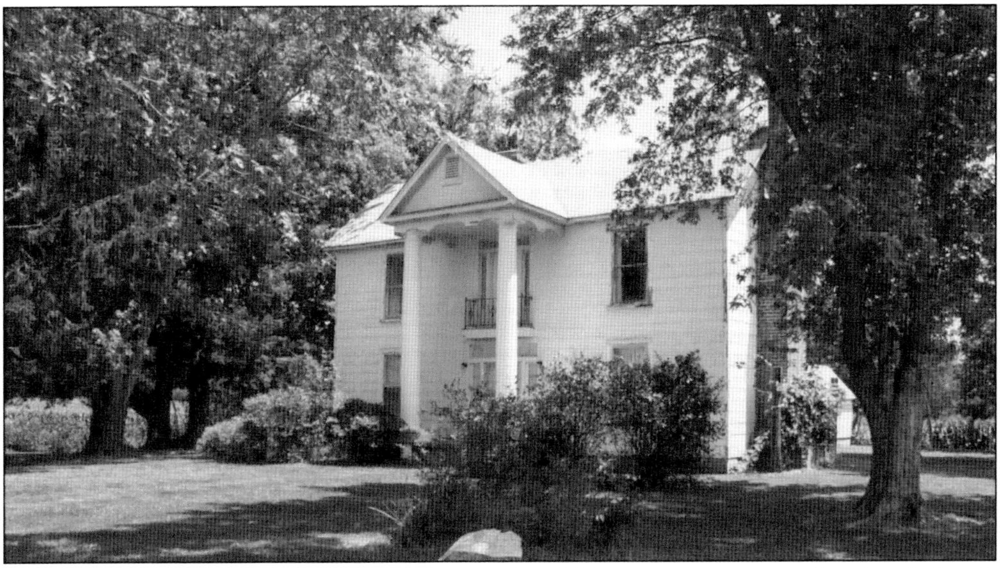

After Union troops invaded South Carolina in the 1860s, many Lowcountry families fled with whatever they could carry with them. Such was the case with Joseph Theus Lee (1811–1898) and his wife, Elise Virginie Erbeau Lee (1821–1886), of Charleston. The Lees bought a tract of farmland off School House Road in Mills River—property that included this Colonial domicile called the Hermitage. The Lees established and operated a private school in Charleston. The couple later taught at Mills River Academy and ran a private school from the Hermitage. (Photograph by the author.)

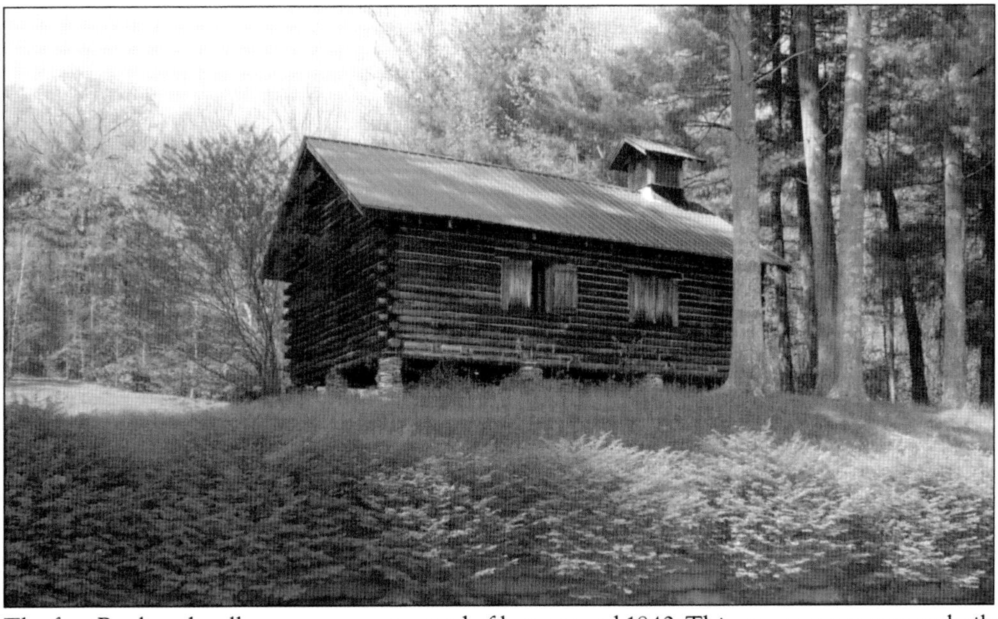

The first Rugby schoolhouse was constructed of logs around 1840. This one-room structure, built by Rugby Middle School shop students in 1982 to replicate the original, serves as a living history classroom and stands behind the contemporary school. (Photograph by the author.)

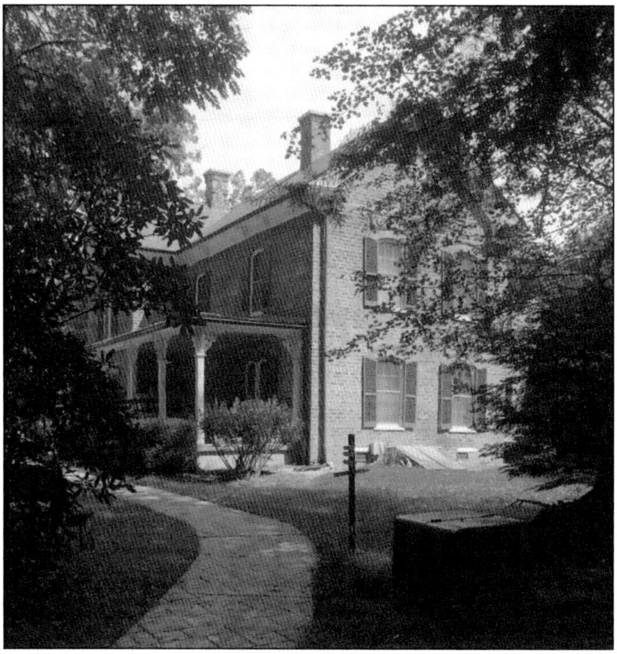

Once a tobacco farm owned by Oliver H. Moss (1822–1904), the Historic Johnson Farm now operates as a heritage education museum owned by Henderson County Public Schools. The site, with its 1880 farmhouse and outbuildings, has been designated a North Carolina Cultural Treasure. Bachelor brothers Vernon (1891–1978) and Leander Johnson (1895–1987) gifted the property to the public school system. Johnson Farm once operated as an agricultural estate and summer retreat where Sallie Leverett Johnson (1866–1958) and her sons Vernon and Leander boarded visitors in the 11-room brick house and the 1923 weatherboarded annex. (Photograph by the author.)

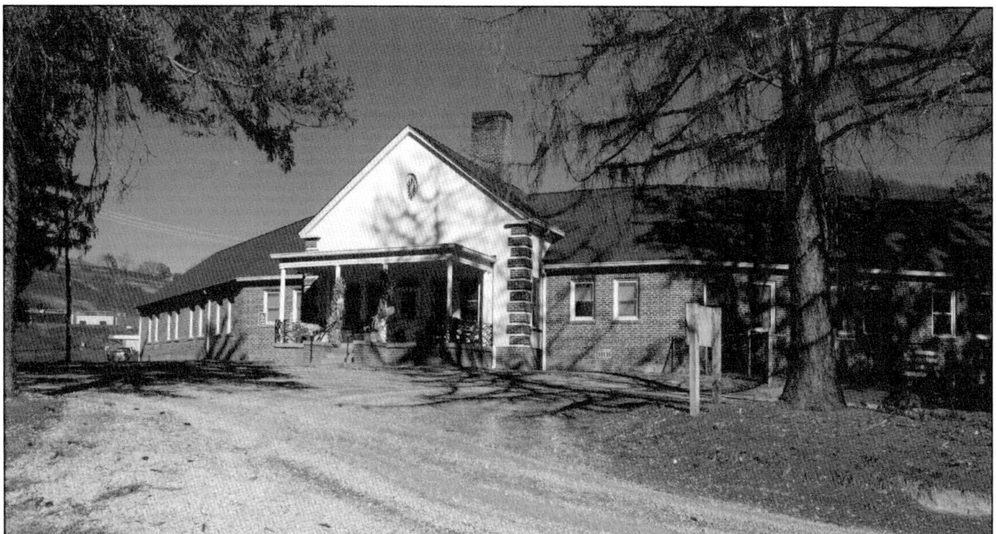

Erle G. Stillwell designed the Henderson County Home—known to many as the "Poorhouse"—in 1933. The building, now abandoned, most recently housed the Stoney Mountain Activities facility and county administrative offices. (Photograph by the author.)

Built for Mary Drake Seagle in 1903, this house replaced a log home. Mary's eldest son, Nathan A. Seagle, financed the building of the house by local craftsmen. Construction began immediately following the death of Nathan's father, Philip C. Seagle. The property passed to Thomas D. Seagle by agreement with his brother Nathan, then to Fannie Elliot Seagle, Mary Katherine Seagle Nelon, and most recently to Alex Nelon, great-grandson of Philip and Mary Seagle. Recent renovations spanned 17 years with an eye to preserving the historical integrity of the ancestral home. (Courtesy of Alex Nelon.)

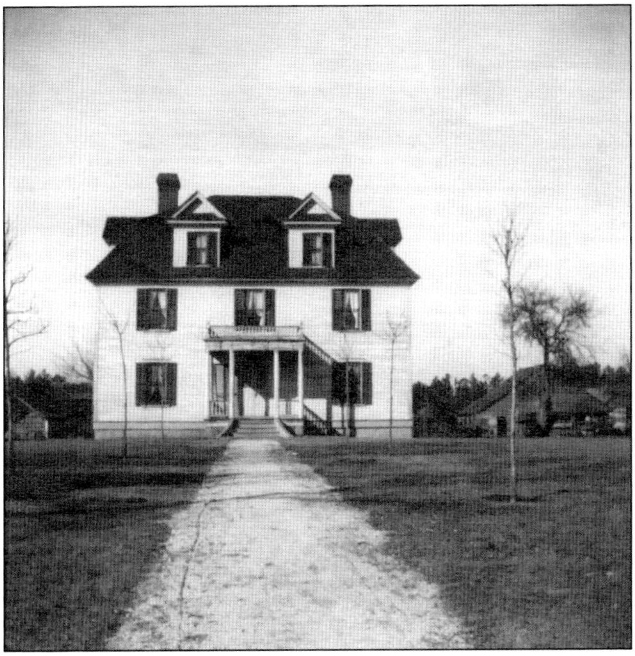

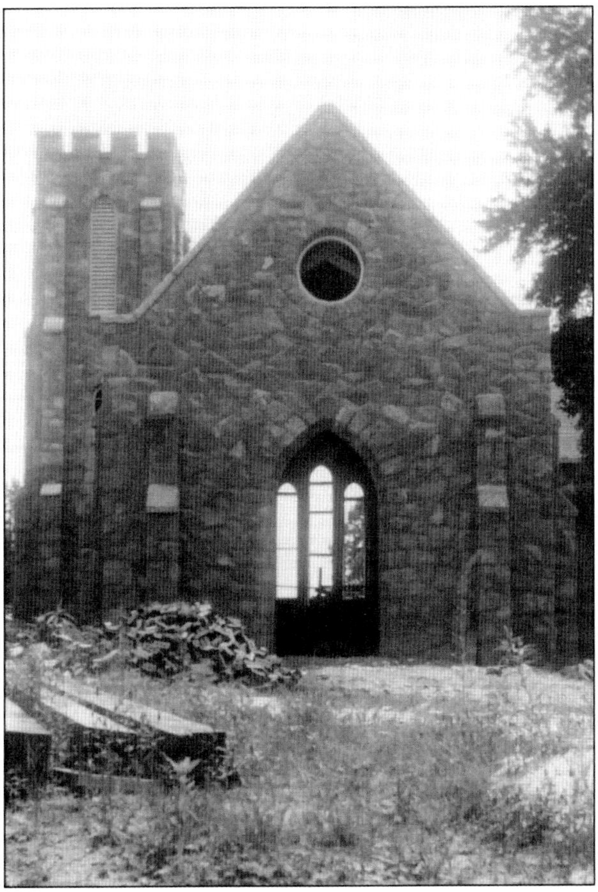

The Reverend John Creighton Seagle (1871–1947) of Rutherford County began building St. Mary's Chapel in Clear Creek before 1940. Progress halted during World War II. John's brother, the Reverend Nathan Adolphus Seagle (1868–1957), resumed construction, completing the chapel in 1955. Under the jurisdiction of St. James Episcopal Church, the chapel was later leased to Mount Pisgah Lutheran Church members, who worshiped there until the late 1980s. St. Mary's then reverted to St. James and the Seagle family. The chapel, known since 2002 as La Capilla de Santa María, hosts a Hispanic congregation. This photograph depicts construction nearing completion. (Courtesy of Alex Nelon.)

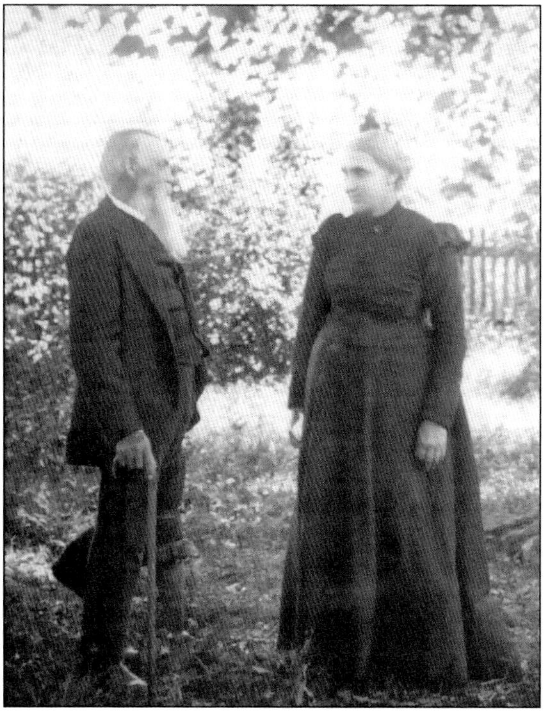

Philip Coon Seagle (1833–1902) and his wife, Mary Serepta Drake Seagle (1837–1914), pose at their home in Clear Creek. Philip lost his left leg while serving with the 23rd North Carolina Infantry in the Confederate army. (Courtesy of Alex Nelon.)

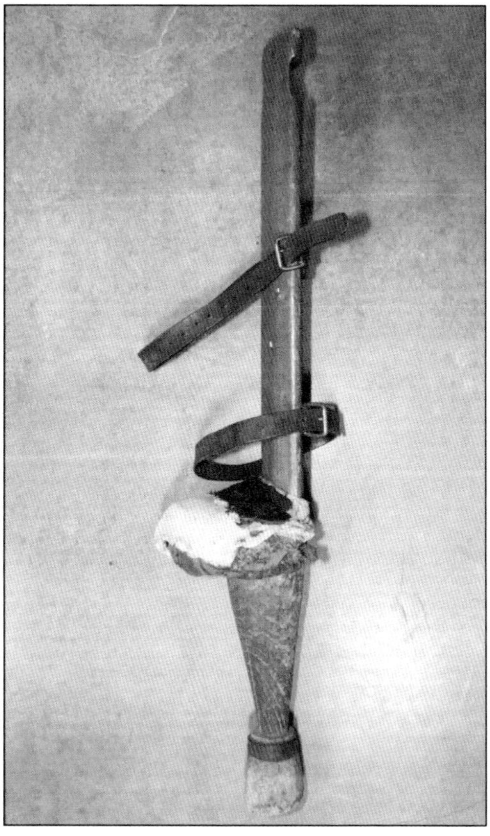

An accomplished cabinetmaker, Philip C. Seagle crafted his own prosthetic leg with belts and buckles as fasteners and a side rail for balance. (Collection of Alex Nelon, photograph by the author.)

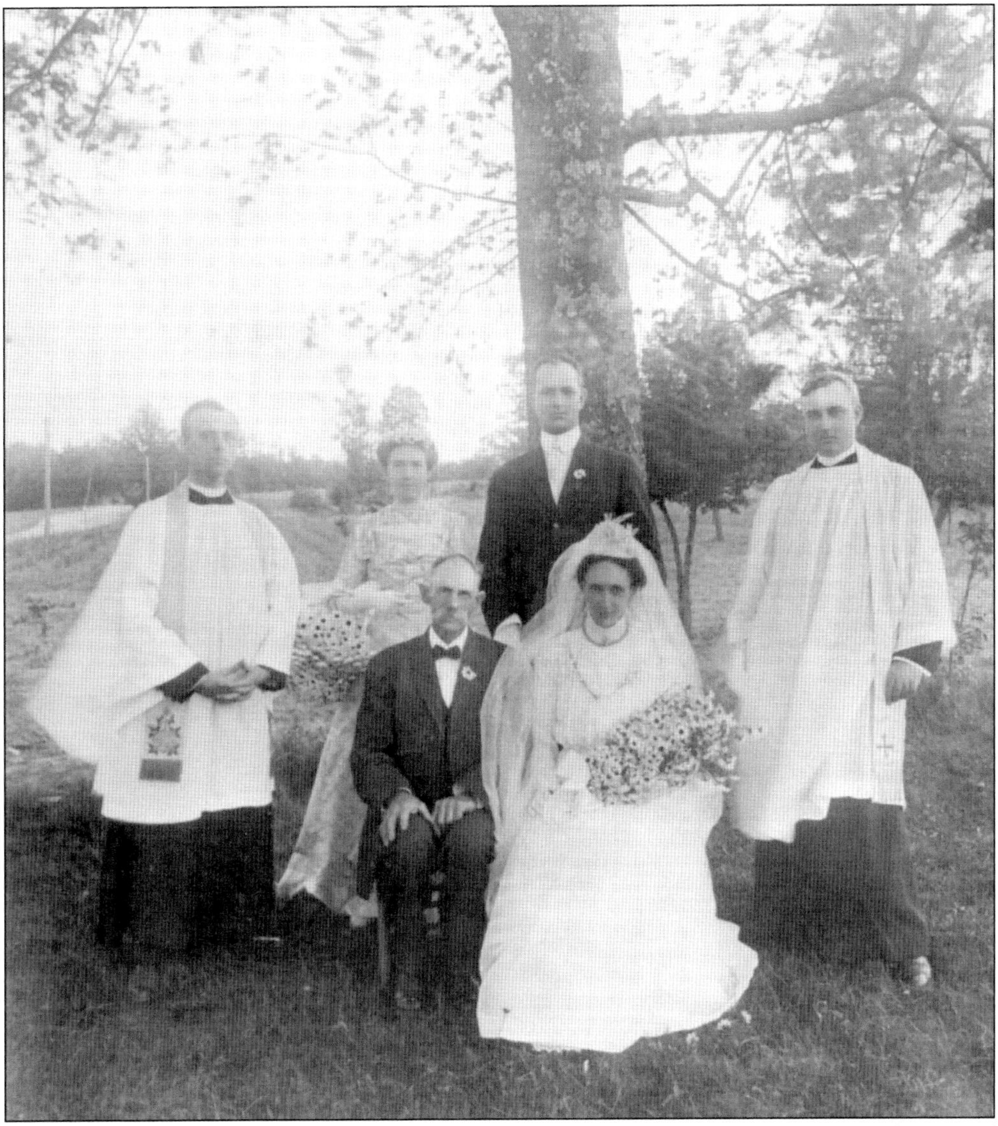

Lee Roy Smith (1846–1921) and Nellie Seagle (1874–1958), seated in the foreground, married in 1910. Standing from left to right are the Reverend Reginald Norton Willcox (1873–1929), Emma Frazier Seagle, Richard Seagle, and the Reverend Nathan Adolphus Seagle. The Reverend Willcox pastored the Episcopal churches of St. James and St. Paul's and the Episcopal missions of Henderson County. (Courtesy of Alex Nelon.)

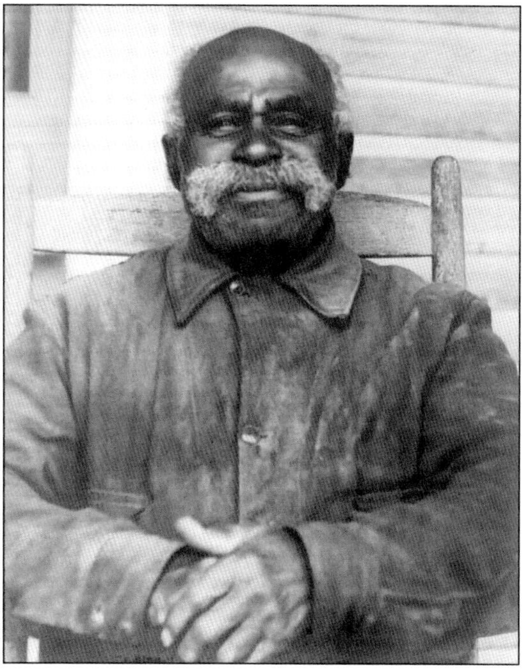

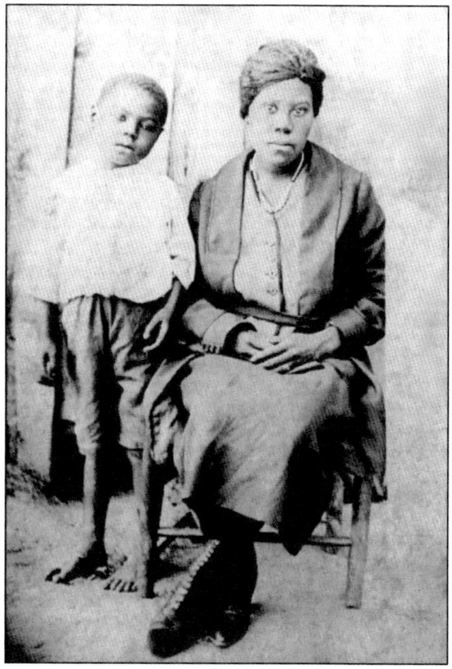

Born to freed slaves, Mack Whiteside (1866–1949) worked as a farmer and miller for most of his life in Clear Creek. Sophia Mills Whiteside (1888–1951), Mack's wife, poses with Abie (1921–1978), one of the Whitesides' nine children. Mack was a trustee of Green Mountain Missionary Baptist Church (1888), which became Mount Zion Baptist Church (below) in 1899. (Above left, courtesy of Alex Nelon; above right, courtesy of Shirley Jackson Davidson; below, photograph by the author.)

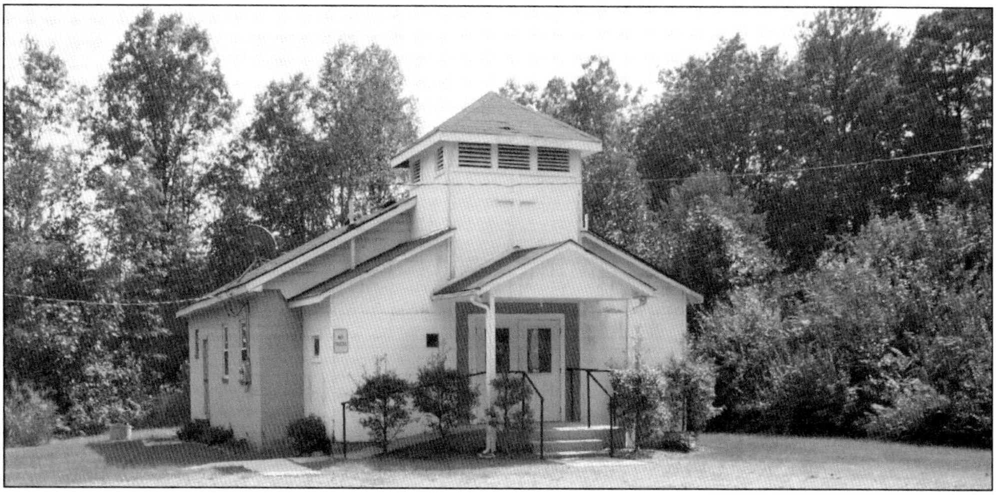

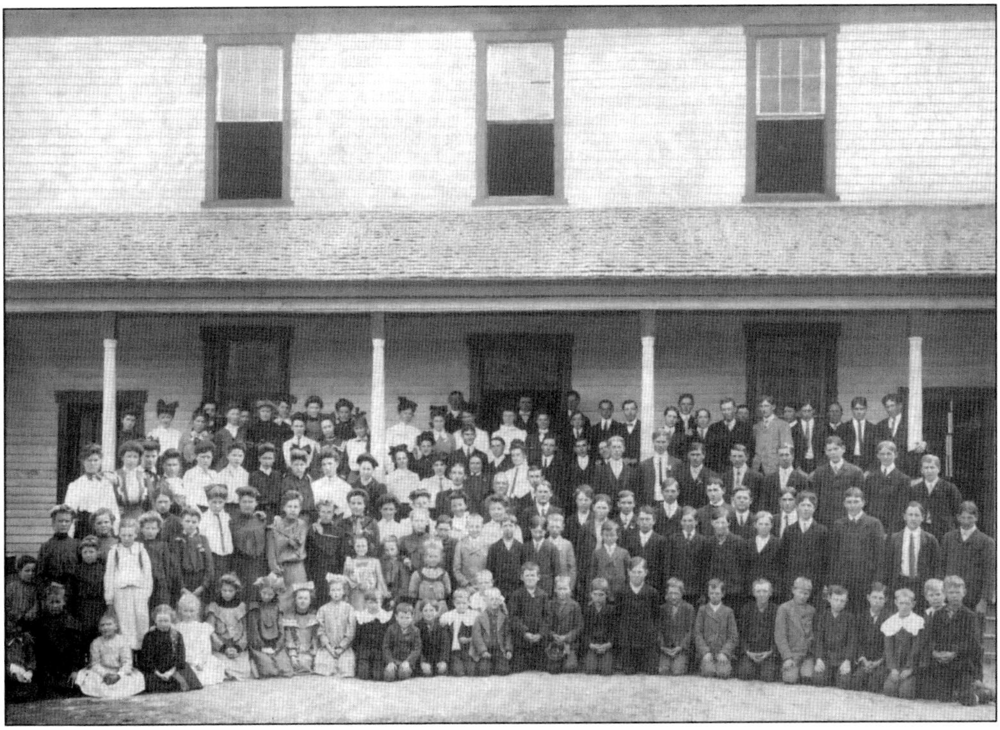

The Fruitland Institute began as the Green Mountain Academy, opened by the Carolina Baptist Association in 1898, for elementary and high school students. The institute closed in the 1930s and operated briefly as a junior college (1933–1934). The Baptist State Convention purchased the property in 1945, thereafter operating the Fruitland Baptist Bible Institute for the training of Baptist ministers. (Courtesy of the Henderson County Genealogical and Historical Society.)

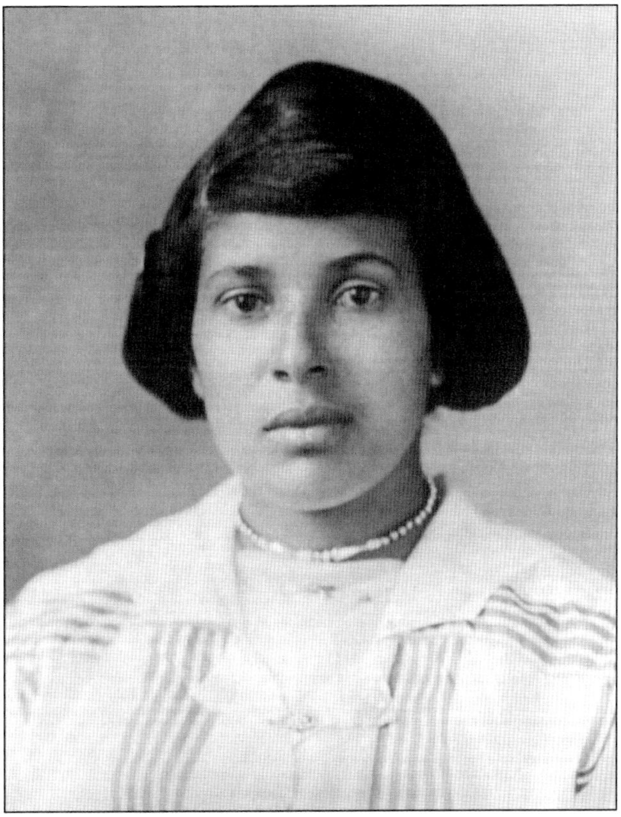

Odie Mills Littlejohn (1891–1968) taught at the Laus School in Edneyville in the early 1900s. Her daughter and son-in-law later converted the building into their home. (Courtesy of Ruth Littlejohn Montgomery.)

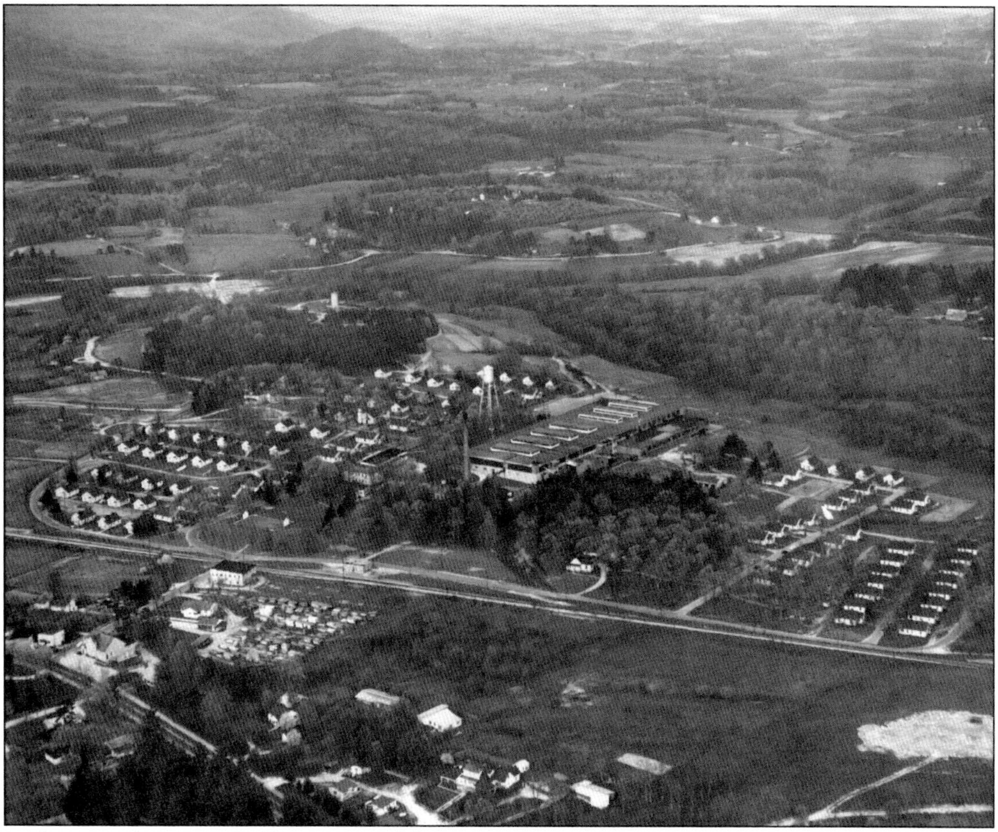

In the sector known as Balfour—named for quarryman William Balfour Troy (1859–1939)—Joseph Ellison Adger Smyth founded Balfour Mills in the early 1920s. Smyth supplied the mill village with cottages, a church, a community center, stores, and a school for the workers' children. International Cellucotton Products Company purchased the operation in the 1940s and changed the name to Berkeley Mills, pictured here. Berkeley Mills merged with Kimberly-Clark Corporation in 1963. (Courtesy of the Henderson County Genealogical and Historical Society.)

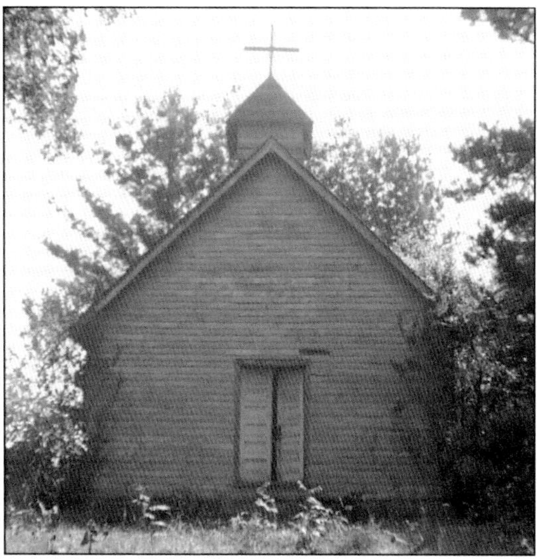

The Episcopal Missionary District of Asheville included St. Matthew's Chapel of Hillgirt, established in 1911 on two and one-half acres of the farmland of William Washington Lyda (1845–1922), sold to the diocese for $1. Fr. Reginald Norton Willcox ministered to the small congregation. The abandoned chapel, pictured in 1964, burned in 1967. (Courtesy of Phillip Heavner.)

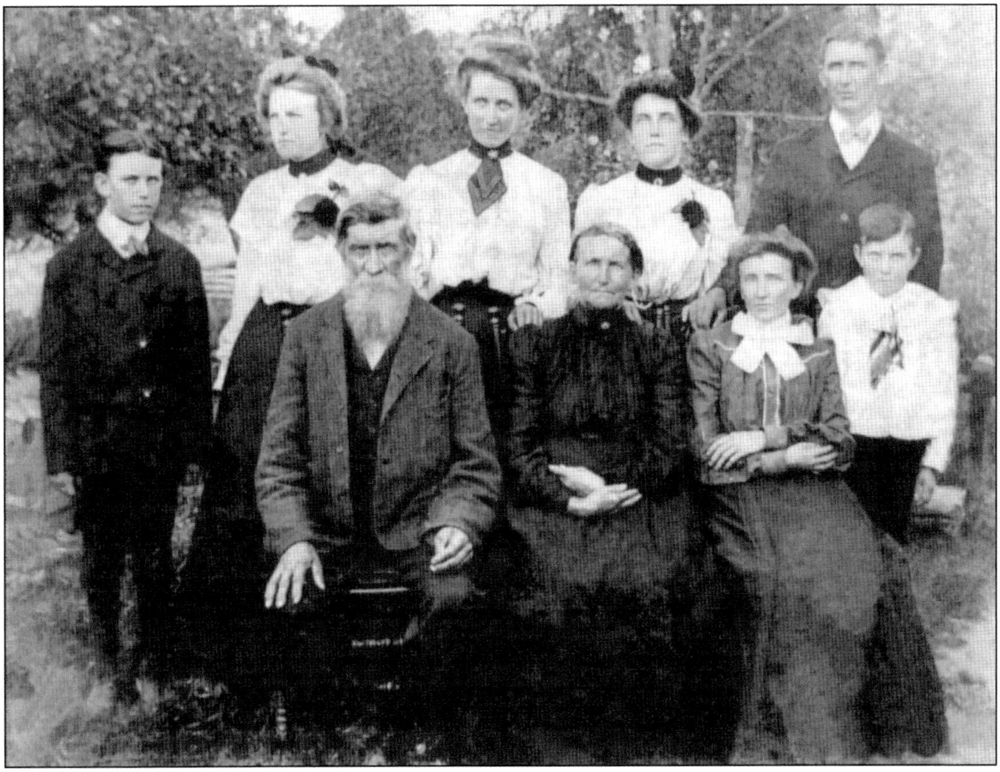

The Lyda family of Hillgirt is, from left to right, (first row) William Washington Lyda, Elizabeth J. Newman Lyda, Bessie Lyda Dunlap, and Holsom Brownlow Lyda; (second row) Samuel Festus "Bill" Lyda, Mollie Lyda Leverett, Nora R. Lyda Edney, Ira Lyda Sims, and Thomas B. Lyda. (Courtesy of Phillip Heavner.)

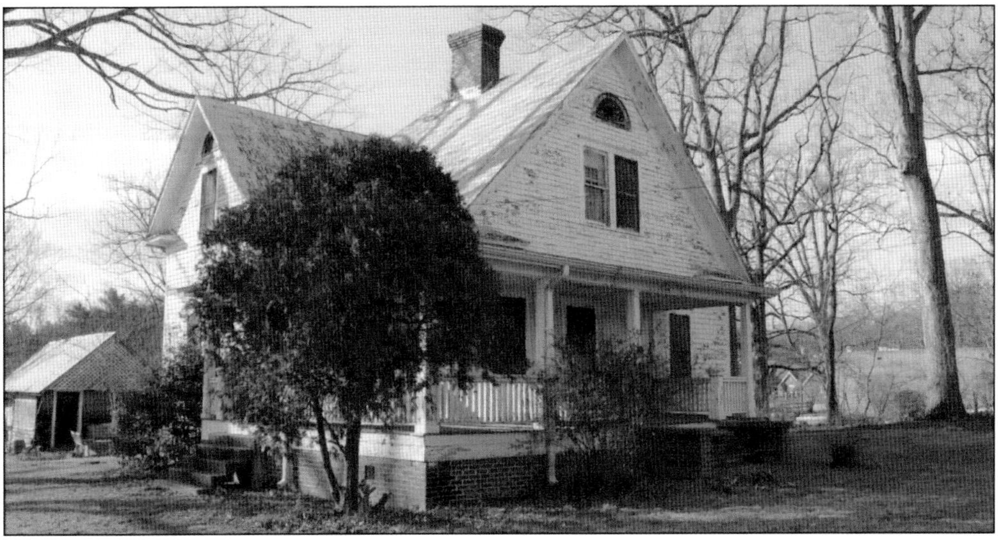

Built in 1900, this was the home of William Edward Poteat (1858–1933) and his wife, Martha L. Vest Poteat (1869–1946), at Fletcher. Poteat, a Southern Railroad executive and superintendent for the Blue Ridge Lime Company, gave land for the Fletcher Methodist Church. John Kern Bagwell (1908–2000) later owned the house. (Photograph by the author.)

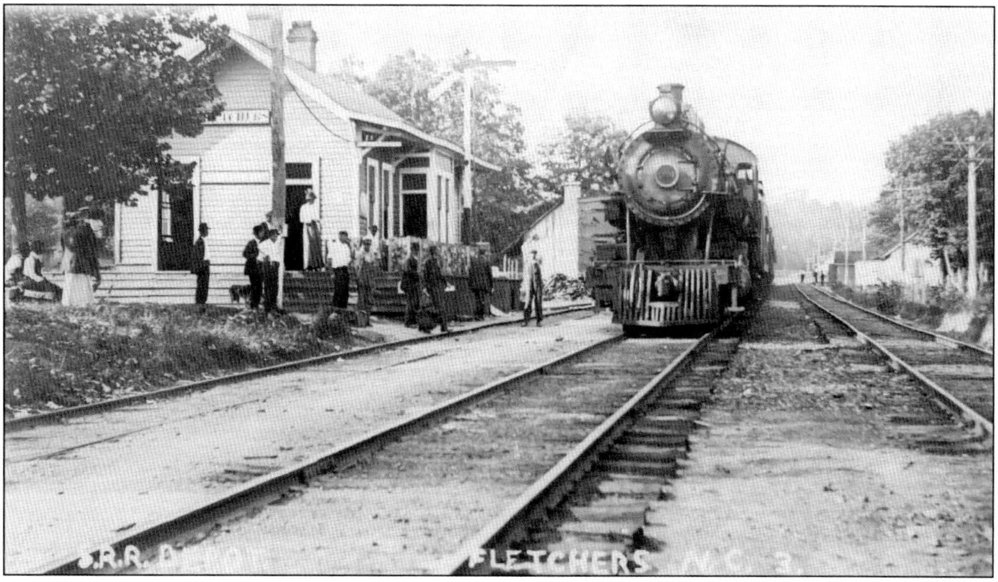

The Fletcher Southern Railroad station was established in the early 1880s. (Courtesy of the Henderson County Genealogical and Historical Society.)

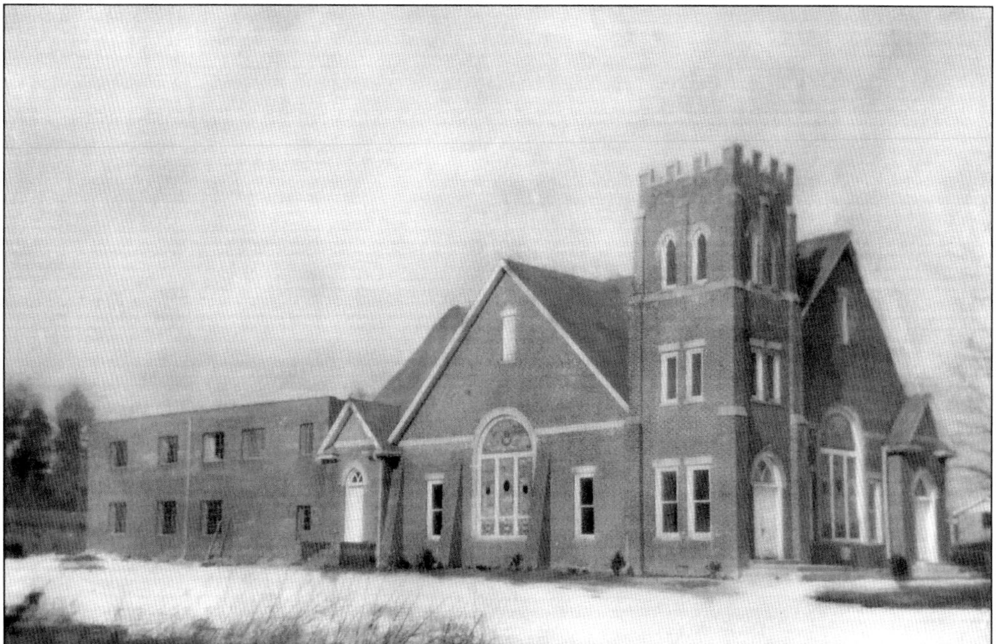

Fletcher First Baptist Church was organized in 1838 as Salem Baptist Church. The current church, pictured here, stands at the second location. (David Wilson photograph, courtesy of Richard Wilson.)

Five

South Henderson County

Crab Creek, Valley Hill, Flat Rock, East Flat Rock, Zirconia, Tuxedo, Macedonia, and Mountain Page

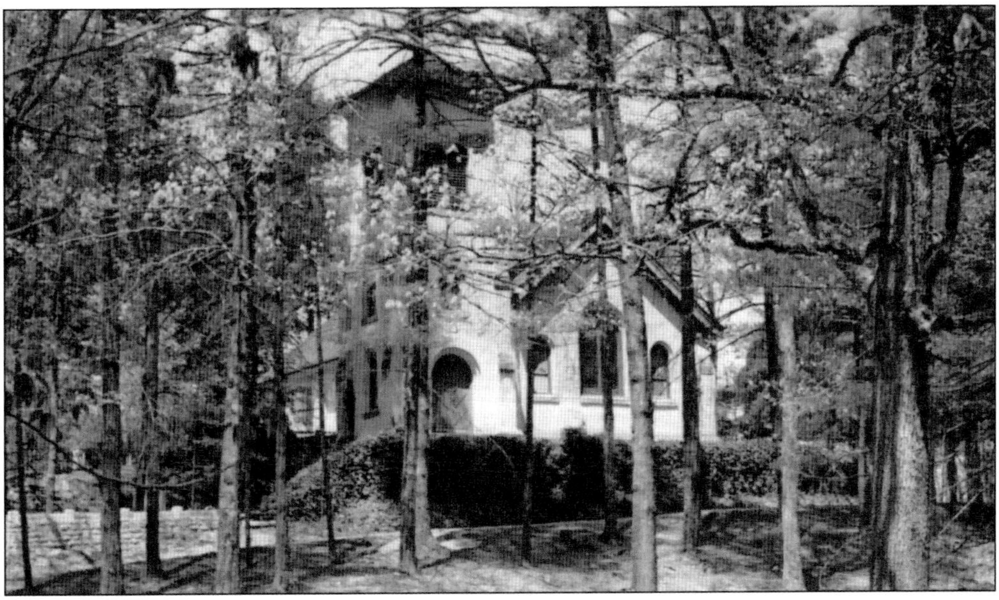

St. John in the Wilderness ranks as the oldest Episcopal church in Western North Carolina. Finding no Anglican churches proximate to Flat Rock, summer residents Charles (1774–1865) and Susan Cole Baring (1763–1845) had a chapel built near their mansion. The inaugural log chapel (built around 1827) burned in a forest fire. A chapel of brick replaced it by 1833. The Barings hired the Reverend Thomas Smith Webb Mott (1800–1869) to serve as rector and to tutor their foster children. In 1836, the Barings deeded the church to the Reverend Levi Silliman Ives, Episcopal bishop of North Carolina. In 1852, Edward C. Jones (1822–1902) designed and oversaw the enlargement of the church, including an Italianate tower and an extension of the nave. The Barings' bodies are interred under the three pews they reserved for their household. (Rev. Reginald Norton Willcox photograph, courtesy of the Henderson County Genealogical and Historical Society.)

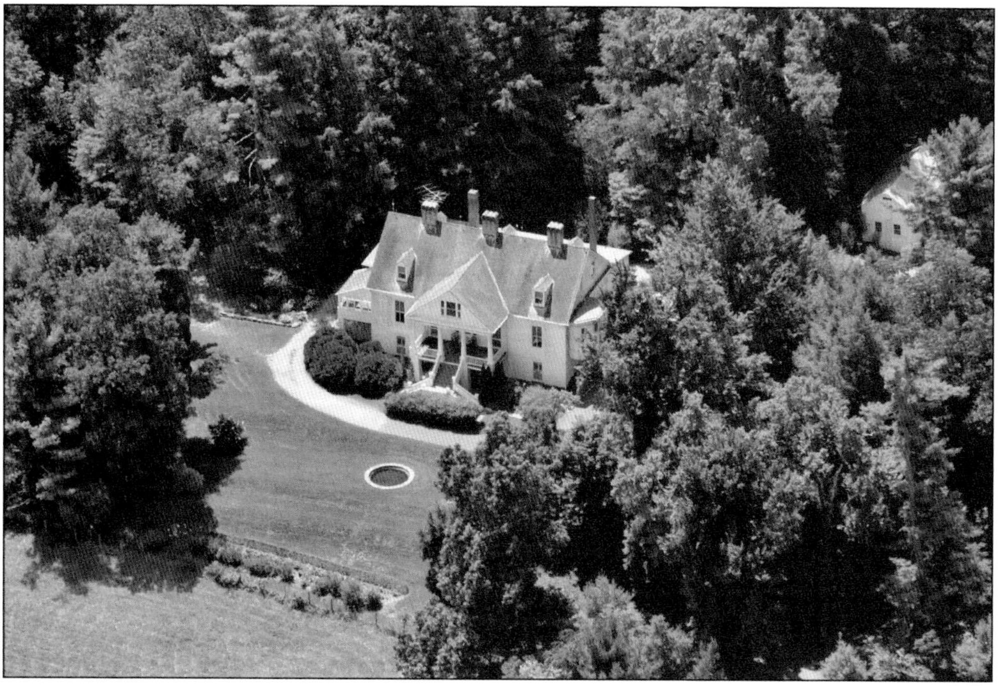

Built for Charlestonian Christopher Gustavus Memminger (1803–1888), the Greek Revival house in the center of this photograph graces the Carl Sandburg Home National Historic Site. Memminger, an attorney, served as the first secretary of the Confederate treasury. Charles F. Reichardt (1819–1864) designed and built the 1839 home, named Rock Hill by Memminger. William Gregg Jr. next owned the estate. Joseph Ellison Adger Smyth later acquired the property and renamed it Connemara to honor his Irish heritage. Carl and Lilian Sandburg lived there from 1945 until Carl's death in 1967. In 1968, the Department of the Interior purchased the property from Carl's widow. (Courtesy of Tim Culberson of Aerial Photo Professionals.)

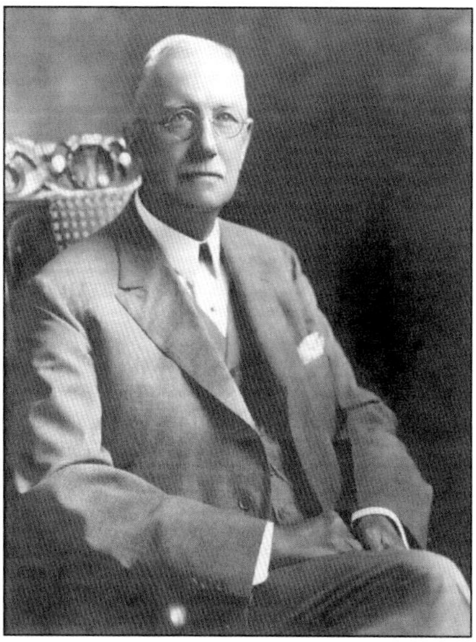

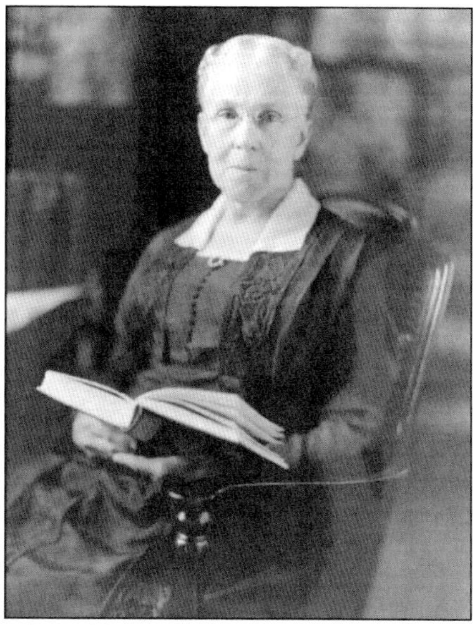

Textile mogul Joseph Ellison Adger Smyth (1847–1942) and his wife, Julia Gambrill Smyth (1849–1927), lived and farmed at Connemara. (Both, courtesy of Larry H. McKay Jr.)

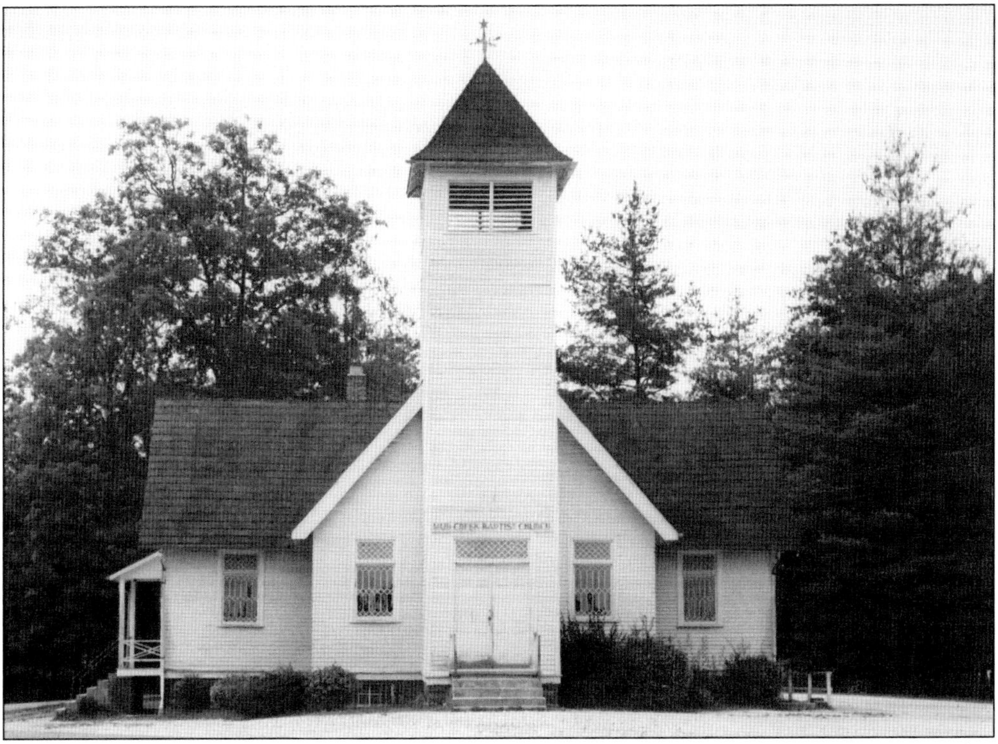

Members of Mud Creek Baptist Church (founded in 1804) first met in log meetinghouses. This sanctuary was erected in 1900. It stood catty-corner to the 1995 church of brick. (Courtesy of Mud Creek Baptist Church.)

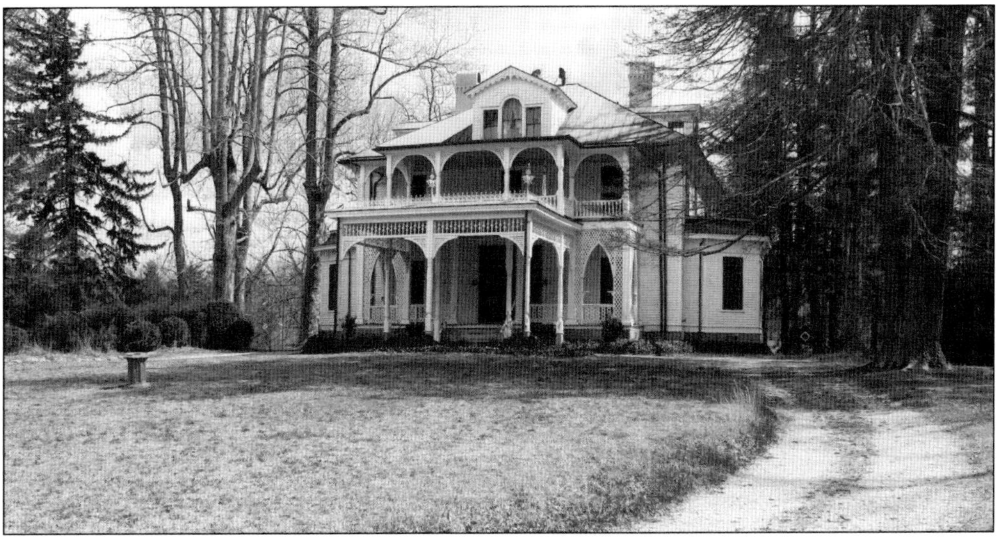

This c. 1847 home, built for James Pringle (1813–1884) at Flat Rock, features an intact kitchen house and slave quarters behind the main house. William Ravenel (1806–1888) bought the property in 1871. One of the property's many successive owners, Augustine T. Smythe (1842–1914), purchased the estate in 1908 and named it Many Pines. Additional owners included Arthur Barnwell, J.H. Parker, Arthur Parker, Charles H. Drayton, Dr. Allard Memminger, Gen. Alex King, Eugene Jervey, and Leonard Phinizy. (Photograph by the author.)

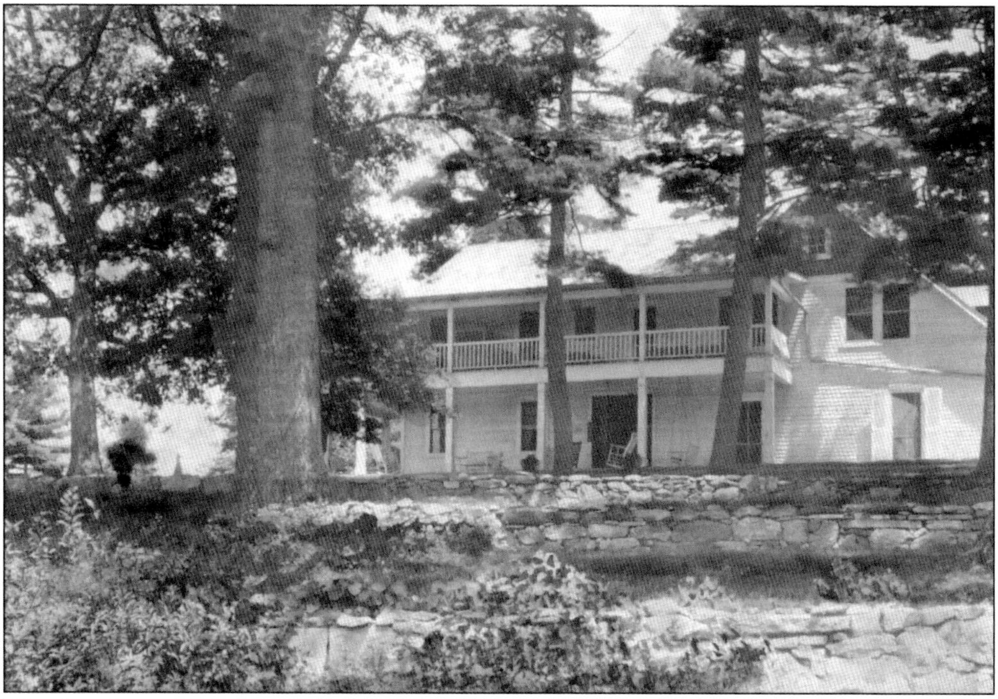

This farmhouse once served as a stagecoach stop alongside Howard Gap Road. Capt. Joseph Ellison Adger Smyth bought the 325-acre estate for his son James Adger Smyth (1873–1928). The younger Smyth named it Faraway Farms. (Courtesy of Larry H. McKay Jr.)

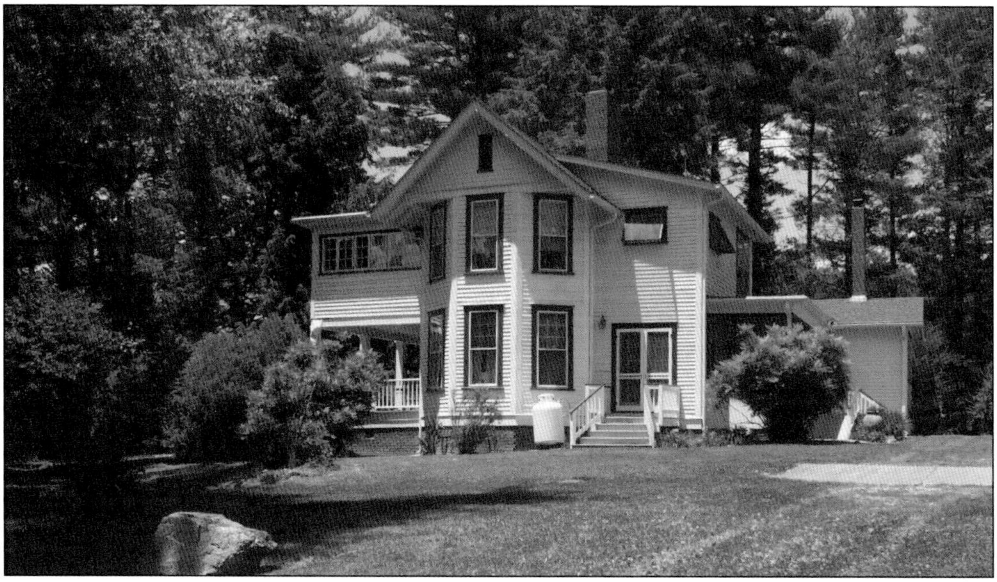

Originally a four-room farmhouse built in the 1890s, Windy Hill was remodeled and enlarged in 1914 by Erle G. Stillwell. Additions included angled bays, guest rooms, porches, and a grand staircase, with a second-level sleeping porch added later. Bought in 1921 by Joseph Ellison Adger Smyth for his daughter Sarah Smyth Hudgens (1880–1973) and her husband, John Allison Hudgens (1872–1946), the estate included approximately 325 acres. A great-granddaughter of J.E.A. Smyth and great-niece of Erle G. Stillwell currently owns the property. (Photograph by the author.)

Summey's or Jordan's mill, later called Henderson County Flour Mill, operates now as Mill House Lodge. The operation belonged first to Peter Summey (1811–1891). In the early 1900s, William C. Jordan (1859–1947) replaced Summey's wooden mill with the existing one of poured concrete and Summey's undershot wheel with an overshot model. Jack and Alexander Ramseur next owned the mill. Judge Mitchell King, Andrew Johnstone, and Henry T. Farmer's names are also included in deeds to this property. The structure has served many functions, from grist-, saw-, and lathe mill to apartments and a motel. (Painting by Dr. William Redin Kirk, courtesy of Stan Shelley.)

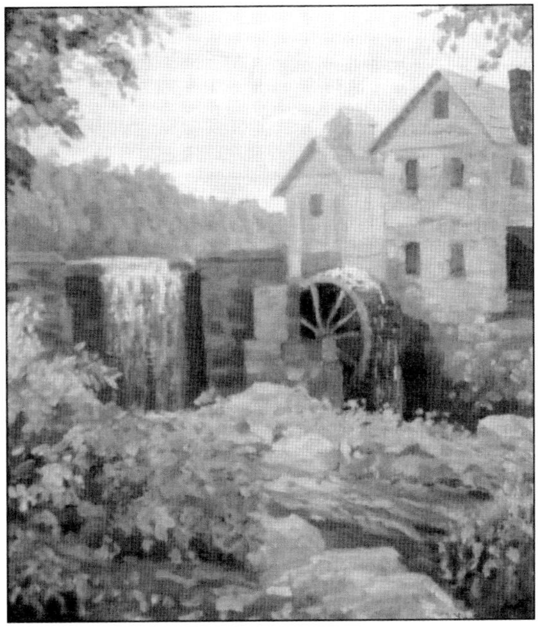

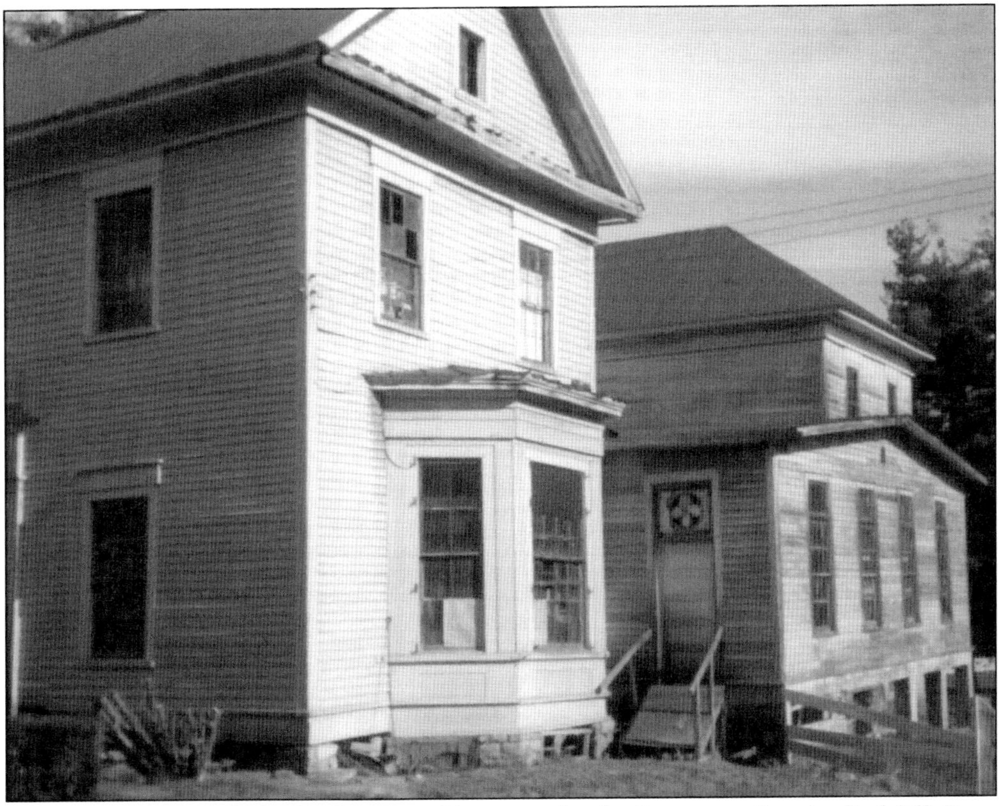

Solitude, the home of Charles Baring and his second wife, Constance Beatrice Radcliffe Dent (1816–1891), was built in 1854 at the mill shoal of Highland Lake. The domicile was moved from its original pad and employed as a clubhouse. It no longer stands. (Courtesy of the estate of Louise H. Bailey.)

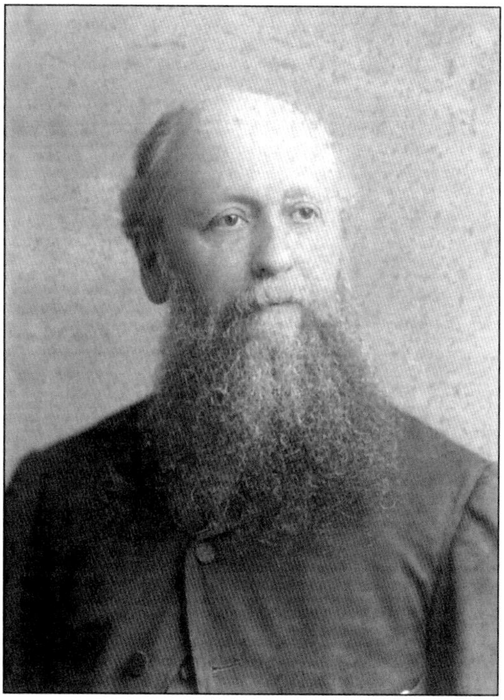

Maj. Theodore Gaillard Barker (1832–1917), a coastal South Carolina rice planter, attorney, and Civil War veteran, married Louisa Preston King (1834–1920) and owned the 1836 Colonial Revival mansion known as Brookland Manor north of the Village of Flat Rock. Major Barker was at one time one of the largest landowners in Henderson County and is the namesake of the community of Barker Heights. Wife Louisa was one of Judge Mitchell King's daughters. (Courtesy of the estate of Louise H. Bailey.)

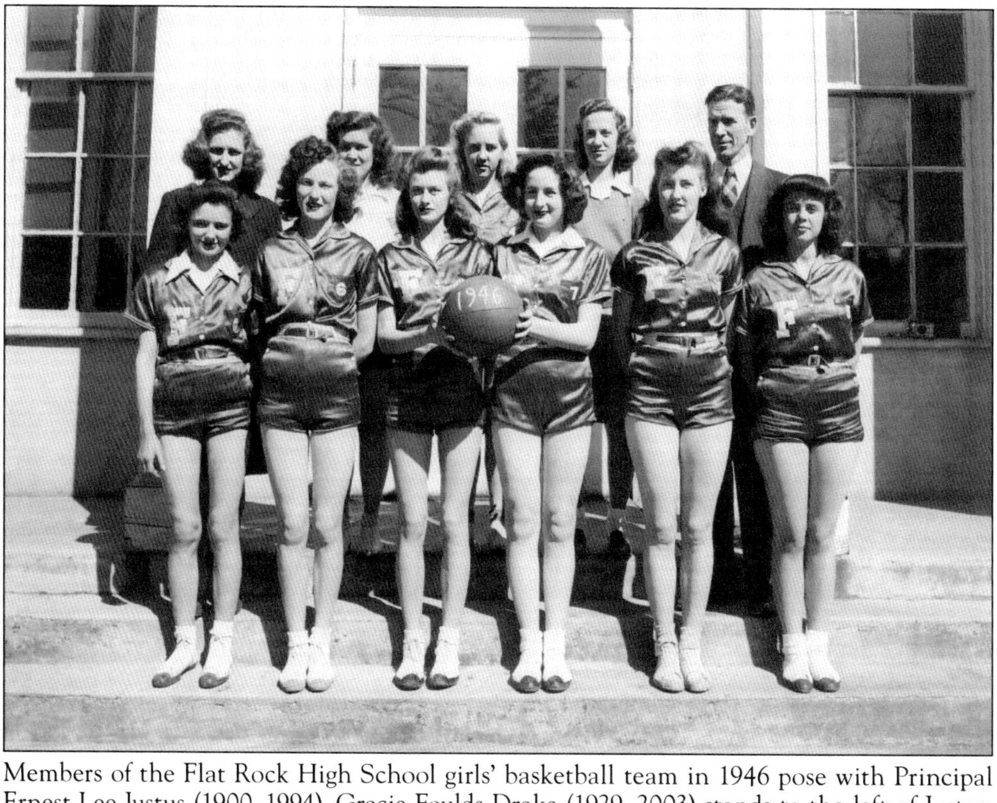

Members of the Flat Rock High School girls' basketball team in 1946 pose with Principal Ernest Lee Justus (1900–1994). Gracie Foulds Drake (1929–2003) stands to the left of Justus. (Author's collection.)

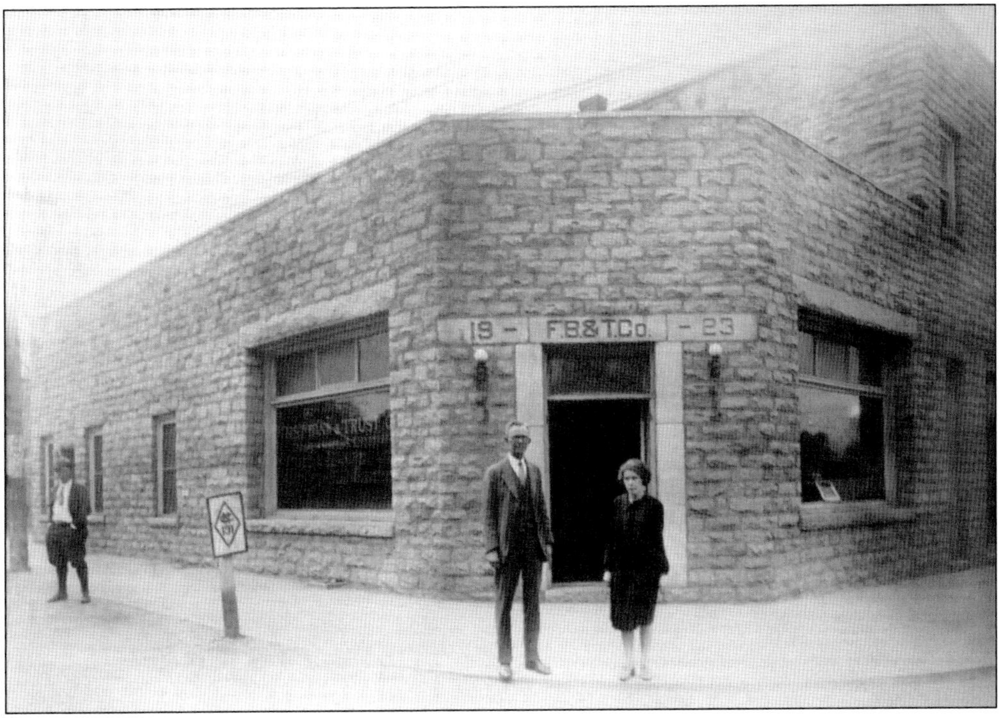

Atlas Otho Jones (1879–1935), register of deeds, and Vera Nora Jones Garner (1904–1970), bookkeeper, pose in front of the First Bank & Trust Company of East Flat Rock at West Blue Ridge Road and Lamplighter Lane. The banking operation, opened in 1923, lasted only 10 years. Sculptor Fred McMullen bought the building in 2011 and converted it into residential quarters and the BenTree Studio. (Courtesy of Fred and Diane McMullen.)

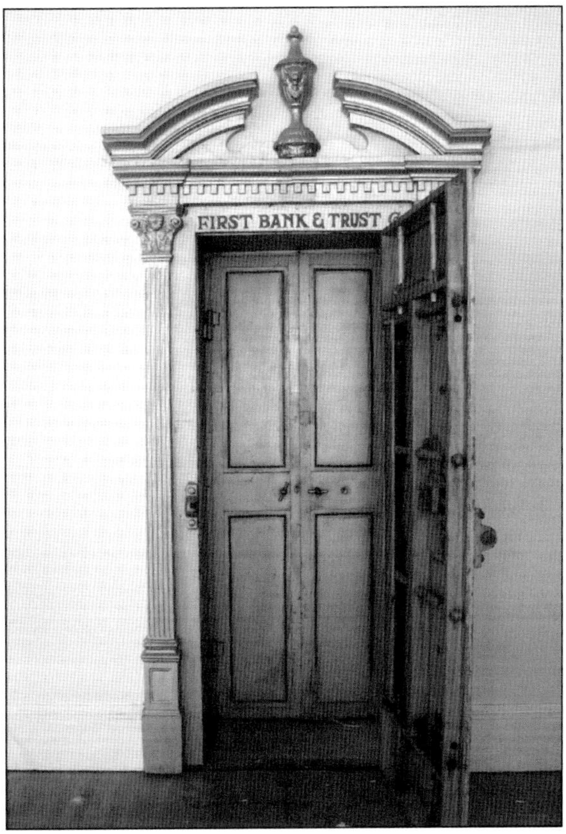

The vault of the former First Bank & Trust Company has been repurposed for storage. (Photograph by the author.)

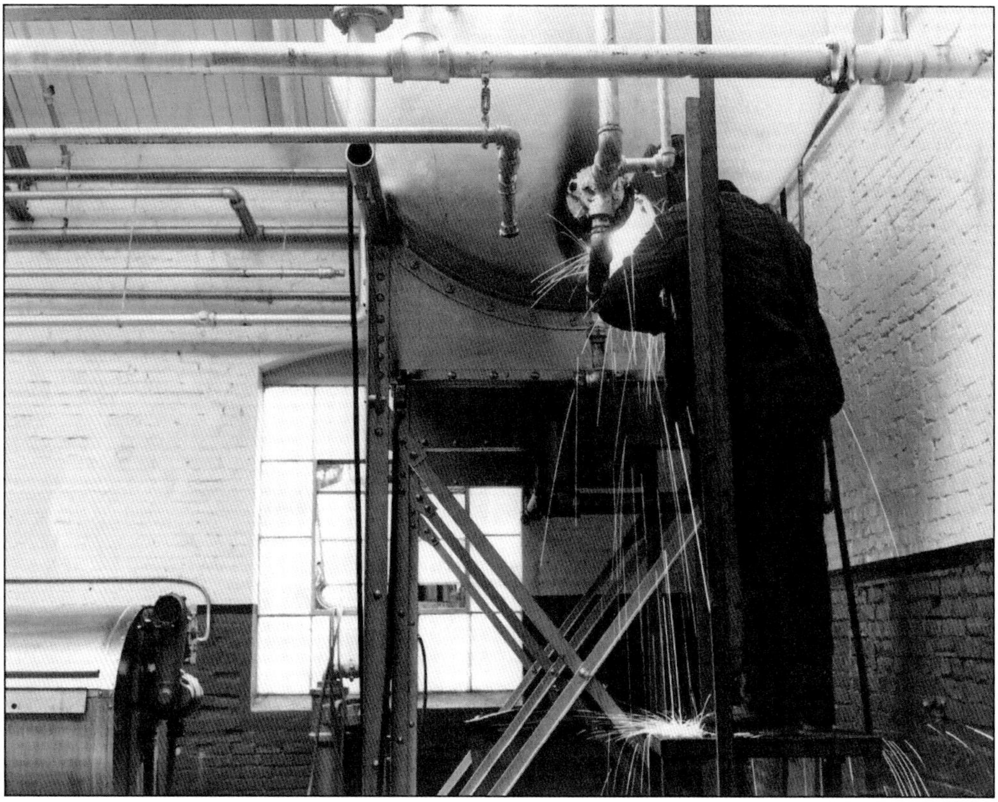

Samuel Leroy King (1920–1963) wields his welder in the dyehouse of the Chipman-LaCrosse Hosiery Mill in East Flat Rock, which began in 1907 as Skyland Hosiery Mill. The operation closed in 1968. (Russell Allen Katzenmoyer photograph, courtesy of the Henderson County Genealogical and Historical Society.)

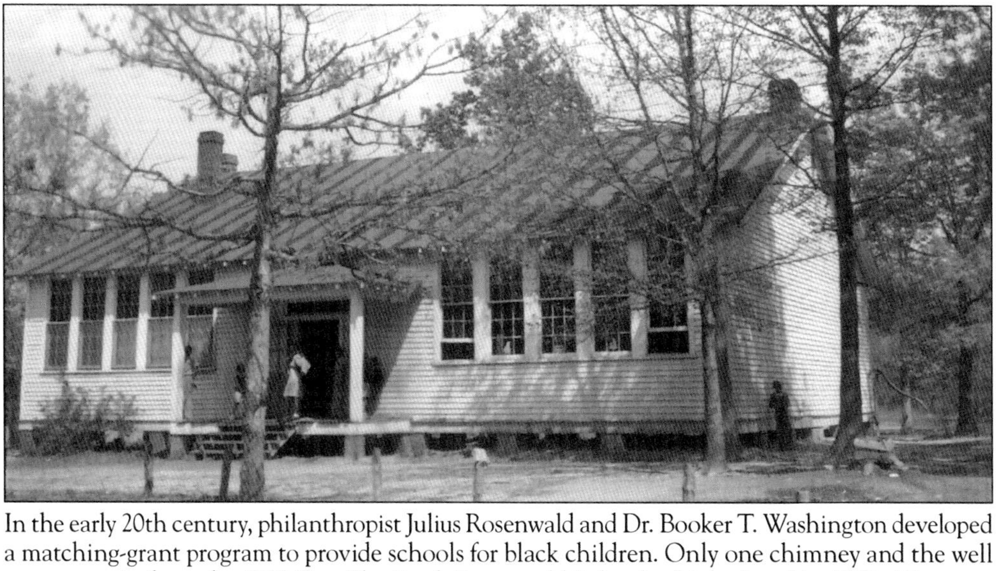

In the early 20th century, philanthropist Julius Rosenwald and Dr. Booker T. Washington developed a matching-grant program to provide schools for black children. Only one chimney and the well pump remain from the 1923 East Flat Rock Rosenwald School, which closed in 1952. (Courtesy of Hortence Potts.)

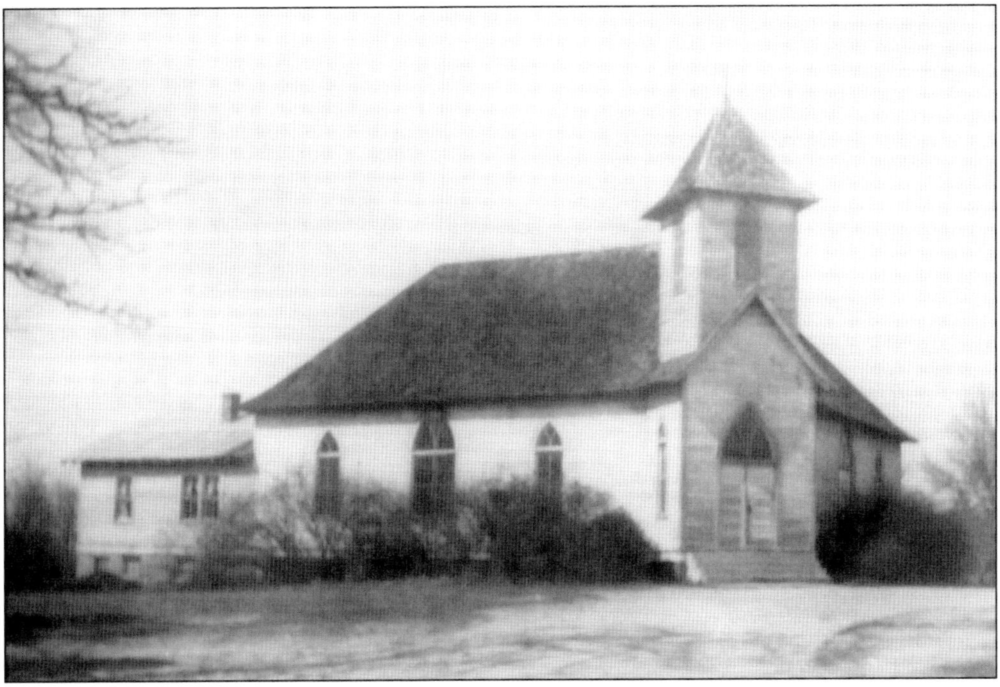

East Flat Rock First Baptist Church was founded in 1909. This photograph of the original (1910) sanctuary dates from 1945. (Courtesy of East Flat Rock First Baptist Church.)

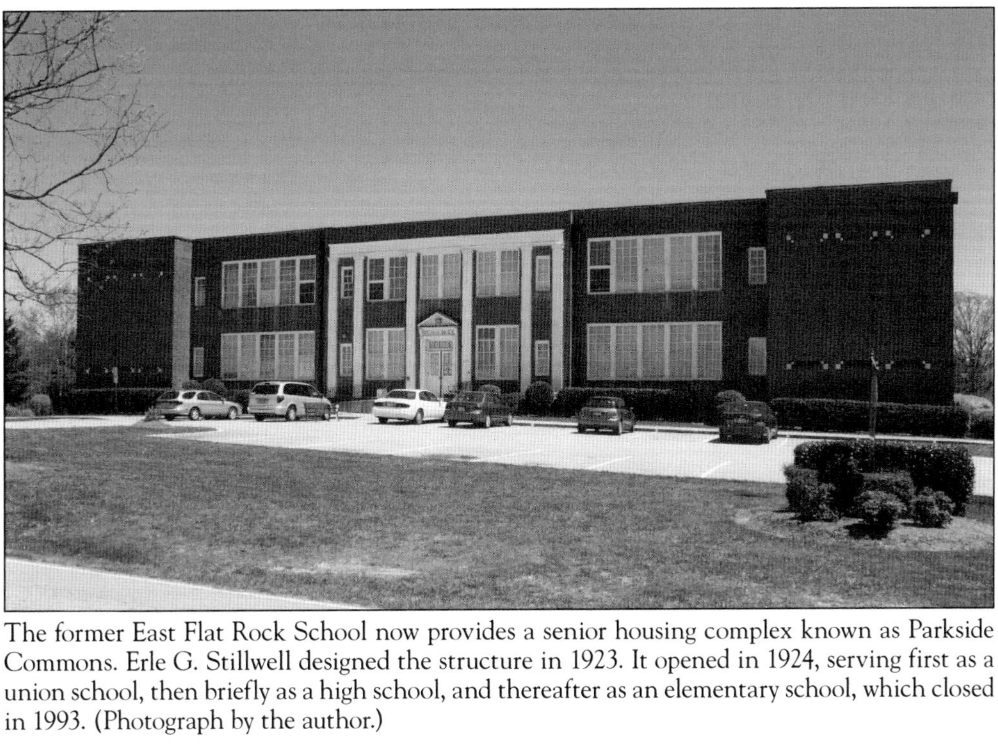

The former East Flat Rock School now provides a senior housing complex known as Parkside Commons. Erle G. Stillwell designed the structure in 1923. It opened in 1924, serving first as a union school, then briefly as a high school, and thereafter as an elementary school, which closed in 1993. (Photograph by the author.)

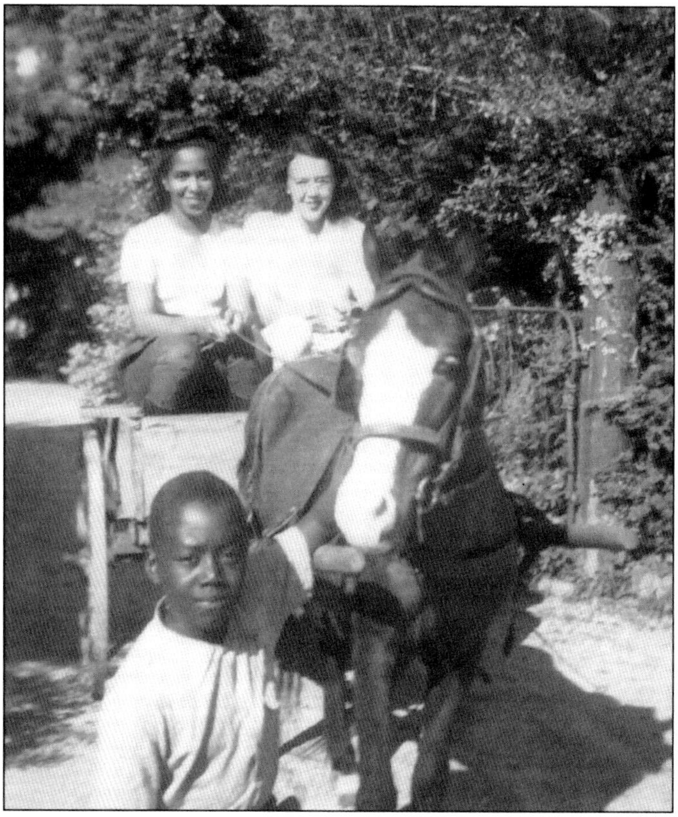

Bobby Simmons leads Wilma King (left) and Hortence Potts on a ride through East Flat Rock in the 1940s. (Courtesy of Hortence Potts.)

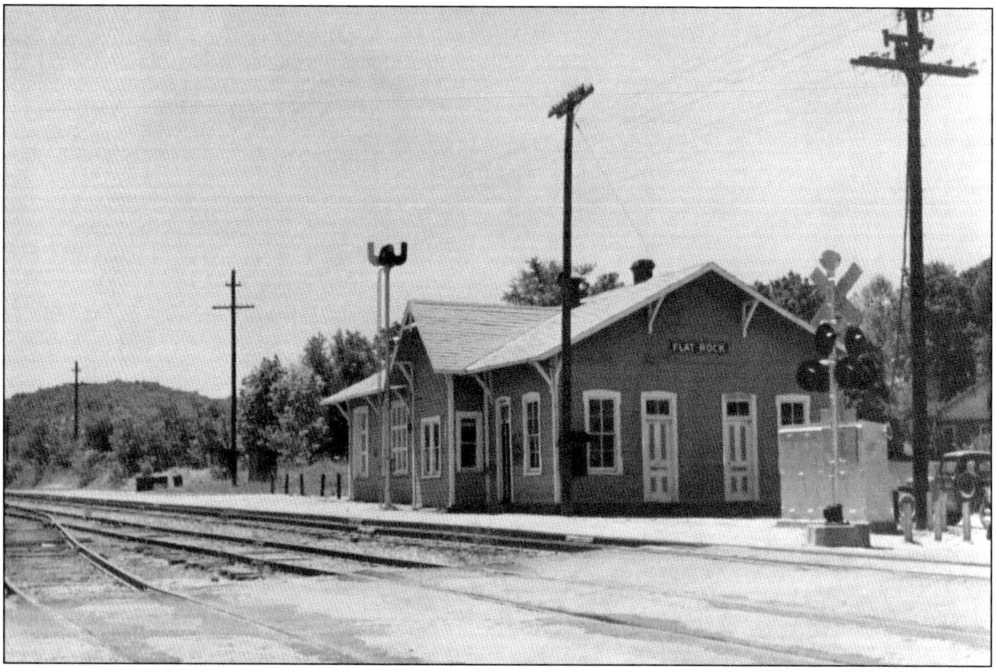

The Flat Rock Southern Railway depot stood in East Flat Rock. (Ed Hunnicutt photograph, courtesy of Ruth Kidd.)

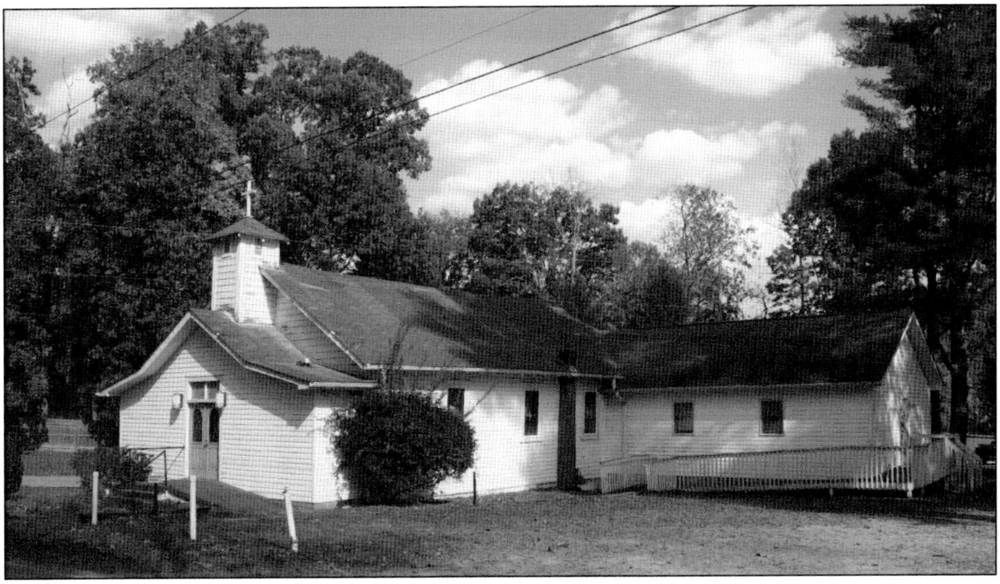

Mud Creek Missionary Baptist Church, established in 1867, was the second black church constituted in Henderson County. Members built the first sanctuary near Bonclarken. The present church, pictured here, stands at Roper and Mine Gap Roads in East Flat Rock. (Photograph by the author.)

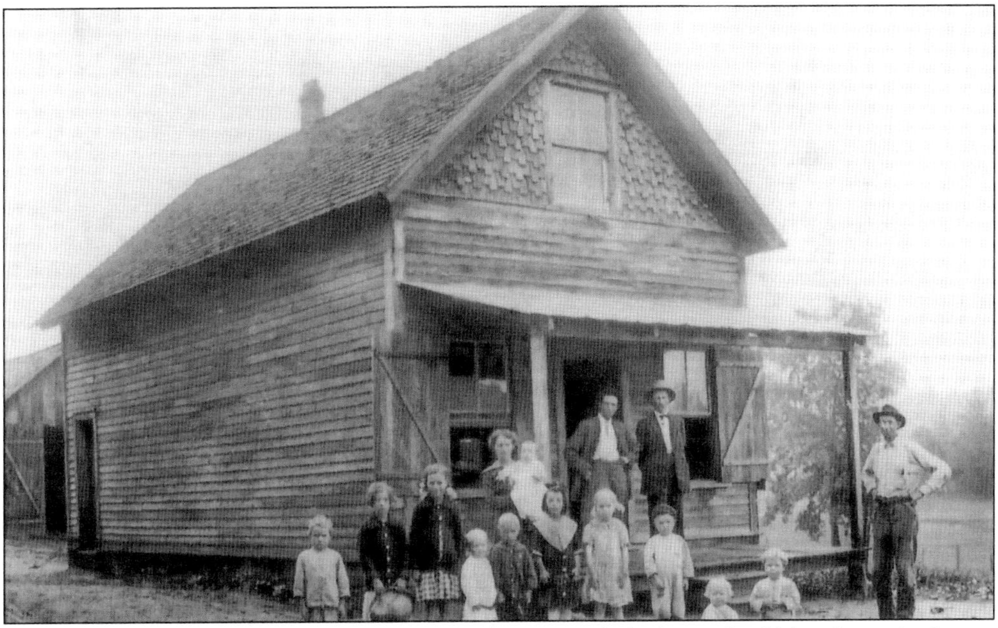

Built in the late 1800s by John Tyler Drake (1876–1927) for his wife, Altha Attie Anderson Drake (1883–1977), and their family, this house has hosted generations of Drakes. Successive family residents sold gasoline, groceries, and milled grain from this property. The homestead, at the point where Kanuga Road changes to Crab Creek Road across from Pleasant Hill Baptist Church, has long been abandoned and now stands on the brink of collapse. (Courtesy of Frank E. Blazey Jr.)

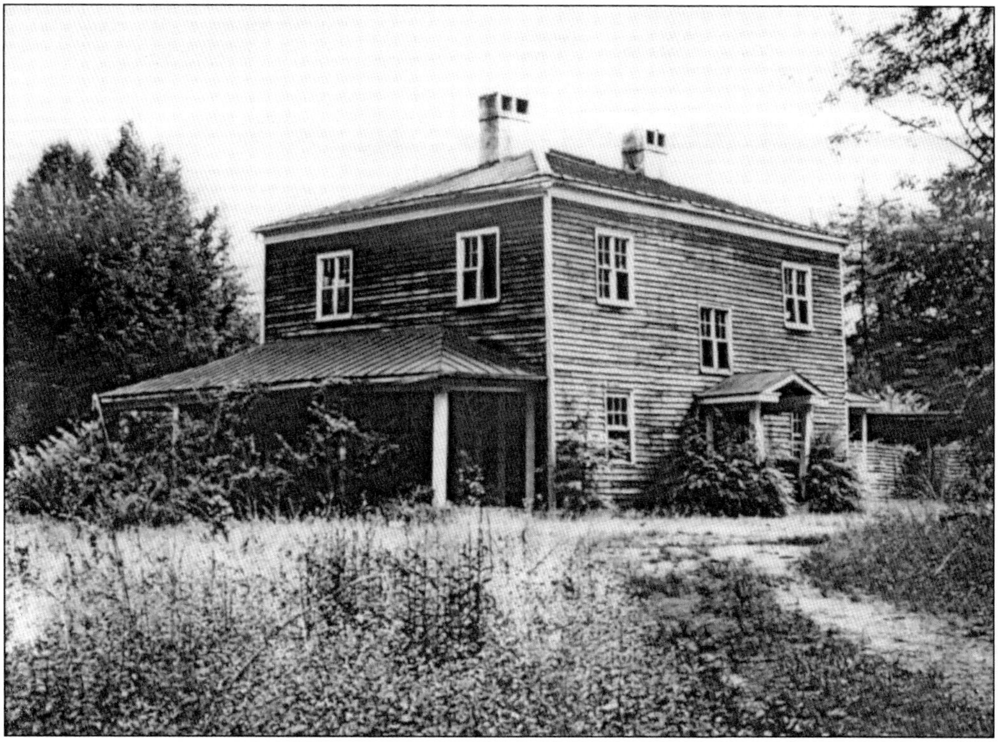

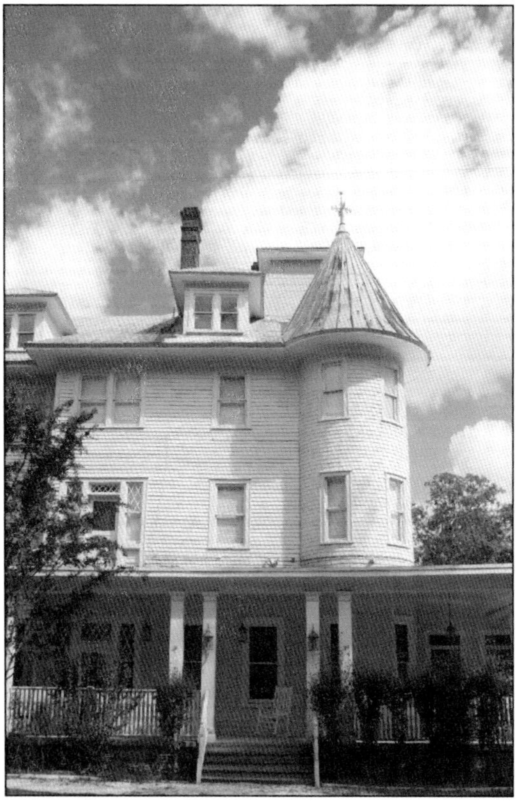

William Coubro Connell (1833–1918) and Agnes McNee Connell (1838–1923) of Scotland bought this manse from Matthew Richard Singleton (1817–1854). Known as Hemlocks, the house was built for Ralph Izard Middleton (1814–1891) in 1838. It has been written that the farm boasted the largest hemlock tree east of the Rocky Mountains. The Connells operated a farm on the property within the present-day Woodhaven subdivision. (Courtesy of the estate of Louise H. Bailey.)

The 1909 Lake View Hotel was later renamed Copper Crest Inn. The Victorian-style edifice looms over a shoreline of Osceola Lake in the Valley Hill community. The now-abandoned 30-room hotel once offered entertainment and gourmet food, including kosher meals. (Photograph by the author.)

The 1901 sanctuary of Pleasant Hill Baptist Church stood alongside Little River Road at the intersection of Kanuga and Crab Creek Roads. This church burned in a suspected arson fire in 1971. A sanctuary of brick replaced it in 1972. (Courtesy of Barbara Willis.)

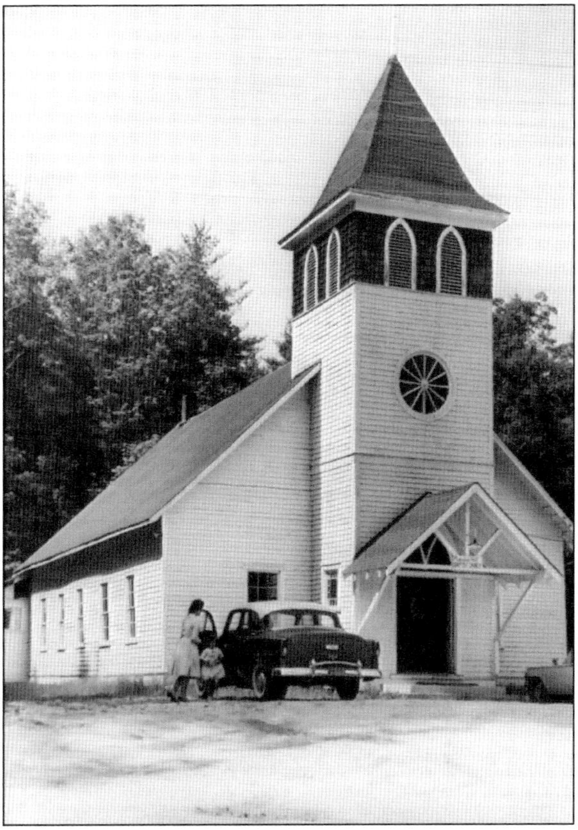

Pleasant Hill Baptist Church burned in 1971. Until members built a new church, the Reverend Jim Dan Willis (1914–1977) at times preached the gospel from a pulpit in the bed of his truck. (Courtesy of Barbara Willis.)

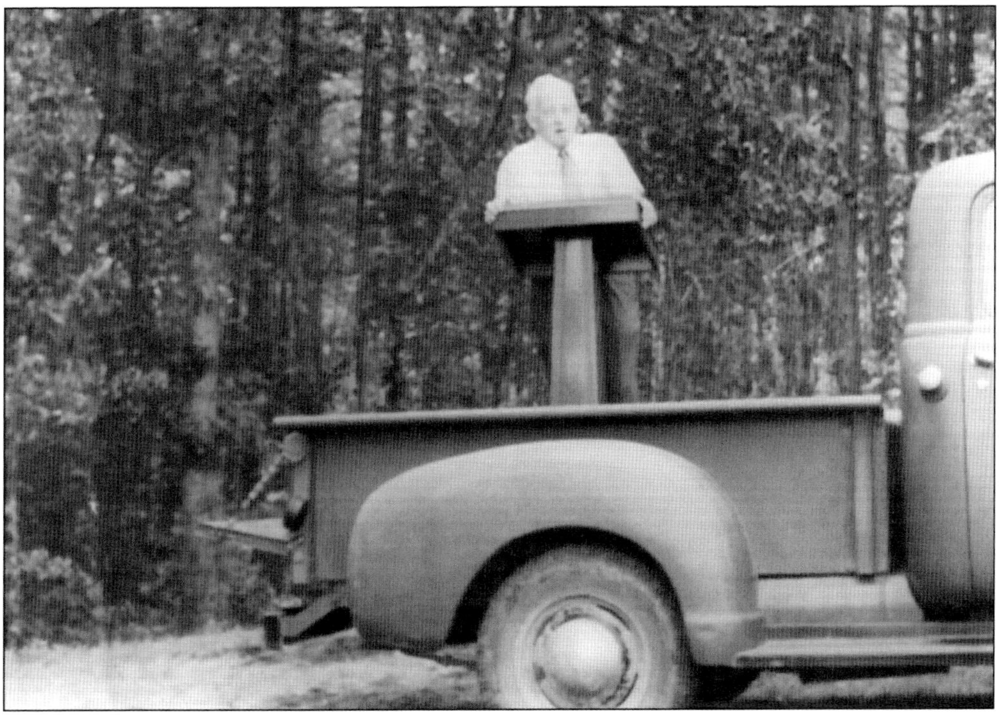

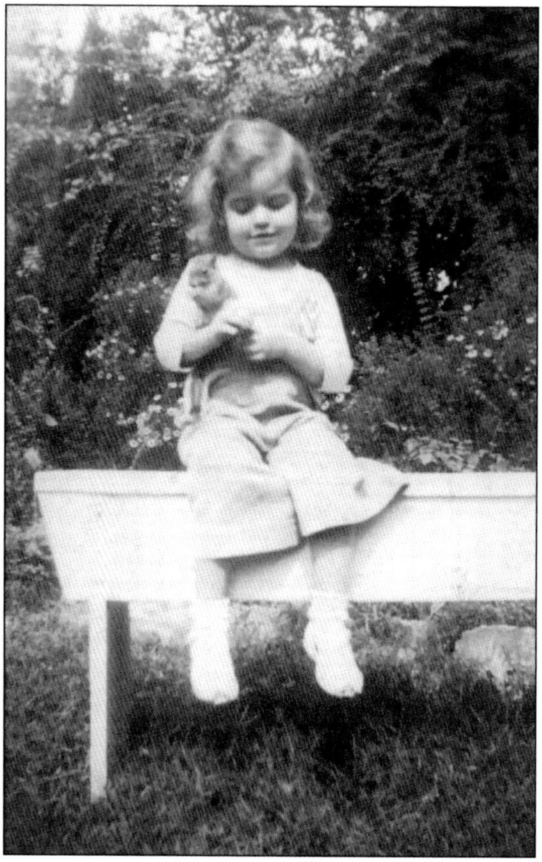

"Penni" Drake (Ruth Anne Drake Thompson) feeds a tame squirrel in Valley Hill. (Courtesy of Sarah Lucille "Sindy" Drake Hamilton.)

The Valley Hill Volunteer Fire Department was founded in 1956 and incorporated in 1958. Pictured from left to right are James C. "Buddy" McCullough, Clyde Peter Griffin, and Ed Young. A vehicle restoration and brake-service company now occupies this building on Willow Road. The new fire department stands catty-corner to it. Valley Hill School can be seen in the top right of this image. (Ed Hunnicutt photograph, courtesy of the Henderson County Genealogical and Historical Society.)

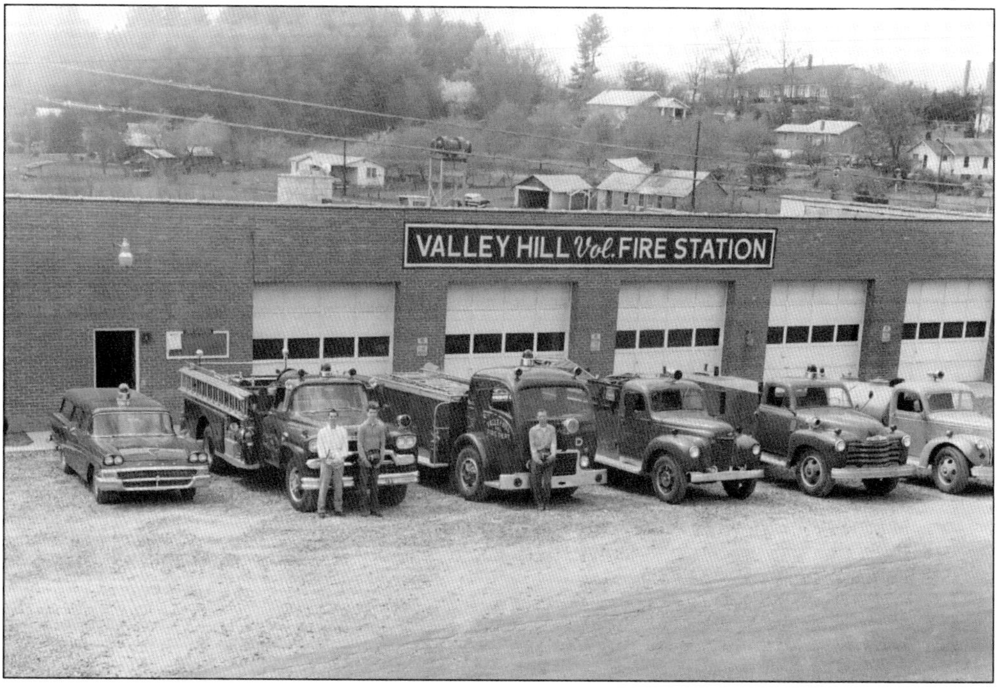

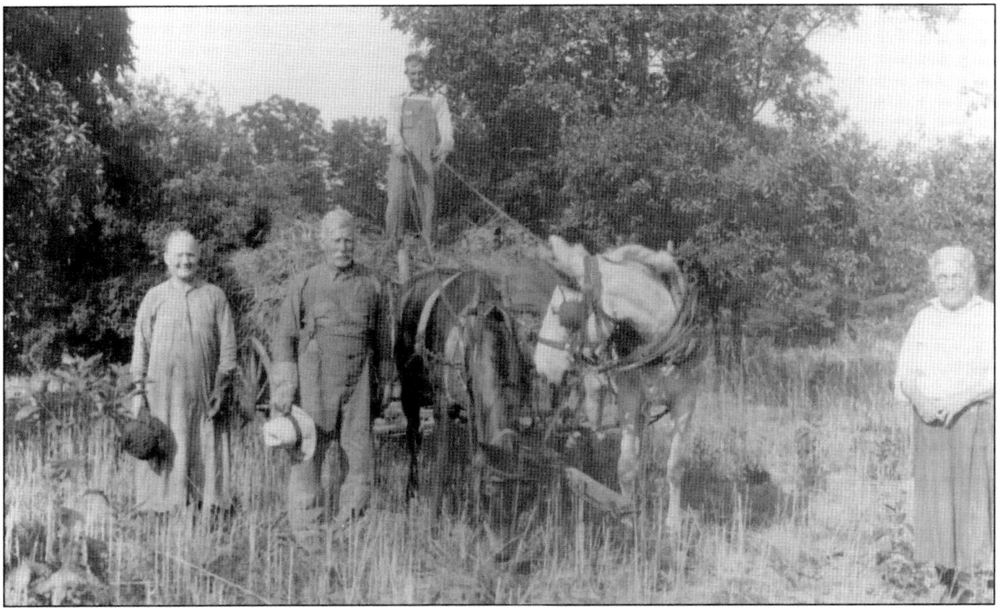

The Stepp family poses at their farm at the foot of Pinnacle Mountain in the Crab Creek sector around 1930. From left to right are Ellen Stepp (1861–1954), Thomas "Uncle Bub" Stepp (1857–1938), and Meredith King (1880–1933) on the wagon drawn by mules named Billy and John, along with Mary Stepp (1855–1941). Old Doc Howe employed Mary as a nanny for his daughters, Jennie and Louise, in Flat Rock. (Courtesy of Jim King and the estate of Louise H. Bailey.)

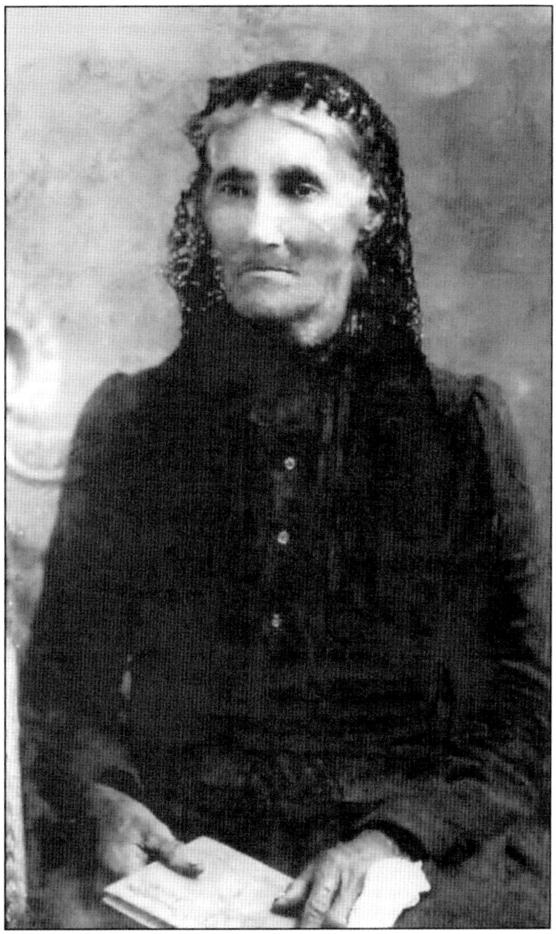

Mary, Ellen, and Thomas Stepp and Rebecca Stepp McCall (1856–1935) were born to Frances "Fanny" Stepp (1827–1905), pictured here, and Thomas Maudern Manders (1826–1891). (Courtesy of the Henderson County Genealogical and Historical Society.)

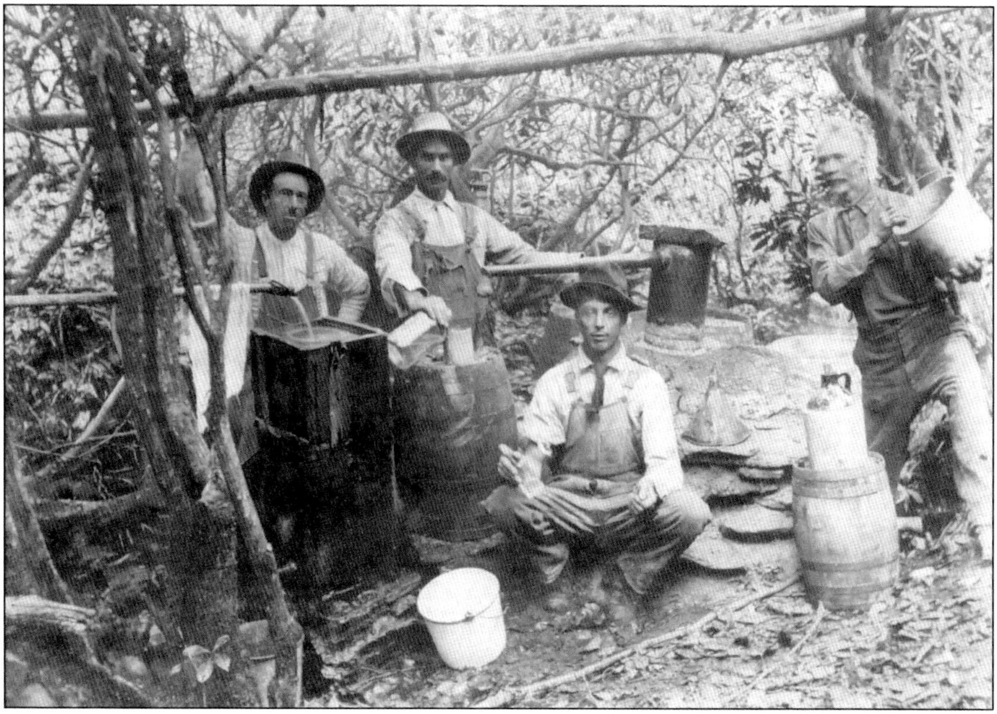

Moonshiners take a moment for a photograph at their distillery operation in the Crab Creek Valley area known as Cathead. From left to right are ? Corn, Tyler Drake, Rufus Brown, and John Bates Brown. (Courtesy of Betty Lakey and the Henderson County Genealogical and Historical Society.)

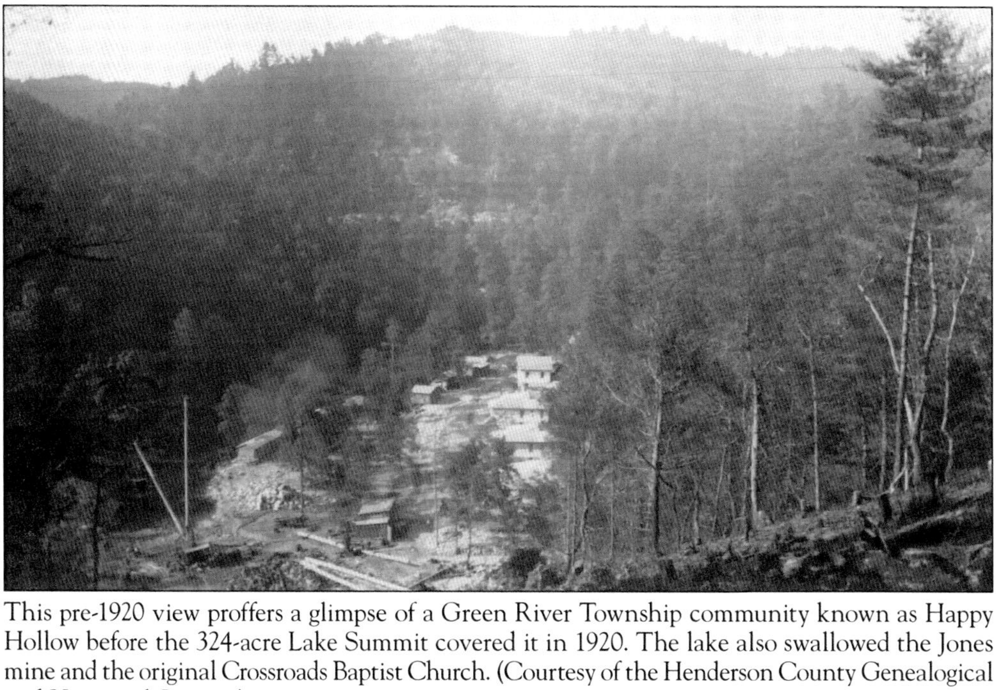

This pre-1920 view proffers a glimpse of a Green River Township community known as Happy Hollow before the 324-acre Lake Summit covered it in 1920. The lake also swallowed the Jones mine and the original Crossroads Baptist Church. (Courtesy of the Henderson County Genealogical and Historical Society.)

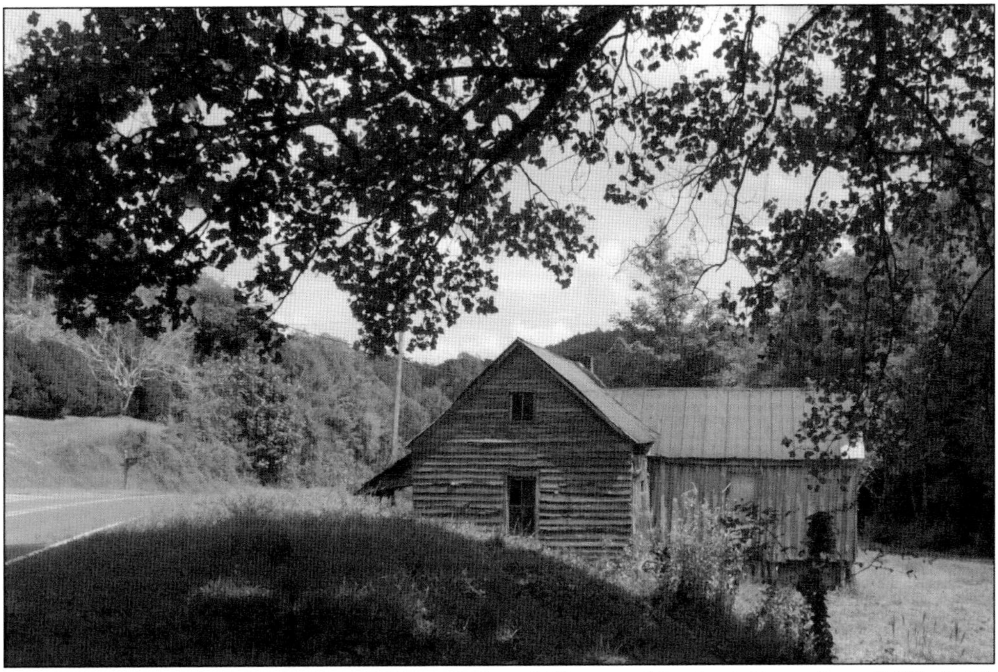

The farm of David Houston Levi (1870–1958) and Florence Elizabeth Revis Levi (1871–1949) now stands abandoned alongside Bob's Creek Road in Green River Township. (Photograph by the author.)

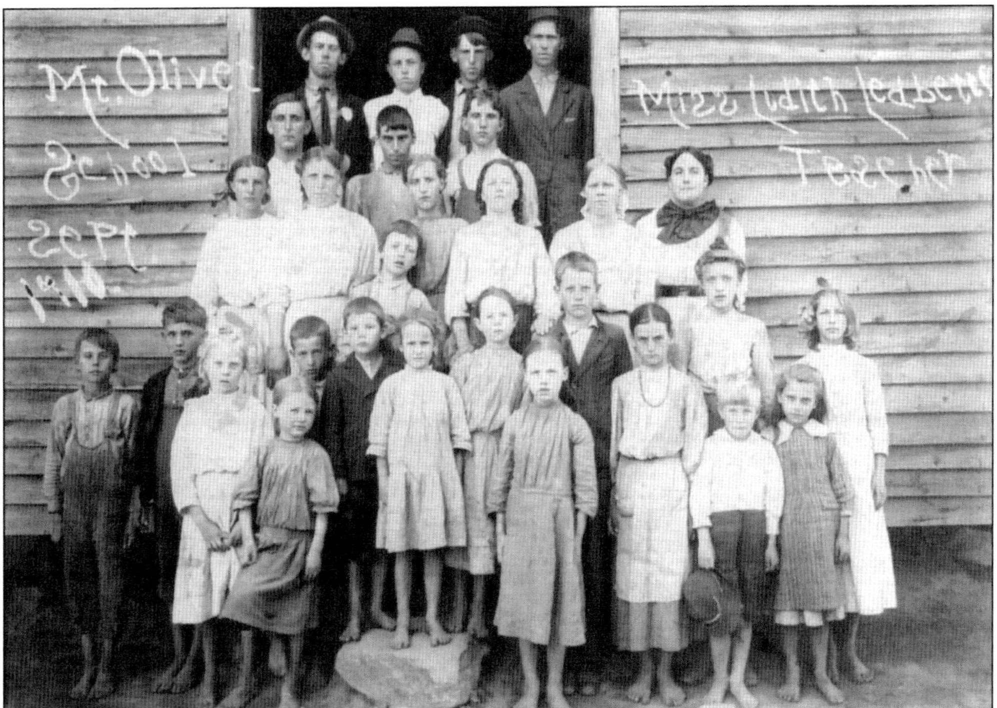

Ludith Ledbetter (Osteen) (1890–1967) poses with her students in 1910 at the Mount Olivet School in Green River Township. (Courtesy of Ella Corn Surrette.)

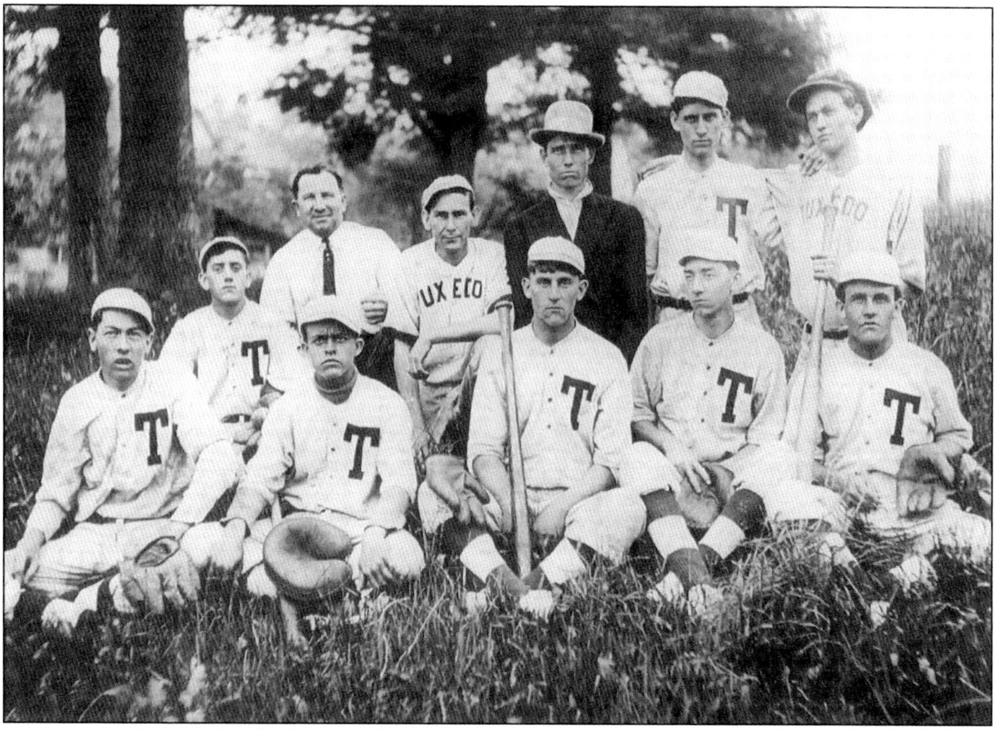

Some of the Tuxedo baseball team players pictured here include Henry Erwin, Donovan Wilkie, Willie Hunnicutt, Frank Corn, Leland Huggins, Cleophas Boone, Dolph Hunnicutt, and Ralph Huggins. (Courtesy of the Henderson County Genealogical and Historical Society.)

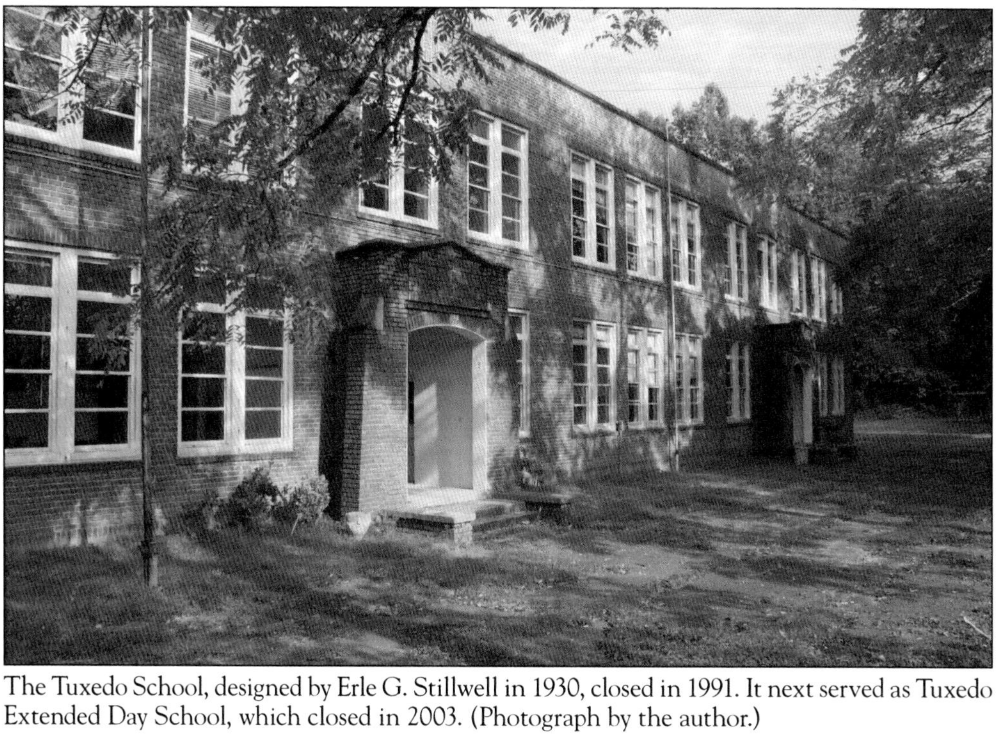

The Tuxedo School, designed by Erle G. Stillwell in 1930, closed in 1991. It next served as Tuxedo Extended Day School, which closed in 2003. (Photograph by the author.)

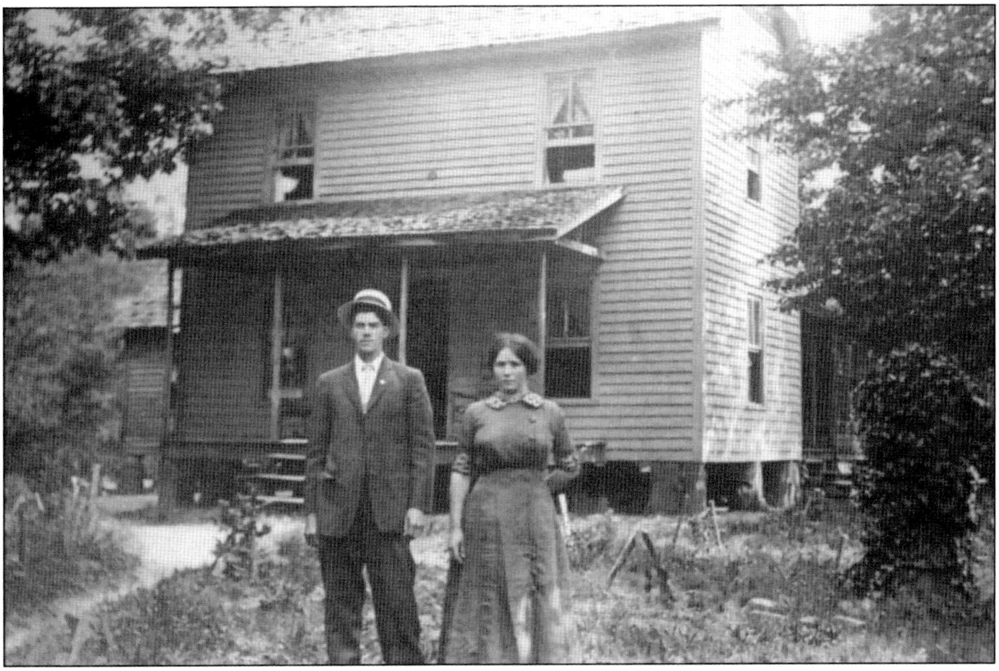

Ulysses Spurgeon Staton (1891–1964) and his wife, Effie Eva Jones Staton (1895–1981), enjoy a quiet moment at their home at Green River Road and Cabin Creek Road in Zirconia. (Courtesy of Fred Beddingfield.)

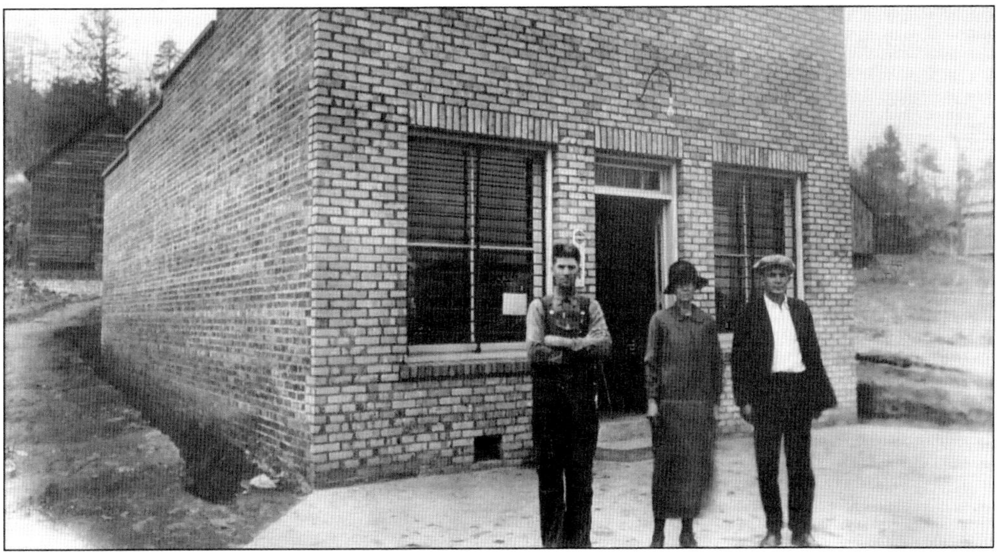

Brothers Ulysses Spurgeon Staton, left, and David Edison Staton (1892–1966) pose with their mother, Rosa Elizabeth Pace Staton Queen (1869–1954), at the Staton Store in Tuxedo. In the early 1920s, U.S. Staton built this general store on the old Greenville Highway. Before the highway was widened, he moved the store a short distance to its current location on Old US Highway 25. Staton sold dry goods, hides, furs, and medicinal herbs. Also a barber who performed dental procedures, Staton operated the store until his death. His wife, Effie, managed the business until her death. Steve and Lisa Waggoner later sold antiques from the store, which now stands abandoned. (Courtesy of Fred Beddingfield.)

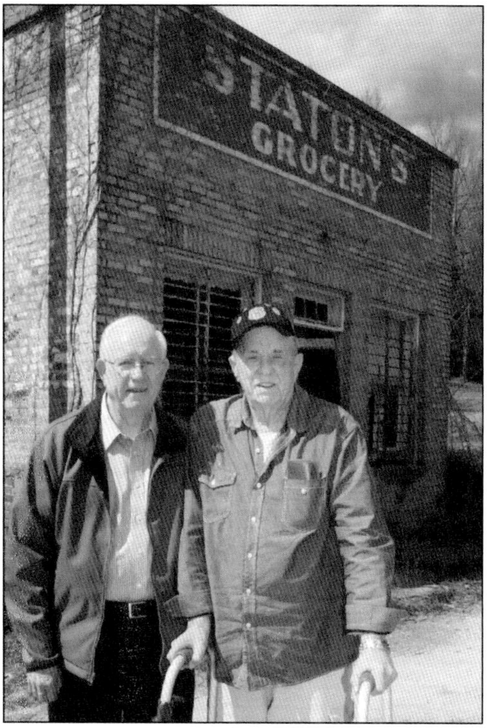

Cousins Rev. David Lewis Staton (left) and Fred Beddingfield (right) reminisce about the old days at the Staton Store in Tuxedo. (Photograph by the author.)

The Green River Manufacturing Company, a textile mill, appears at the center of this aerial view of Tuxedo. The original, wood-frame Tuxedo First Baptist Church can be seen to the lower left of the mill complex, with Lake Summit in the background. (Courtesy of the Henderson County Genealogical and Historical Society.)

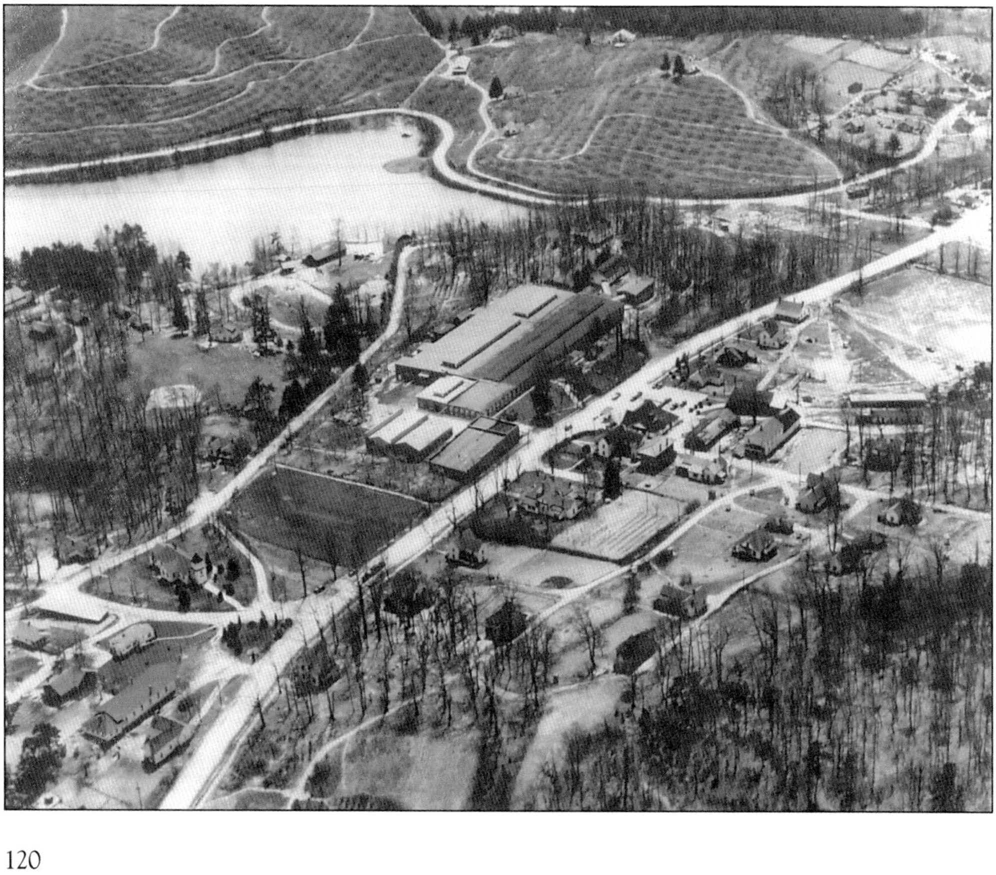

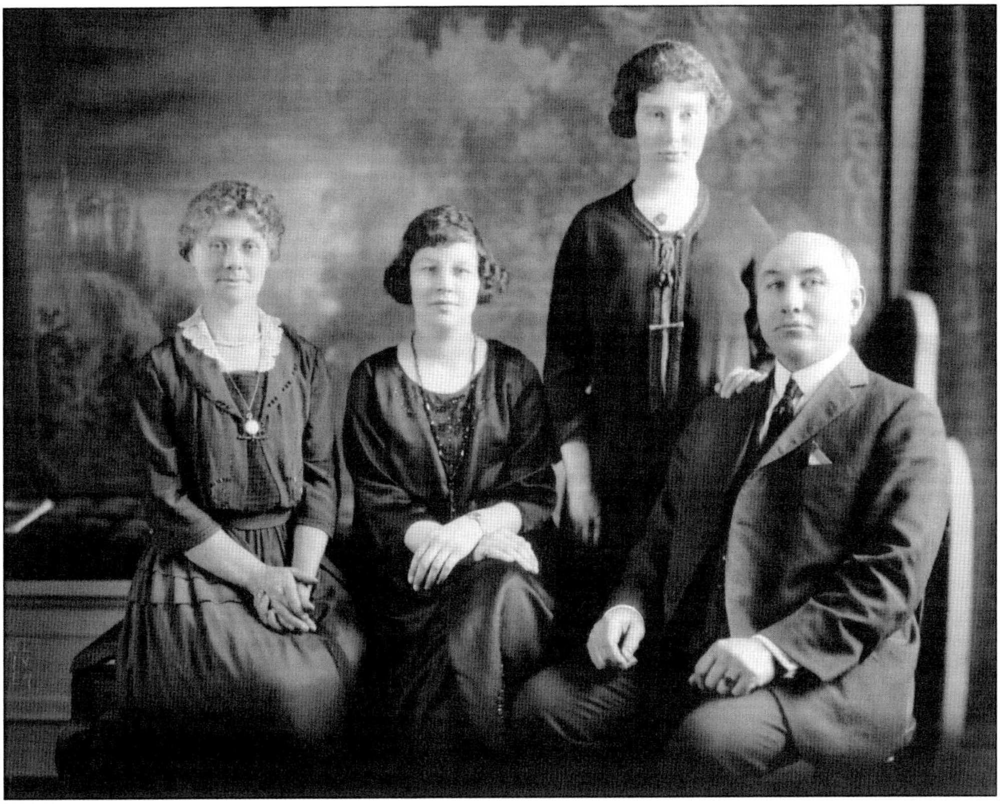

Robert William Boys (1869–1949), his wife, Charlotte (1891–1967), and granddaughters pose for a portrait. Boys owned the Green River Manufacturing Company, which he renamed Green River Mills, Inc. (C.H. Oak Collection, courtesy of the Henderson County Genealogical and Historical Society.)

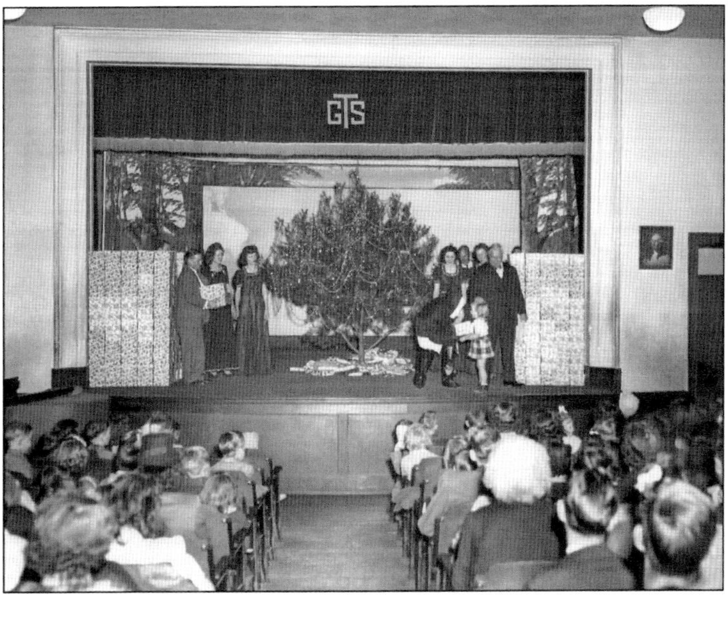

Robert Waring Boys (1901–1977), son of Robert William Boys, presents Christmas gifts to students at Tuxedo School on behalf of his Green River Mills. (Ed Hunnicutt photograph, courtesy of the Henderson County Genealogical and Historical Society.)

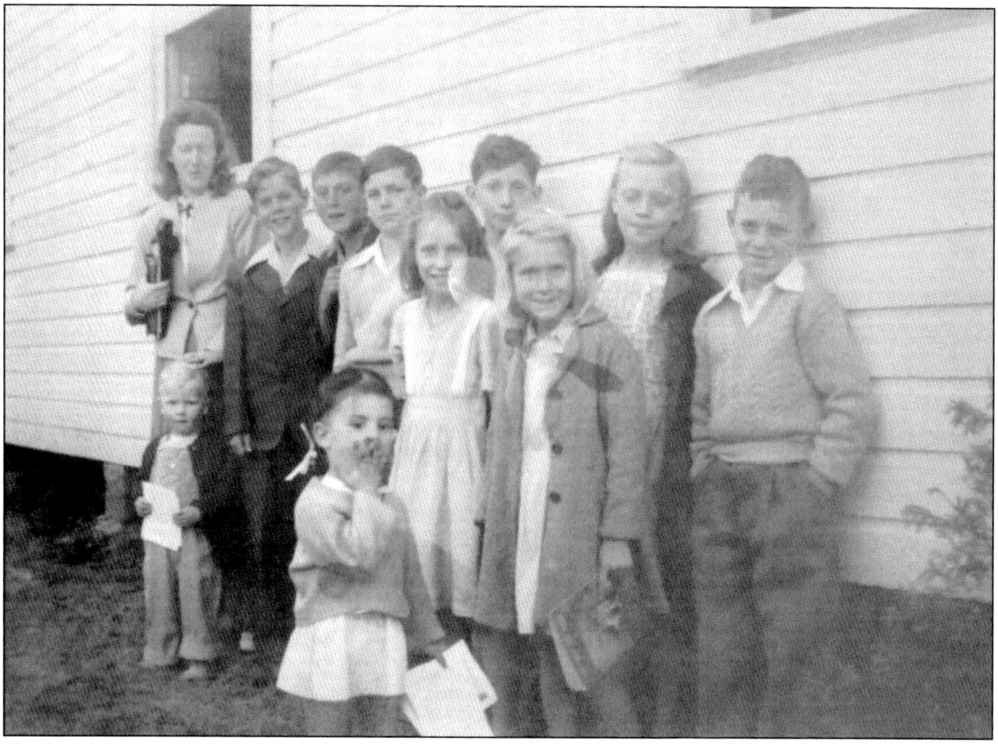

Fannie Morgan taught Sunday school at Green River Baptist Church. Pictured in 1947 are, from left to right, Fannie Geneva Levi Morgan (1912–2010) with her son Robert at her feet, Fred Beddingfield, Joe Burns, David Lewis Staton, Carolyn Osteen, Wayne Beddingfield, Anna Lou Burns, Janey Ward, and Steve Staton. Ella Corn stands in the foreground. (Courtesy of Ella Corn Surrette.)

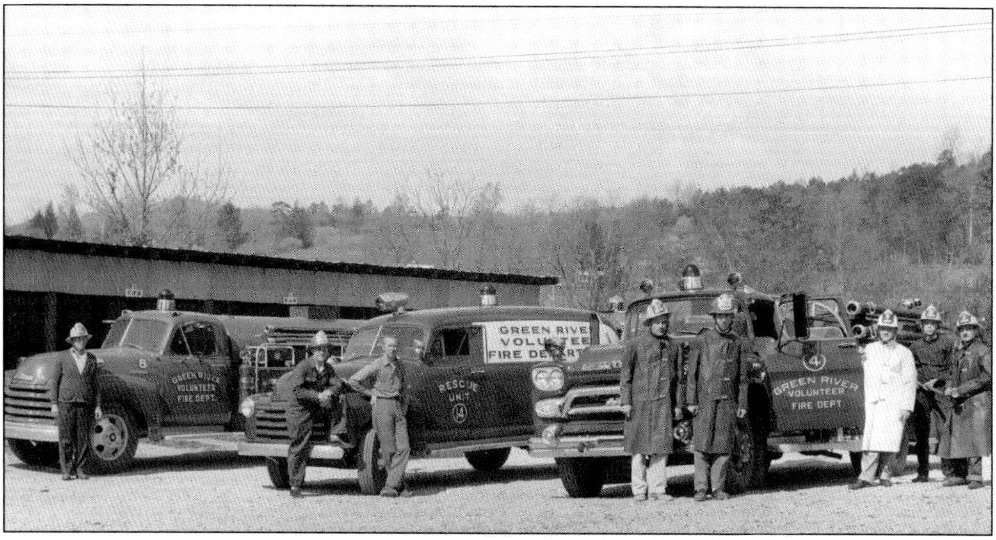

Members of the Green River Volunteer Fire Department pictured here are, from left to right, Ollie Caldwell, Jack Erwin Sr., James Osteen, Carl Taylor, Harold Bradley, Clyde Ballard, Jack "Jackie" Erwin Jr., and Alfred Coggins. (Ed Hunnicutt photograph, courtesy of the Henderson County Genealogical and Historical Society.)

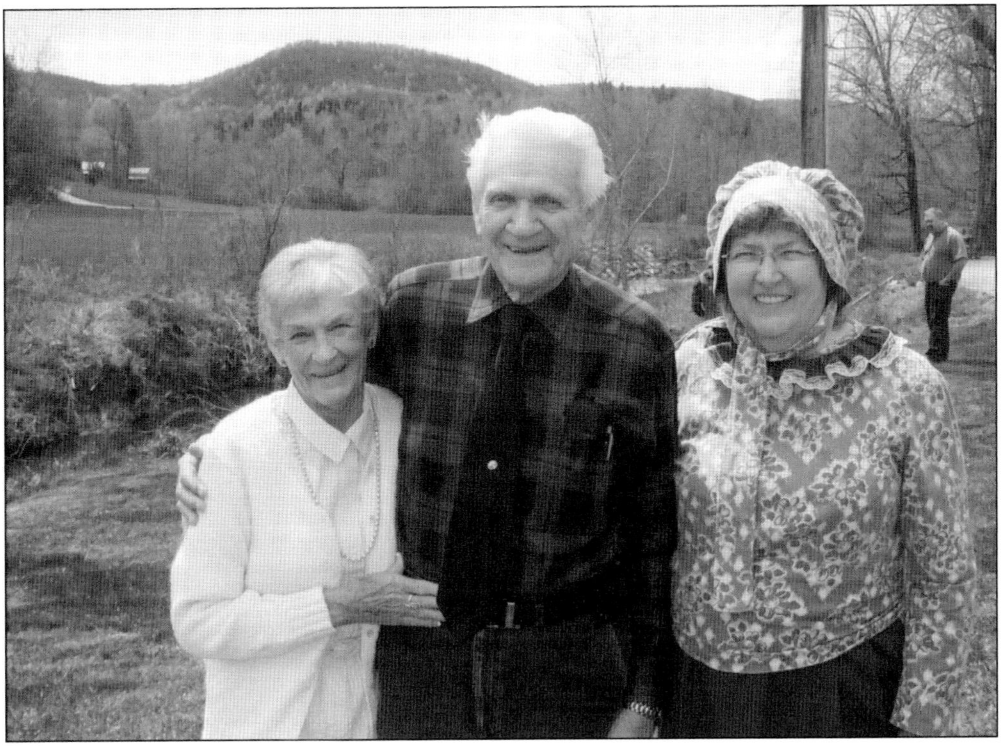

Arnetta Osteen Mullinax (left); her husband, Garland Mullinax; and Mary Lois Maybin celebrate Old-Timey Day at Cedar Springs Baptist Church. (Photograph by the author.)

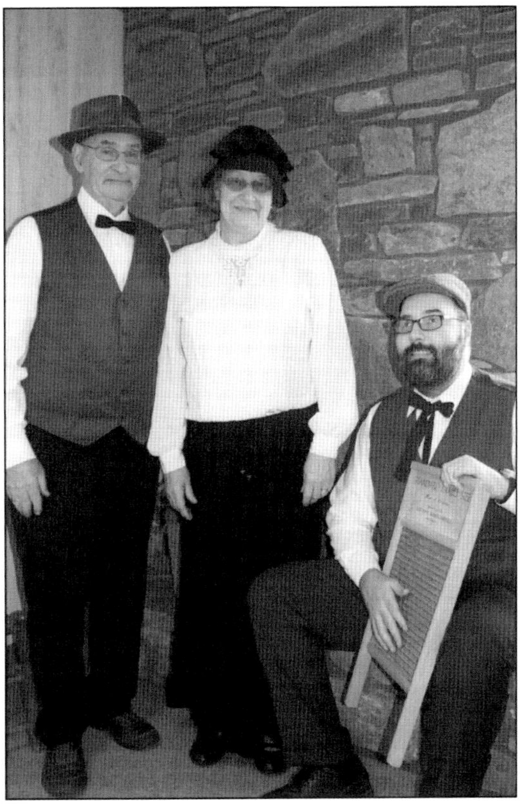

Ballard and Maybin family roots run deep in Henderson County. Robert Elias Ballard, his wife, Pearl Jane Maybin Ballard, and their son Gary Craig Ballard are talented musicians. Pictured here, they celebrate an Old-Timey Day event at Cedar Springs Baptist Church in Green River Township. (Photograph by the author.)

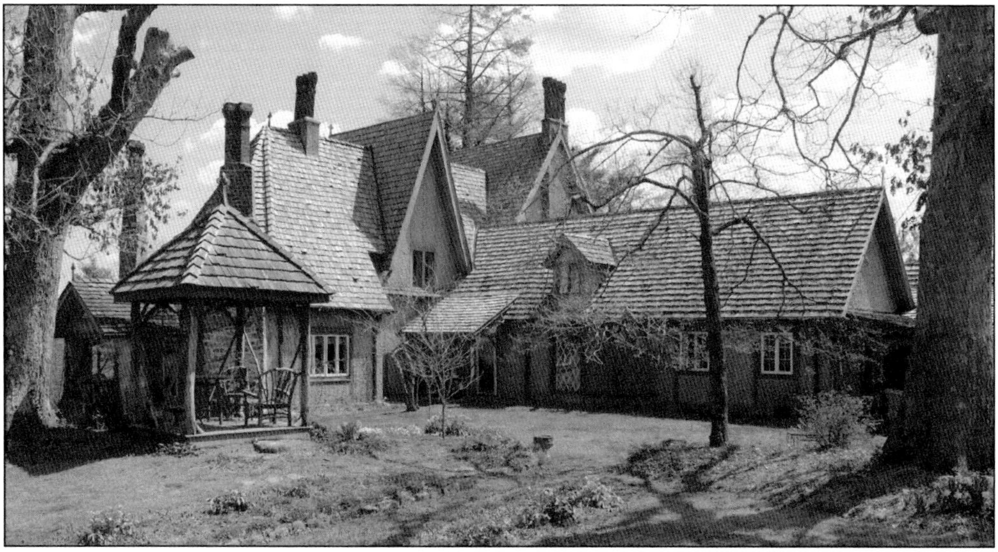

The House of Seven Gables in Macedonia was known also as the Top, High Gables, the House of Gray Gables, and High Holde. This English-style c. 1889 home was built for Leonard Hewett (1866–1912), an immigrant from the Isle of Wight, and his wife, Eliza Fry Maury Hewett (1857–1910) of Kentucky. The Copisa Orchard once covered the outlying acres. (Photograph by the author.)

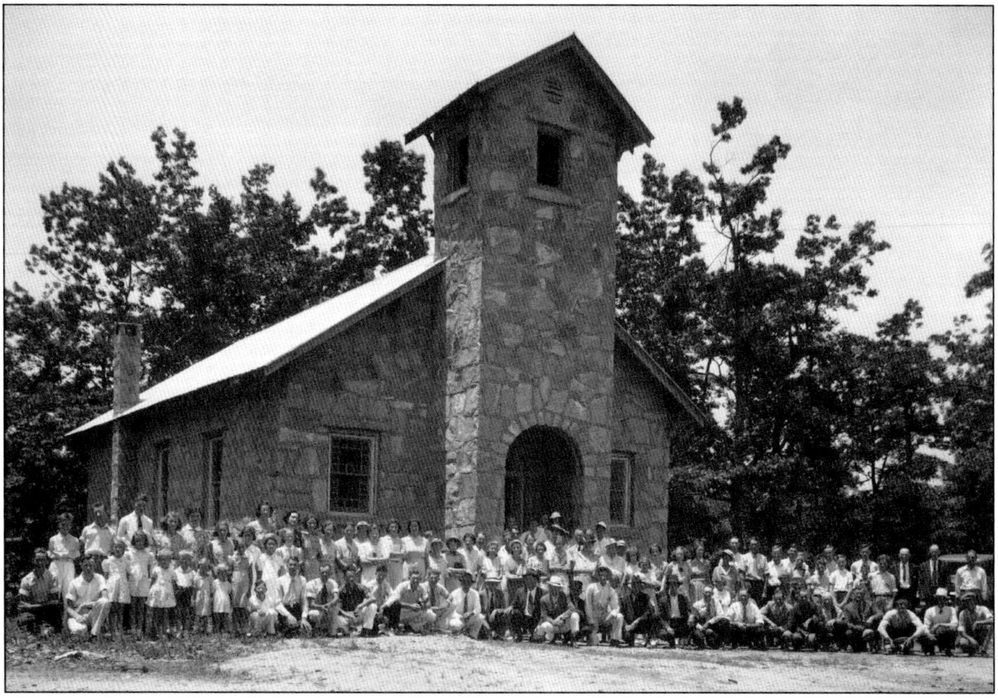

Mountain Page Baptist Church was established around 1785. Church members quarried and laid the granite blocks to build the sanctuary pictured here in 1936. The rock sanctuary succeeded an earlier construction of wood. The community of Mountain Page, one of the earliest settlements in what became Henderson County, lies between Macedonia and the Polk County line. (Courtesy of the Baker-Barber Collection, Community Foundation of Henderson County, Henderson County Public Library.)

Index

Originally sheathed in copper paint, the galvanized tin dome atop the historic Henderson County Courthouse sports a statue of Themis, the Greek goddess of divine justice and law and the mother of the fates. This casting of Lady Justice counts as one of only three in the United States missing an important item: the blindfold the statue is supposed to be wearing. For more than 100 years, Themis has watched the evolution of Henderson County from her lofty perch. In 1987, city leaders set forth a provision that no structure can be taller than the dome of the historic courthouse. (Photograph by the author.)

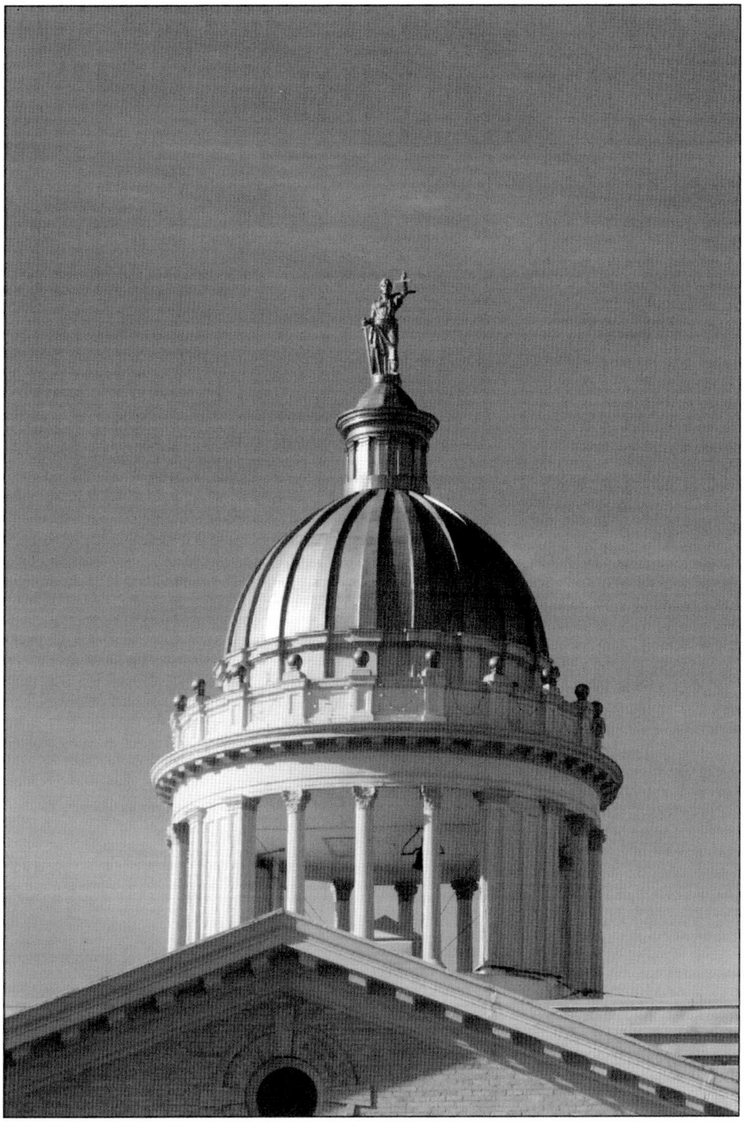

Also by Terry Ruscin

A History of Transportation in Western North Carolina
Glimpses of Henderson County, North Carolina
Hidden History of Henderson County, North Carolina
Hendersonville & Flat Rock: An Intimate Tour